PERSPECTIVES ON CRIME AND JUSTICE

Joseph A. Schafer, Series Editor

Institutional Sexual Abuse in the #MeToo Era

Edited by Jason D. Spraitz
and Kendra N. Bowen

Southern Illinois University Press | Carbondale

Southern Illinois University Press
www.siupress.com

24 23 22 21   4 3 2 1

Publication of this book has been underwritten by the
Elmer H. Johnson and Carol Holmes Johnson
criminology fund.

Library of Congress Cataloging-in-Publication Data
Names: Spraitz, Jason D., [date] editor. | Bowen, Kendra N.,
[date] editor.
Title: Institutional sexual abuse in the #MeToo era / edited by
Jason D. Spraitz and Kendra N. Bowen.
Description: Carbondale : Southern Illinois University Press,
[2021] | Series: Perspectives on crime and justice | Includes
bibliographical references and index.
Identifiers: LCCN 2020044449 (print) |
LCCN 2020044450 (ebook) | ISBN 9780809338238 (paperback) |
ISBN 9780809338245 (ebook)
Subjects: LCSH: Sex crimes. | MeToo movement.
Classification: LCC HV6556 .I57 2021 (print) |
LCC HV6556 (ebook) | DDC 364.15/30973—dc23
LC record available at https://lccn.loc.gov/2020044449
LC ebook record available at https://lccn.loc.gov/2020044450

Printed on recycled paper ♻

Contents

Institutional
Sexual
Abuse
in the
#MeToo Era

Introduction: Examining Institutional Sexual Abuse during the #MeToo Era

Jason D. Spraitz and Kendra N. Bowen

#MeToo Movement

Tarana Burke started the "Me Too" movement long before it gained national attention. As has been outlined in *New York Times* profiles and CNN articles, Burke was the director of a youth camp in the late 1990s. One day, a 13-year-old girl began telling Burke about being sexually victimized by her mother's boyfriend (Criss, 2018). After a few minutes, Burke stopped the young girl and said that another counselor would be able to provide better assistance. In thinking about the interaction, Burke said, "I didn't have a response or a way to help her in that moment, and I couldn't even say 'me too'" (Garcia, 2017, para. 2).

Nearly ten years later, Burke created a nonprofit organization named Just Be Inc. to assist sexual assault victims (Garcia, 2017). She devoted herself to providing support and finding resources for these victims and dubbed her commitment to helping young women of color "Me Too." In an interview with CNN, Burke said of this original Me Too movement,

> On one side, it's a bold, declarative statement that, "I'm not ashamed," and "I'm not alone." . . . On the other side, it's a statement from survivor to survivor that says, "I see you, I hear you, I understand you and I'm here for you or I get it." (Criss, 2018, para. 15)

Her work continues today.

Yet, in mid-October 2017, Burke's Me Too movement was unknowingly appropriated by actress Alyssa Milano when she tweeted, "If you've been sexually harassed or assaulted write 'me too' as a reply to this tweet" (Santiago & Criss, 2017). As a result, the #MeToo hashtag went viral. Of Milano's tweet, Burke said, "Initially I panicked . . . I felt a sense of dread, because something that was part of my life's work was going to be co-opted and taken from me and used for a purpose that I hadn't originally intended" (Garcia, 2017, para. 19).

Those fears were valid. Despite the fact that #MeToo literally became an overnight sensation, Burke did not receive credit for what she had created. Black women, Latinx women, and other women of color soon came to Burke's defense (Garcia, 2017). A couple days later Milano reached out to Burke, and within a week Milano was on morning talk shows publicly crediting Burke as the founder of Me Too.

Now, more than three years after Milano's tweet, Burke wants to make sure that Me Too is more than a hashtag: "This is a movement about the 1 in 4 girls and the 1 in 6 boys who are sexually abused every year and who carry those wounds into adulthood" (Criss, 2018, para. 5). In part, the History and Vision statement of the Me Too movement points out that

> our vision from the beginning was to address both the dearth in resources for survivors of sexual violence and to build a community of advocates, driven by survivors, who will be at the forefront of creating solutions to interrupt sexual violence in their communities.
>
> In less than six months, because of the viral #metoo hashtag, a vital conversation about sexual violence has been thrust into the national dialogue. What started as local grassroots work has expanded to reach a global community of survivors from all walks of life and helped to de-stigmatize the act of surviving by highlighting the breadth and impact of sexual violence worldwide. (Me Too Movement, n.d.)

With this book, we intend to join this vital conversation by amplifying the knowledge the contributing authors have about sexual abuse, violence, and harassment in various institutional settings.

Institutional Sexual Abuse

Institutional sexual abuse is defined in many ways. For example, Gallagher (2000) suggested that sexual abuse in the workplace is, plainly, "the sexual abuse of [people] by persons who work with them" (p. 795). But Sullivan and Beech (2002) noted that the concept of institutional sexual abuse should not be limited simply to the workplace; rather, they argued that the location can be interchangeable. No matter the location, though, a disparate power dynamic must exist between offender and victim in which the abuser uses their power as a tool of harm (Wolfe et al., 2003).

Spraitz (2018) has argued that institutional sexual abuse occurs when the abusers "use the authority and power given to them in order to victimize others" (p. 226). Additionally, Spraitz claimed, "institutional abuse is prolonged when those who have the ability to stop it from happening fail to act in the best interests of the victims" (p. 226). This book reveals that there is much more to institutional sexual abuse than what these definitions suggest. Yet, the power dynamic exists. The recent reinvigoration of the #MeToo movement has given victims the support to disclose the abuse they have suffered and to take back their power.

While not exhaustive, the content in this volume covers several areas: schools and universities, the foster care system, the entertainment industry, journalism and the advertising industry, social media, sports, and political, religious, and correctional institutions. The contributing authors examine what has been uncovered in these areas and discuss ways that sexual abuse can be eliminated and prevented in the future.

Summary and Overview of the Book

The first two chapters focus on institutional sexual abuse as it relates to #MeToo in university settings. In chapter 1, Mia Gilliam and Shelly Clevenger note that college-age women are sexually victimized more frequently than non-college-age women, but only recently have a growing number of those outside higher education started to realize the vulnerabilities and dangers that these college-age women face. Further, the authors provide support for the argument that not all college women are victimized equally, especially Black women, bisexual women, transgender women, and sorority women. This leads into the presentation of their first case study, an overview of #CarryThatWeight, which Emma Sulkowicz started while a student at Columbia University. Gilliam and Clevenger highlight two additional cases: a traveling art exhibit dubbed "What Were You Wearing?" that has appeared on various college campuses, and Julie Libarkin's compilation of more than 700 substantiated claims of sexual misconduct and abuse lodged against faculty, staff, and administrators at universities throughout the United States. Each case study is a concrete example of how education and advocacy can be used to raise awareness of institutional sexual abuse on college campuses. Gilliam and Clevenger use these examples and their overview of prior research to call for more strategies and policies that will effect positive change on campuses.

Continuing the discussion of sexual abuse in higher education in chapter 2, Nicole Bedera provides a timely discussion of how #MeToo has helped alter the landscape. Bedera notes that approximately 20 percent of undergraduate women are victims of sexual assault and argues that we must consider the institutional role the university plays in order to understand this violence. To do so, Bedera explains the history of Title IX legislation, provisions instituted during the Obama administration, and current rollbacks of those provisions under Betsy DeVos's tenure with the U.S. Department of Education. In addition, Bedera provides two case studies of victim-survivors she has interviewed as part of her larger research efforts. Both women were inspired by the #MeToo movement to share their stories. Bedera ends the chapter with a discussion of several ideas for short-term and long-term change: greater promotion of gender equality, banning fraternities, bystander intervention training, prevention programming like "Flip the Script," and introducing policies that take a survivor-centered and trauma-informed approach.

In chapter 3, Amina Zarrugh provides insight into #MeToo and politics. Zarrugh details the history of sexual abuse and sexual harassment in not only the United States but also the United Kingdom. As such, the chapter is full of historical context, such as a discussion of the sexual harassment allegations made against then Supreme Court nominee Clarence Thomas by Anita Hill and the resulting congressional hearings as well as accusations against British Parliament members. Zarrugh brings the Thomas–Hill hearings full circle with a case study examining the 2018 sexual assault allegations against then Supreme Court nominee Brett Kavanaugh by Christine Blasey Ford. She closes her chapter by noting that #MeToo has great potential to move beyond its current status as a social movement and become a bona fide legal movement.

Jason D. Spraitz and Kendra N. Bowen provide in chapter 4 an in-depth discussion of #MeToo as it relates to religious institutions. Using as a common thread a recent grand jury report from Pennsylvania that examined clergy sexual abuse throughout the state, Spraitz and Bowen focus on several issues, including the prevalence of sexual abuse in the Catholic Church, grooming behaviors of abusive clergymen, and theoretical underpinnings of the abuse. Their chapter also highlights reports of abuse from evangelical religious institutions and offers a case study on the origins of the #ChurchToo movement. A second case study looks at the impact #ChurchToo had in one evangelical megachurch. Spraitz and Bowen conclude with a discussion of the various responses that have resulted from multiple religious institutions in the wake of a growing number of abuse disclosures.

Reneè Lamphere begins chapter 5 by looking at abuse in the foster care system, describing the correlation that exists between an extensive history of repeated abuse of foster care youths and the likelihood that they experience placement instability. For example, girls in foster care who have had a sexual abuse history experience changes in placement more than twice as often as those who have not experienced abuse. Additionally, sexually abused foster care youths start having sex at a younger age and are less likely to use protection or contraception. Lamphere also notes that approximately 60 percent of child sex trafficking victims were once in foster or group homes. She closes the chapter with a discussion of the role the guardian ad litem plays in helping victims of child sexual abuse in the foster care system and the positive impact that figure can have on the lives of these survivors.

Lamphere and Matthew Hassett address institutional sexual abuse in the U.S. correctional system in chapter 6, presenting in-depth information on the known sexual victimization rates in jails and prisons throughout the country. They note that prison and jail sexual abuse not only is underreported but also has been normalized in our culture, mainly through portrayals of prison violence in entertainment media. Lamphere and Hassett compare current #MeToo responses to the passage of the Prison Rape Elimination Act in 2003. This act had bipartisan political support and pledged zero tolerance for sexual victimization while providing federal research money for evaluations of its effectiveness. In addition, Lamphere and Hassett present several short case studies, including a lawsuit that incarcerated victims have filed against the Central California Women's Facility, as well as insights on prison sexual abuse and violence from a currently incarcerated man.

Chapter 7 provides an overview of #MeToo and institutional abuse in the entertainment industry, specifically Hollywood, from Ashley Wellman. Wellman begins her chapter by discussing the near-instant attention that A-list stars, such as Alyssa Milano, brought to the #MeToo movement over a decade after Tarana Burke coined the term. In addition, Wellman notes that many actresses and actors are reluctant to report their abuse because they fear retaliation that will halt their career, yet some alleged abusers continue to receive accolades and awards. Wellman conducts a deep dive into the case of high-powered Hollywood executive Harvey Weinstein in which she details the allegations against him and the status of court proceedings. A second case study of a sexually abusive actor highlights Bill Cosby. Wellman follows these case studies up with a discussion of the difficulties that victimized male actors must deal with when deciding to disclose their abuse; she mentions as an example the ridicule that Terry Crews faced when he talked about his victimization history. Through all of this, Wellman sees hope in the way that celebrities amplify the message of #MeToo—their platform has already led to the creation of #TimesUp—but cautions that more work needs to be done.

In chapter 8, Pamela J. Forman, Anne M. Nurse, and Lake D. Montie address #MeToo in the world of sport. This chapter focuses on two well-known cases of institutional sexual abuse: the Jerry Sandusky scandal at Pennsylvania State University and the abuse perpetrated by Larry Nassar while he was a staff member of the USA Gymnastics team and Michigan State University. Their analysis of each case provides an in-depth explanation of the institutional failures that led to Sandusky's and Nassar's prolonged sexual abuse. Additionally, Forman, Nurse, and Montie discuss the role that hegemonic masculinity plays in the culture of sport and how it serves to silence young male and female victims alike. While Michigan State and Penn State have attempted to show their newfound commitment to public safety in the aftermath of these scandals, Forman, Nurse, and Montie report that more work is needed at local university and federal levels to ensure the safety of all participants.

Jacqueline Lambiase, Tracy Everbach, and Carolyn Bronstein discuss sexual abuse in advertising and journalism in chapter 9. The authors note that mass media companies are in an interesting position, reporting the #MeToo disclosures while also dealing with allegations and accusations made by journalists and creatives in advertising technology who have been sexually violated within their institution. Lambiase, Everbach, and Bronstein cover tremendous ground in this chapter and provide two highly detailed case studies. The first focuses on the sexual harassment allegations against Fox News chairman and CEO Roger Ailes and his subsequent removal. The second case study examines Andy Rubin's exit from Google as well as several additional credible allegations of sexual harassment levied against other Google executives. In closing the chapter, Lambiase, Everbach, and Bronstein point out that the responses to sexual abuse within the institutions of advertising and journalism have included voices of advocates from different racial, ethnic, socioeconomic, gender, and sexual backgrounds.

The final chapter, from Tania G. Levey, examines the sexual harassment and threats of violent victimization that are generated via social media platforms. For example, as #MeToo grew, Levey notes that it was the most-used advocacy hashtag in 2018 on Instagram. Levey's chapter explores the power and ability that social media companies use to challenge current norms and power structures despite dealing with their own innumerable and constant cases of abuse, harassment, and threatening behavior. A discussion of Facebook and Twitter policies ensues with a focus on how social media and its users can be protected as platforms evolve and become even greater forces for social change. Levey acknowledges that the ability to police every behavior does not exist and leaves the reader wondering if the social change harnessed through social media will be progressive or regressive; we do not know the answer yet.

Together these chapters show the breadth of institutional sexual abuse and how it is not limited to careers in the political arena or the advertising industry. They demonstrate that both an A-list movie star and a first-year university student may be sexually victimized and that protections against victimization and protocols to respond to it are lacking in nearly every industry and institution. Last, these chapters detail extensive institutional complicity and allegations of cover-ups that only serve to protect organizations. But, the #MeToo movement has the ability to help change this situation by providing victims with the courage and support to draw attention to the abuse that occurred and by creating prevention policies and holding abusers accountable in the aftermath of the victimization. Now it is important for others, especially those in positions of power, to help victims seek justice, to work with organizations to improve their policies and protocols, to work with researchers to identify and implement the best evidence-based practices, and to believe victims. We know how daunting it is for victims of sex crimes to disclose the abuse that they have suffered, especially when the abuser is supported by strong institutional norms that would rather handle accusations and allegations discreetly behind closed doors. Yet, the #MeToo movement, and all of its ancillary movements, has shown the strength of community and how much more powerful victims, advocates, and allies are when the community speaks truth to power. It is now incumbent upon us all to carry the momentum of #MeToo forward in order to improve all institutions.

References

Criss, D. (2018, November 30). *The media's version of #MeToo is unrecognizable to the movement's founder, Tarana Burke.* CNN. https://www.cnn.com/2018/11/30/us/tarana-burke-ted-talk-trnd/index.html

Gallagher, B. (2000). The extent and nature of known cases of institutional child sexual abuse. *British Journal of Social Work, 30*(6), 795–817. https://doi.org/10.1093/bjsw/30.6.795

Garcia, S. E. (2017, October 20). The woman who created #MeToo long before hashtags. *New York Times.* https://www.nytimes.com/2017/10/20/us/me-too-movement-tarana-burke.html

Me Too Movement (n.d.). *History & Inception.* https://metoomvmt.org/get-to-know-us/history-inception/

Santiago, C., & Criss, D. (2017, October 17). *An activist, a little girl and the heart-breaking origin of "Me Too."* CNN. https://www.cnn.com/2017/10/17/us/me-too-tarana-burke-origin-trnd/index.html

Spraitz, J. D. (2018). Institutional sexual abuse. In C. M. Hilinski-Rosick & D. Lee (Eds.), *Contemporary Issues in Victimology: Identifying Patterns and Trends* (pp. 225–244). Lexington Books.

Sullivan, J., & Beech, A. (2002). Professional perpetrators: Sex offenders who use their employment to target and sexually abuse the children with whom they work. *Child Abuse Review, 11*(3), 153–167. https://doi.org/10.1002/car.737

Wolfe, D. A., Jaffe, P. G., Jette, J. L., & Poisson, S. E. (2003). The impact of child abuse in community institutions and organizations: Advancing professional and scientific understanding. *Clinical Psychology: Science and Practice, 10*(2), 179–191. https://doi.org/10.1093/clipsy/bpg021

I. Institutions of Higher Learning

1. Sexual Abuse in Higher Education and the Impact of #MeToo

Mia Gilliam and Shelly Clevenger

The #MeToo movement has gained momentum and raised awareness nationwide, and this is perhaps no more apparent than on college campuses. College students have embraced the movement and have come forward with their own stories of harassment and sexual assault. #MeToo has been discussed in classrooms, and students have rallied outside of class in support of survivors and mobilized to form a network of community within the college campus. The #MeToo movement has shown survivors, particularly those on campus, that they are not alone and has given them a way to connect with one another. It has also exposed the structural problems and years of sexual harassment and sexual assault committed by men within the rape culture that exists in the United States.

Historically, the public has viewed college as a safe place for young people to live and learn (Fisher et al., 2010). This public perception has been changing, however, and the #MeToo movement is contributing to greater change. As the media reports the increase in the number of sexual assaults on college campuses, society is beginning to realize the dangers that young people face regarding sexual victimization in higher education (Hunter, 2005; Wilcox et al., 2007).

Women ages 18–24 have higher rates of sexual victimization than any other age group, and the victimizations often are unreported to police (Sinozich & Langton, 2014). While in college, women are often more vulnerable to sexual victimization than women in the general population (Fisher et al., 2000; Gross et al., 2006; Koss et al., 1987; White & Smith, 2009). For these reasons, the #MeToo movement has relevance for the women on college campuses.

This chapter will explore sexual violence on college campuses, with the goal of illustrating that this violence has been a long-standing issue, although one not frequently acknowledged until recent decades. With amplification from the #MeToo movement, it has become an area of national concern. First, we will present an overview of the scholarly research on sexual assault in higher education, showcasing prevalence of sexual assault and how women are disproportionately victimized. We will follow this up with a discussion about the reporting of sexual assault, or lack thereof, as this is often the most underreported crime, and how #MeToo may be able to affect this situation. We will also examine the reaction of universities to sexual violence on college campuses and the related policies and strategies that have been employed to combat this issue. Finally, we will discuss suggestions for future change and the overall impact of the #MeToo movement.

The History of Sexual Abuse in Higher Education

Sexual assault on college campuses was first studied by Kirkpatrick and Kanin (1957). They administered a self-report survey to 291 female college students, asking participants about their experiences with sexually aggressive behaviors. They found that 55.7 percent of women surveyed had experienced aggressive attempts at sexual intimacy, 21 percent had experienced attempted/forced sexual intercourse, and 6 percent had experienced physical pain and/or threats to gain acquiescence. While this research showed that a high number of female college students experienced sexual victimizations, it was not until 1982 that the next piece of major research regarding sexual victimization of college students was published. This is likely because most of the scholarly criminological research during the 1960s and 1970s was not focused on feminist issues, such as the victimization of women, but rather on issues relating to male offending and victimizations.

Koss and Oros (1982) developed the first modern measure of sexual victimization on college campuses with the Sexual Experiences Survey (SES). This survey measured not only rape but also other types of sexual victimization, such as sexual assault and sexual coercion. Koss et al. (1987) conducted the first national study to examine college sexual victimization using the SES. They investigated the prevalence of sexual assault among college students in a sample of 6,159 students attending institutions across the United States. The researchers asked college women about their lifetime sexual victimization since the age of 14. They were interested in measuring instances of rape and sexual assault but also of sexual coercion and unwanted sexual contact. This was the first study to examine those constructs. Results suggested that 27.5 percent of college women had experienced the legal definition of rape. They also found that 53.7 percent of women surveyed had experienced sexual coercion in their lifetime, and 46.3 percent reported that they had experienced sexual victimization within the last year. In addition, 6.5 percent of women reported that they were raped within the last year, and 10.1 percent reported an attempted rape. This research, like the study conducted thirty years previously, revealed that college women experienced high rates of sexual violence.

Subsequent researchers have used modified versions of the SES to investigate the extent of sexual violence on college campuses. Most studies reveal the prevalence rates for sexual violence on college campuses range between 10 percent and 30 percent of female students. Gidycz and Hanson (1995) examined sexual violence at a large midwestern university and found that 10 percent of women there had experienced a completed or attempted rape. Schwartz and Pitts's study (1995) revealed that 10.5 percent of women reported experiencing a rape while in college. Expanding on the research of Koss et al. (1987), Fisher et al. (2000) created the National College Women Sexual Victimization study, one of the most comprehensive studies on unwanted sexual experiences to date. It addressed several methodological issues with the SES that allowed for more in-depth information to be collected. For example, the 2000 sexual victimization study incorporated follow-up questions. After participants answered each general question regarding an unwanted sexual experience, they were asked to provide additional information. There were questions about the perpetrator, about the type of contact that occurred, and whether the incident was attempted or completed. Asking these follow-up questions allowed Fisher and colleagues to classify each incident based on the details provided by the respondents and in accordance with the legal definition of a completed rape. Fisher et al. sampled 4,446 college women who provided information regarding unwanted sexual experiences. They found that approximately one in four respondents had experienced an event that met the legal definition of rape, and 15.5 percent of respondents had experienced another sexual victimization other than rape (Fisher et al., 2000). The finding that one in four college women had been raped is often cited nationally when discussing how many women experience college sexual victimizations.

Sinozich and Langton (2014) conducted a national study to examine sexual violence on college campuses and utilized the National Crime Victimization Survey, the National Intimate Partner and Sexual Violence Survey, and the Campus Sexual Assault Study. They found that women aged 18 to 24 had the highest rate of victimization for rape and sexual assault compared to all other female age groups from 1995 to 2013. The National Crime Victimization Survey victimization rate from 2007 to 2013 was 4.7 per 1,000 females aged 18 to 24. The 2011 National Intimate Partner and Sexual Violence Survey reported that 2 percent of all women had experienced unwanted sexual contact within the past 12 months (Black et al., 2011). Finally, the 2007 Campus Sexual Assault Study found that 14 percent of sampled females, who were between 18 and 25 years old, had experienced a completed sexual assault since they began college (Krebs et al., 2009).

Sinozich and Langton's study (2014) allowed respondents to be identified as students (that is, enrolled in a college, university, trade school, or vocational school) or as nonstudents. They found that the rate of rape and sexual assault was 1.2 times higher for nonstudents than for students, which was not something that has been seen previously. This was one of the first large-scale studies to examine this population, and it might indicate that it is the age of the individuals and not just the college environment that could be impacting victimization. However, it is important to note that student victimization (80 percent) was far more likely than nonstudent victimization (67 percent) to not be reported to the police. Moreover, student victims were approximately twice as likely to believe that the incident was not important enough to report.

Some groups of college students may be at greater risk for sexual assault than others. Research shows that Black women, bisexual women, and sorority women are at greater risk (Cantor et al., 2015). Transgender, gay, lesbian, queer, and gender-nonconforming students experienced nonconsensual sexual assault at a rate of 1 in 3, which is higher than the national average (compared to 1 in 4 women and 1 in 17 men). The 2015 U.S. Transgender Survey (James et al., 2016) found that 47 percent of respondents reported sexual assault within their lifetime but were reluctant to report to institutions, such as their universities, out of fear of discrimination and humiliation for being transgender.

Case Study: #CarryThatWeight

In April 2013, Emma Sulkowicz (who identifies as nonbinary and uses gender-neutral they/them pronouns; Tolentino, 2018), then a sophomore at Columbia University, reported that they had been raped by a fellow student in their dorm room on the first day of the 2012–2013 academic year (Bazelon, 2015). What began as a consensual sexual encounter became violent when the perpetrator allegedly choked and anally penetrated them (Tolentino, 2018). In response to the clearing of their alleged rapist in a hearing by Columbia University, Sulkowicz pledged to carry a mattress around campus until they graduated or the accused rapist was expelled (Bazelon, 2015). Sulkowicz explained that the mattress was a symbol for the mental weight endured daily by rape victims. In September 2014, Sulkowicz began carrying a 50-pound mattress, which was the same size as those in Columbia's dorms, everywhere they went on campus. This became part of their senior thesis for a visual arts degree, a piece titled *Mattress Performance (Carry That Weight)*. They carried the weight every day, including to their graduation ceremony in May 2015.

The protest was not received by all as empowering or positive. The student whom Sulkowicz accused of rape filed a lawsuit against Columbia University, the university president, and the art professor supervising the thesis. The lawsuit alleged that the accused was being subjected to gender-based harassment as a result of the *Mattress Performance* being accepted for college credit as Sulkowicz's thesis. The suit was dismissed (Kutner, 2016). There were also those on the Columbia campus who were outraged by Sulkowicz's protest, because the alleged rapist had been found "not responsible" by the university in 2013. Some saw it as a "smear campaign" aimed at harming the individual who was accused. However, other students thought the protest was brave for calling attention to the issues of campus sexual violence. A survey of students at Columbia University that asked about the legacy of Sulkowicz's protest found that 40 percent of students surveyed thought it had a negative impact on campus life; 36 percent said it was positive, as it raised awareness about the issue of rape on college campuses; and 23 percent were neutral. Another positive impact of this campaign was that one-fifth of students said that it altered the way that they date (Hegdahl, 2017),

Regardless of the divisive nature that this protest had on Columbia University's campus, Sulkowicz's actions sparked a national conversation and renewed energy akin to the #MeToo movement. Many students took up the cause, resulting in a trending Twitter hashtag, #CarryThatWeight, and over 130 mattress demonstrations across campuses nationwide (Nathanson, 2014). #CarryThatWeight also drew national attention to the issue of consent as well as to nonbinary individuals.

Underreporting of Sexual Violence in Higher Education

Through the #MeToo movement, society has learned that there are many women who survived sexual violence but may not have reported or told anyone about their victimizations. This is particularly the case for college women, many of whom participated in #MeToo. The underreporting of sexual assault is common and can be attributed to a multitude of factors. One of the most influential factors is the victim's fear of others' responses upon disclosure. While responses can be positive and supportive from family, friends, and the public, reaffirming an individual's choice to come forward (this was often seen with the disclosures on social media with #MeToo), there are also negative social reactions to someone disclosing a victimization, such as victim blaming and disbelief (Ullman, 1996). Other negative reactions include purposeful attempts to harm victims and to make them feel responsible and guilty for their victimization. These can be unintentional yet still harmful responses that were initially meant to be supportive (Herbert & Dunkel-Schetter, 1992). Friends and family, as well as society in general, may not understand the reality of sexual victimization, and the comments that others make or the things they say to survivors may reflect that. There has been a backlash to the #MeToo movement in terms of survivors experiencing hateful and derogatory comments (often on the Internet) and in the way prominent government officials have minimized the experiences of survivors publicly.

Often, the social responses that victims receive are dependent upon the circumstances surrounding the event. For example, officers were less likely to arrest a suspect if the victim did not immediately report the assault or had engaged in some form of "misconduct" (Frazier & Haney, 1996). "Misconduct" could include anything from hitchhiking to being alone at a bar or wearing what the officers perceived as a skimpy wardrobe. There is a view of a stereotypical victim that is ingrained in the larger rape culture of the United States and in the public consciousness. A stereotypical "innocent" victim is generally viewed as a female who was raped by a stranger who had a weapon (and as a result has sustained obvious physical traumas), she reported the crime immediately, and she appeared clearly distraught during the investigation and trial (Maier, 2011). Women who are not defined as "innocent" victims are often considered to have contributed to their own victimization. This is especially the case for female college students, who are often falsely viewed as contributing to their own victimization based on dressing in a certain way, drinking alcohol, taking drugs, walking alone, or being out at a party or a bar.

Case Study: "What Were You Wearing?"

In response to the accusations and victim-blaming statement "What were you wearing?," an art exhibit addresses just that question in an attempt to show people what survivors of rape and sexual assault were wearing. The project was created in 2013 by Jen Brockman, the director of the University of Kansas Sexual Assault Prevention and Education Center, and Dr. Mary A. Wyandt, who oversees the programming at the rape education center at the University of Arkansas. It showcases clothing items that survivors were wearing at the time of their attack along with a statement about the item and the victimization. The variety of items and range of sizes, from children's to adult clothing, highlight the fact that many different people of all ages in all types of apparel are sexually victimized.

The aim of this exhibit is to draw attention to the fact that it is not what one wears that leads to victimization. In recognizing that people were victimized in regular, everyday, non-sexy clothing, those who visit this exhibit might see themselves in the survivor stories as those not "asking" to be victimized. The exhibit has been on other campuses as well (Vagianos, 2017). It is relevant in the #MeToo movement era as it shows that survivors of sexual violence are everywhere and can be anyone wearing anything.

Reactions to Sexual Abuse in Higher Education

Despite its frequent and prevalent occurrence, rape on college campuses was not labeled by public and government officials as a "social problem" until the late 1980s (Sloan & Fisher, 2011), and it was not until the 1990 Crime Awareness and Campus Security Act, renamed the Clery Act in 2000, that campus safety came to the forefront of federal legislation. The Clery Act requires colleges and universities throughout the United States to make crime incidents that occurred on campus publicly available for all to see and to report not only campus crime but also incidents that occur in residential and commercial areas near campus (Dobbs et al. 2009). The act includes a clause calling for punishment of institutions that do not participate. However, research has indicated that campus crime is often highly underreported due to confusion pertaining to jurisdiction, ineffective and inefficient organizational management, and student and offender confidentiality concerns (Wilcox et al., 2007).

The Clery Act was designed to decrease sexual victimization rates on college campuses by increasing public awareness. An unintended outcome was that institutions received pressure from the public to protect students and offer effective crime prevention programs (Sloan & Fisher, 2011). Yet while the Clery Act encourages the development of sexual violence policies and prevention programs, there are no specific requirements or descriptions of what such programs should look like (Vladutiu et al., 2011). The result is that each institution must design and implement its own programs and policies regarding sexual victimization.

In the wake of the #MeToo movement, more survivors are coming forward (Halper, 2018; McCrackin, 2019). A potentially positive outcome of this movement may be an overall cultural shift in the way that higher education handles sexual assault cases.

Case Study: List of Sexual Misconduct Cases

Julie Libarkin, director of Michigan State University's Geocognition Research Lab, collected and verified cases of sexual misconduct by staff, faculty, and administrators at universities across the nation. Case information is recorded in a Google document that can be viewed by anyone. In order to be included on Libarkin's list, the case must have public documentation as well as institutional information, such as findings by the university, settlements, and legal facts entered into record. The compilation contains over 700 substantiated cases of sexual misconduct. The earliest case on the list dates to 1917, while the majority are from the twenty-first century. Many of the individuals on the list are faculty members, but deans, vice presidents, and presidents of universities are also included. Many cases ended with the resignation of the individual; others resulted in firings; and the majority involved settlements between the university and the victim. In 2016 and 2018, 22 public institutions paid over $10.5 million dollars in 59 settlement cases that involved sexual misconduct (Flaherty, 2018).

This list, which has now been widely circulated, exposes what many universities would like to hide from view: that there are sexual predators who work at the university who are victimizing students, staff, and faculty. The #MeToo movement is giving momentum and attention to this list.

Programs to Combat Sexual Abuse in Higher Education

One of the ways that the #MeToo movement may be able to help reduce incidents of sexual abuse in higher education is through the programming that is offered. Since the passage of the Clery Act, many U.S. colleges and universities have implemented some type of rape prevention program to combat the growth of sexual abuse. One of the most common types of programs implemented is a risk reduction program. It aims at decreasing a woman's risk for victimization and includes tactics such as education and self-defense training (Lonsway et al., 2009).

Women are the targeted population for these projects because they are at the greatest risk for victimization. Ullman's research (2007) revealed that some self-defense and other forms of rape avoidance programs were inconsistent in lowering victimization rates. Yet, most evaluations have demonstrated decreases in victimization and revictimization from these types of initiatives, while other risk reduction program evaluations have found increases in self-protective behaviors (Gidycz et al., 2006; Orchowski et al., 2008). Orchowski and colleagues (2008) also found increases in women's resistance self-efficacy and assertive sexual communication behaviors after participating in a risk reduction program. Still, Gidycz and colleagues (2015) found that risk reduction programs are insufficient as the only resource to reduce campus sexual assault. Most survivors are victimized by someone whom they know and are unprepared to combat the assault. Even if potential targets learn self-defense and practice protective behaviors and proactive communication in dating, that does not mean that they will not be victimized. Many of the stories of survivors who have come out of the #MeToo movement illustrate that nothing could have prepared them for their victimization.

Most institutions have utilized a combination of rape prevention and risk reduction programs (Katz & Moore, 2013; Lonsway et al., 2009; Ullman, 2007). Rape prevention programs are designed to target and change the behaviors and rape-supportive attitudes of potential perpetrators (Lonsway et al., 2009). They have been moderately successful at altering attitudes regarding rape (Morrison et al., 2004). However, since they account for only a small number of programs, there have been few evaluations of them, making the results inconclusive (Lonsway et al., 2009). Research has shown that focusing sexual assault education efforts on those men who have been identified as "high risk" has also resulted in increased perpetration of sexual violence (Stephens & George, 2009).

Community-based prevention programs, focused on bystander education, are also recommended to help prevent sexual violence on college campuses. Numerous bystander education programs have emerged in the past few decades, including but not limited to Bringing in the Bystander (Banyard et al., 2004), SCREAM peer education (McMahon et al., 2014), and the Mentors in Violence Prevention Program (Katz et al., 2011). Any third-party witness (that is, not the victim or perpetrator) to a sexual assault is considered a bystander. When bystanders intervene in the situation on behalf of victims, they become responsive bystanders. The overarching goal of bystander education programs is to encourage pro-social attitudes and behaviors regarding sexual assault and to foster a safe communal environment. These programs generally include education on sexual assault prevalence rates and on high-risk situation indicators and strategies to assist the safety as a bystander.

Research on bystander education has shown that program participants improved in measures of rape myth acceptance and knowledge of sexual misconduct and showed significant increases in pro-social bystander attitudes, bystander efficacy, and self-reported bystander behaviors. The increases endured at 4-month and 12-month follow-ups (Banyard et al., 2007). One meta-analysis of in-person bystander education programs found a small but significant effect on rape-supportive attitudes and a decrease in rape proclivity (Katz & Moore, 2013). Another bystander intervention program evaluation resulted in less self-reported sexual aggression and an impact on men's perceptions of peer intervention when encountering others engaging in inappropriate behavior (Gidycz et al., 2011).

In 2011, Vladutiu and colleagues conducted a systematic review of eight literature review articles, published between 1993 and 2005, that examined dissertations and peer-reviewed journal articles evaluating the effectiveness of higher education–based sexual violence prevention programs in the United States. Their findings indicated that there were certain considerations that should be included for effective programming. For example, interventions targeting single-gender audiences are more effective at improving rape attitudes, behavioral intent, rape awareness, rape knowledge, rape empathy, and rape myth acceptance. Lectures, rape scenario videos, films, interactive dramas, role playing, presentations by rape survivors, workshops, and worksheets/brochures are some tools and strategies that have been used effectively to educate students about risk reduction strategies, gender-role socialization, sexual assault education, human sexuality, rape myths, rape deference, rape awareness, and/or self-defense.

In the era of #MeToo, it is important to consider how to best implement programs for education of all students, as well as faculty and staff. Much of the literature on prevention programs has focused on students as the targeted audience; however, focus should also be on the education of those who interact with students, as students may be at risk of harm from faculty and staff. Some universities, but not all, make training mandatory for all those employed by the university. More attention needs to be paid to the sexual misconduct of university faculty and employees and prevention of sexual assault of students, as well as staff, in future training efforts.

Conclusion

The women's liberation movement had a profound impact on situations involving sexual violence as the media began to depict such violence as a serious issue worthy of further discussion and helped to de-sensationalize some rape myths that existed in society. However, it is the #MeToo movement that has made sexual assault a topic of household discussion and arguably began a revolution in the way society sees sexual victimization. This has translated into the lived college student experience. #MeToo has made it possible for college students who have been victimized to voice their story without fear, as they now know that they are not alone.

A potential positive impact for students currently enrolled in college, as well as those entering higher education, is that the stigma related to sexual assault victimization is diminishing in response to the #MeToo movement because of the support that survivors are experiencing. That does not mean that there is not adversity for survivors or that all resistance has been eliminated, as was evidenced by the reaction of some to the high-profile testimony of Dr. Christine Blasey Ford and the eventual outcome of the confirmation of Justice Brett Kavanaugh to the U.S. Supreme Court in the fall of 2018. However, the many voices of survivors and the exposure of sexual assault and misconduct is a positive step toward bringing an end to the stigma. Young people currently in college will be the next generation of leaders and advocates; their understanding of sexual violence is arguably at a much deeper level as a result of the #MeToo movement and the awareness that it brings to victimization.

References

Banyard, V. L., Moynihan, M. M., & Plante, E. G. (2007). Sexual violence prevention through bystander education: An experimental evaluation. *Journal of Community Psychology, 35*(4), 463–481. https://doi.org/10.1002/jcop.20159

Banyard, V. L., Plante, E. G., & Moynihan, M. M. (2004). Bystander education: Bringing a broader community perspective to sexual violence prevention. *Journal of Community Psychology, 32*(1), 61–79. https://doi.org/10.1002/jcop.10078

Bazelon, E. (2015, May 29). Have we learned anything from the Columbia rape case? *New York Times Magazine.* https://www.nytimes.com/2015/05/29/magazine/have-we-learned-anything-from-the-columbia-rape-case.html

Black, M. C., Basile, K. C., Breiding, M. J., Smith, S. G., Walters, M. L., Merrick, M. T., Chen, J., & Stevens, M. R. (2011). *The national intimate partner and sexual violence survey (NISVS): 2010 summary report.* National Center for Injury Prevention and Control.

Cantor, D., Fisher, B., Chibnall, S., Townsend, R., Lee, H., Bruce, C., & Thomas, G. (2015). *Report on the AAU Campus Climate Survey on Sexual Assault and Sexual Misconduct.* Association of American Universities. http://www.aau.edu/uploadedFiles/AAU_Publications/AAU_Reports/Sexual_Assault_Campus_Survey/Report on the AAU Campus Climate Survey on Sexual Assault and Sexual Misconduct.pdf

Dobbs, R. R., Waid, C. A., & Shelley, T. O. (2009). Explaining fear of crime as fear of rape among college females: An examination of multiple campuses in the United States. *International Journal of Social Inquiry, 2*(2), 105–122.

Fisher, B., Cullen, F., & Turner, M. (2000). *The sexual victimization of college women.* National Institute of Justice.

Fisher, B. S., Daigle, L. E., & Cullen, F. T. (2010). What distinguishes single from recurrent sexual victims? The role of lifestyle-routine activities and first-incident characteristics. *Justice Quarterly, 27*(1), 102–129. https://doi.org/10.1080/07418820902763061

Flaherty, C. (2018, September 20). Beyond naming to shame. *Inside Higher Ed.* https://www.insidehighered.com/news/2018/09/20/why-one-academic-spends-hoursweek-putting-together-spreadsheet-documented

Frazier, P. A., & Haney, B. (1996). Sexual assault cases in the legal system: Police, prosecutor, and victim perspectives. *Law and Human Behavior, 20*(6), 607–628. https://doi.org/10.1007/BF01499234

Gidycz, C. A., & Hanson, K. (1995). A prospective analysis of the relationships among sexual assault experiences: An extension of previous findings. *Psychology of Women Quarterly, 19*(1), 5–29. https://doi.org/10.1111/j.1471-6402.1995.tb00276.x

Gidycz, C. A., Orchowski, L. M., & Berkowitz, A. D. (2011). Preventing sexual aggression among college men: An evaluation of a social norms and bystander intervention program. *Violence against Women, 17*(6), 720–742. https://doi.org/10.1177/1077801211409727

Gidycz, C. A., Orchowski, L. M., Probst, D. R., Edwards, K. M., Murphy, M., & Tansill, E. (2015). Concurrent administration of sexual assault prevention and risk reduction programming: Outcomes for women. *Violence against Women,* *21*(6), 780–800. https://doi.org/10.1177/1077801215576579

Gidycz, C. A., Rich, C. L., Orchowski, L., King, C., & Miller, A. K. (2006). The evaluation of a sexual assault self-defense and risk-reduction program for college women: A prospective study. *Psychology of Women Quarterly, 30*(2), 173–186. https://doi.org/10.1111/j.1471-6402.2006.00280.x

Gross, A., Winslett, A., Roberts, M., & Gohm, C. (2006). An examination of sexual violence against college women. *Violence against Women, 12*(3), 288–300. https://doi.org/10.1177/1077801205277358

Halper, J. D. (2018, December 14). In wake of #MeToo, Harvard Title IX office saw 56 percent increase in disclosures in 2018, per annual report. *Harvard Crimson.* https://www.thecrimson.com/article/2018/12/14/2018-title-ix-report/

Hegdahl, R. (2017). *Two years on, "Mattress Girl" is still a divisive issue for Columbia students.* The Tab. https://thetab.com/us/columbia/2017/02/20/mattress -girl-performance-columbia-4028

Herbert, T. B., & Dunkel-Schetter, C. (1992). Negative social reactions to victims: An overview of responses and their determinants. In L. Montada, S. Filipp, & M. J. Lerner (Eds.), *Life crises and experiences of loss in adulthood* (pp. 497–518). Lawrence Erlbaum Associates.

Hunter, D. (2005). Campus safety: What every college student needs to know. *Women in Business, 57*(2), 16–17.

James, S. E., Herman, J. L., Rankin, S., Keisling, M., Mottet, L., & Anafi, M. (2016). *The Report of the 2015 U.S. Transgender Survey.* National Center for Transgender Equality.

Katz, J., Heisterkamp, H. A., & Fleming, W. M. (2011). The social justice roots of the Mentors in Violence Prevention model and its application in a high school setting. *Violence against Women, 17*(6), 684–702. https://doi.org/10.1177 /1077801211409725

Katz, J., & Moore, J. (2013). Bystander education training for campus sexual assault prevention: An initial meta-analysis. In R. Maiuro (Ed.), *Perspectives on college sexual assault: Perpetrator, victim, and bystander* (pp. 183–196). Springer Publishing.

Kirkpatrick, C., & Kanin, E. (1957). Male sex aggression on a university campus. *American Sociological Review, 22*(1), 52–58. https://doi.org/10.2307/2088765

Koss, M. P., Gidycz, C. A., & Wisniewski, N. (1987). The scope of rape: Incidence and prevalence of sexual aggression and victimization in a national sample of higher education students. *Journal of Consulting and Clinical Psychology, 55*(2), 162–170. http://dx.doi.org/10.1037/0022–006X.55.2.162

Koss, M. P., & Oros, C. J. (1982). Sexual experiences survey: A research instrument investigating sexual aggression and victimization. *Journal of Consulting and Clinical Psychology, 50*(3), 455–457. http://dx.doi.org/10.1037/0022–006X.50.3.455

Krebs, C. P., Lindquist, C. H., Warner, T. A., Fisher, B. S., & Martin, S. L. (2009). College women's experiences with physically forced, alcohol or drug-enabled, and drug-facilitated sexual assault before and since entering college. *Journal of American College Health, 57*(6), 639–47. https://doi.org/10.3200/JACH.57.6.639–649

Kutner, M. (2016, April 25). Lawsuit against Columbia over "mattress protest" returns to court. *Newsweek.* https://www.newsweek.com/paul-nungesser -lawsuit-columbia-sulkowicz-452241

Lonsway, K. A., Banyard, V. L., Berkowitz, A. D., Gidycz, C. A., Katz, J. T., Koss, M. P., & Ullman, S. E. (2009, January). *Rape prevention and risk reduction: Review of the research literature for practitioners.* VAWnet: The National Online Resource Center on Violence against Women.

Maier, S. L. (2011). Sexual assault nurse examiners' perceptions of the revictimization of rape victims. *Journal of Interpersonal Violence, 27*(2), 287–315. https:// doi.org/10.1177/0886260511416476

McCrackin, C. (2019, February 13). Campus impacts of #MeToo. *Auburn Plainsman.* https://www.theplainsman.com/article/2019/02/campus-impacts-of-metoo

McMahon, S., Postmus, J. L., Warrener, C., & Koenick, R. A. (2014). Utilizing peer education theater for the primary prevention of sexual violence on college campuses. *Journal of College Student Development, 55*(1), 78–85. https://doi.org /10.1353/csd.2014.0001

Morrison, S., Hardison, J., Mathew, A., & O'Neil, J. (2004). *An evidence-based review of sexual assault preventive intervention programs.* Department of Justice.

Nathanson, R. (2014, December 1). How "Carry That Weight" is changing the conversation on campus sexual assault. *Rolling Stone.* http://www.rollingstone .com/politics/news/how-carry-that-weight-is-changing-the-conversation-on -campus-sexual-assault-20141201

Orchowski, L. M., Gidycz, C. A., & Raffle, H. (2008). Evaluation of a sexual assault risk reduction and self-defense program: A prospective analysis of a revised protocol. *Psychology of Women Quarterly, 32*(2), 204–218. https://doi.org /10.1111/j.1471–6402.2008.00425.x

Schwartz, M. D., & Pitts, V. L. (1995). Exploring a feminist routine activities approach to explaining sexual assault. *Justice Quarterly, 12*(1), 9–31. https://doi.org /10.1080/07418829500092551

Sinozich, S., & Langton, L. (2014, December). *Rape and sexual assault victimization among college-age females, 1995–2013.* Bureau of Justice Statistics. http://www. bjs.gov/content/pub/press/rsavcaf9513pr.cfm

Sloan, J., III, & Fisher, B. (2011). *The dark side of the ivory tower: Campus crime as a social problem.* Cambridge University Press.

Stephens, K. A., & George, W. H. (2009). Rape prevention with college men: Evaluating risk status. *Journal of Interpersonal Violence, 24*(6), 996–1013. https:// dx.doi.org/10.1177/0093854806297117

Tolentino, J. (2018, February 12). Is there a smarter way to think about sexual assault on campus? *New Yorker*. https://www.newyorker.com/magazine/2018/02/12/is-there-a-smarter-way-to-think-about-sexual-assault-on-campus

Ullman, S. E. (1996) Social reactions, coping strategies, and self–blame attributions in adjustment to sexual assault. *Psychology of Women Quarterly, 20*(4), 505–526. https://doi.org/10.1111/j.1471–6402.1996.tb00319.x

Ullman, S. E. (2007). A 10-year update of "Review and Critique of Empirical Studies of Rape Avoidance." *Criminal Justice and Behavior, 34*(3), 411–429. https://doi.org/10.1177/0093854806297117

Vagianos, A. (2017, September 4). *Art exhibit powerfully answers the question "What were you wearing?"* HuffPost. https://www.huffingtonpost.com/entry/powerful-art-exhibit-powerfully-answers-the-question-what-were-you-wearing_us_59baddd2e4b02da0e1405d2a

Vladutiu, C. J., Martin, S. L., & Macy, R. J. (2011). College- or university-based sexual assault prevention programs: A review of program outcomes, characteristics, and recommendations. *Trauma, Violence, & Abuse, 12*(2), 67–86. https://doi.org/10.1177/1524838010390708

White, J., & Smith, P. Hall. (2009). Covariation in the use of physical and sexual intimate partner aggression among adolescent and college-age men: A longitudinal analysis. *Violence against Women, 15*(1), 24–43. https://doi.org/10.1177/1077801208328345

Wilcox, P., Jordan, C. E., & Pritchard, A. J. (2007). A multidimensional examination of campus safety victimization, perceptions of danger, worry about crime, and precautionary behavior among college women in the post-Clery era. *Crime & Delinquency, 53*(2), 219–254. https://doi.org/10.1177/0097700405283664

2. Finding the Strength to Speak Out, Waiting to Be Heard: #MeToo on College Campuses

Nicole Bedera

According to the most commonly cited statistics, one in five women will be sexually assaulted during their undergraduate careers (Cantor et al., 2019; Krebs et al., 2007). This is not new—the rate of sexual assault on college campuses has not changed much over the past 60 years (Adams-Curtis & Forbes, 2004)—but increased attention from the federal government and the #MeToo movement might be giving college campuses the push they need to do something about that statistic.

It is a strange time to consider the promise of #MeToo for college campuses. As I write, the Trump administration—and specifically the Department of Education, with Secretary Betsy DeVos at its helm—threatens to undo many of the gains made for survivors on college campuses in the past ten years. Soon after assuming leadership, DeVos and her administration reversed the legal guidance on Title IX instated by the Obama administration, which had brought campus sexual assault into the national spotlight. More recently, the DeVos administration released a proposed policy (Department of Education, 2018) that strengthens rights for those accused of sexual misconduct in ways that defy judicial precedence and would allow universities to place new (and perhaps insurmountable) barriers in the way of survivors seeking justice. Due to the reversal and the proposed policy change, the future of survivors on college campuses is uncertain and the legal landscape tumultuous.

Still, something about the chaos surrounding issues of campus sexual violence is clarifying. It allows us to see the ideological shifts over the past decade that endure in the face of a formidable challenge. Despite strong pressure from the federal government for universities to revert back to ignoring the realities of sexual violence on campus, more students than ever are reporting sexual mal-treatment (Musu-Gillette et al., 2016), and the conversation about how best to support students coming forward is robust and compassionate. Most importantly, in the face of losing their rights on campus, thousands of students and alumni have taken to social media to share their stories of campus sexual violence with the tagline #MeToo. Regardless of the political landscape, we are better equipped than ever to end sexual violence on campus—all we have to do is listen to the survivors speaking up.

Why College Campuses?

At first, it can be hard to understand why college sexual violence gets so much attention. Activists and politicians focus on rates of sexual violence on college campuses, but there is reason to believe that women who attend college are at a lower risk of sexual violence over the course of their lifetimes compared to women who never step foot on campus (Axinn et al., 2018). To be certain, the high rate of violence off campus should not diminish the experiences of students. However, there is another reason sexual violence that occurs in a college context deserves our attention: universities create environments that permit—or perhaps even encourage—sexual violence to occur.

It is impossible to understand college sexual violence without considering the role of university organizations in its commission. The majority of those who commit college sexual assault are not random perpetrators—they are easily traced back to specific university organizations and practices that support them. These organizations are single-sex and male-dominated, such as fraternities and men's athletic teams. Their members perpetrate sexual violence at much higher rates than other men on campus (Foubert et al., 2007; Franklin et al., 2012; Young et al., 2016). They also intentionally exclude women and embrace traditional no-tions of masculinity, including, at times, the specific encouragement of violence against women (Martin, 2016; Sanday, 2007). While we might expect universities to decry or even abolish organizations so clearly tied to violence, they do the op-posite. Masculine organizations remain powerful on campus and are permitted to control many social resources (for example, access to alcohol, party spaces, university reputation) without substantial oversight by universities themselves, enabling sexual violence to occur with little repercussion (Armstrong et al., 2006; Wade, 2017a). These organizations (and the violence they perpetrate) are further empowered through seemingly benign university traditions such as encour-aging alumni donations, which are most reliably collected from male alumni who remember their days of fraternities and football fondly (Martin, 2016). The source of college sexual violence—particularly in a large university environment—is relatively clear, but historically, little has been done to address it. That is, until recently.

A History of Title IX and Campus Sexual Violence

Campus sexual violence first entered the national discourse in the 1980s. At that time, stories of sexual abuse at our most prestigious institutions of higher education splashed the covers of magazines and the front pages of newspapers. Spurred by innovations in survey methodology (Koss & Gidycz, 1985; Koss & Oros, 1982), researchers offered up data supporting what feminist organizations had known for years: sexual violence was a common occurrence in the lives of young women, and college women were among the most vulnerable (Brownmiller, 1975; New York Radical Feminists, 1974).

The efforts in the 1980s did not succeed in abolishing sexual assault on campus. After facing immense backlash, the issue slowly retreated from the public consciousness, with many Americans forgetting about the realities of sexual violence at universities altogether. However, there were still notable gains on college campuses that resulted from feminist activism in the 1980s. Most obviously, the definitions of sexual assault and harassment expanded in federal law, aligning more closely with women's experiences of sexual violence and paving the way for more college women to name their maltreatment. Congress passed the Violence against Women Act, which funded women's centers on college campuses that provided survivors with direct services like counseling. Colleges also became beholden to the Jeanne Clery Act, which obliges universities to be accountable to their students about the crime that occurs on campus and in the surrounding communities. Best known for requiring universities to report statistics relating to campus crime, the Clery Act also compelled universities to instill procedures for sexual violence prevention and response. These gains laid the foundation for the discussion we are having about college sexual assault today. But, 1980s feminists did not stop there. Even after the first wave of activism to combat campus sexual assault had come to its end in the public eye, a small handful of persistent actors continued to fight to understand and stop the violence that occurred.

All of these changes were central in providing the legal and organizational groundwork necessary for student activists to bring campus sexual violence back into the national spotlight in the 2010s. As chronicled most prominently in *The Hunting Ground* (Dick & Ziering, 2016), student activists demanded their universities take sexual violence seriously through lawsuits filed with the U.S. Department of Education. To do so, activists depended on a modern interpretation of a law that predated the public discussion of campus sexual violence: Title IX.

Title IX is an educational amendment to the Civil Rights Act. Originally passed in 1972, it states in its entirety, "No person in the United States shall, on the basis of sex, be excluded from participation in, be denied the benefits of, or be subjected to discrimination under any education program or activity receiving Federal financial assistance" (20 U.S.C. Sec. 1681, Title IX, 1972). Prior to 2013, the law had been applied primarily to desegregation of public universities on the basis of gender and to equal representation of men's and women's sports across all levels of public education. But based on changes to the definition of sexual harassment following feminist activism in the 1980s, there was reason to believe epidemic levels of sexual violence on campus could constitute a "hostile environment" for women and, accordingly, meet the standards of sex-based discrimination prohibited through Title IX.

Bolstering student activists' case was a short document released by the Department of Education during the Obama presidency—what has come to be known as the "Dear Colleague Letter" of 2011. Drawing upon the Clery Act, the Dear Colleague Letter made the above argument explicit and informed universities that they could sacrifice their access to federal funding if they did not take appropriate measures to prevent and respond to sexual assault on campus. In short, the Dear Colleague Letter unequivocally labeled university inaction to campus sexual assault a form of sex-based discrimination.

The argument used by activists and the Obama administration was well made. Researchers have connected sexual violence to a number of negative outcomes in female college students. Sexual assault survivors exhibit lower academic performance and a higher risk of dropping out (Jordan et al., 2014). In fact, one study found that a history of sexual assault is the best-known predictor for women's college GPAs (Baker et al., 2016). The toll on academics is easy to understand when the psychological impact of adult sexual trauma is so severe. Victims of sexual assault face higher rates of depression, anxiety, sleep problems, sexual problems, and dissociation. These risks are even more pronounced when their universities minimize the severity of their trauma or refuse to take proper measures to address sexual violence on campus (Smith & Freyd, 2013, 2014, 2017).

In the early 2010s, university inaction regarding sexual assault was by far the most common response, and it still might be. But as student survivors began to realize how common these neglectful experiences were, they organized. Through groups like Know Your IX and End Rape on Campus, student survivors across the country shared their stories with one another and taught each other how to demand more through filing complaints with the Department of Education (Dick & Ziering, 2016). In doing so, they caught the attention of high-ranking White House officials. In 2014, the Obama administration created the White House Task

Force to Protect Students from Sexual Assault. A few months later, the Obama administration released more comprehensive guidelines for universities to respond to campus sexual violence. At the same time, it announced federal investigation into 50 schools based on the complaints filed by student activists. Since then, well over 200 colleges and universities have been investigated by the federal government for failing to meet the needs of student survivors, as legally mandated by Title IX. Universities have responded rapidly. Over the next few years, many implemented affirmative consent policies, added preventive education on sexual violence, offered resources to student survivors, and more clearly articulated their policies for adjudicating claims of sexual misconduct (Badke et al., 2016).

The actions of the Obama administration—and the universities making changes in its wake—were not without controversy. In 2014, few people knew that campus sexual violence rates were so high, and to them the Obama administration's actions felt like an overreaction. Even those confronted with the numbers were reluctant to believe them or take them seriously, often rationalizing young men's sexual predation as part of a "normal" college experience or blaming young women for their own sexual victimization through vilifications of "hookup culture." The Obama administration's embrace of affirmative consent was particularly controversial, leading critics to try to delegitimize collegiate definitions of rape. They accused women of making "false reports" of sexual assault, even when the encounters they reported clearly violated their university's sexual misconduct policy. These critiques resonated with Betsy DeVos, whose intention to roll back the advances in Title IX policy became central in discussions of her confirmation as the secretary of the Department of Education for the Trump administration.

Quickly after taking office, DeVos's administration rescinded every guideline the Obama administration had implemented to address campus sexual assault, including the Dear Colleague Letter of 2011. The DeVos administration has also proposed its own policy about the management of sexual misconduct, which is overwhelmingly focused on protecting men from allegations of sexual violence. While many universities have not yet changed their sexual misconduct policies to align with the DeVos administration's goals, the implication of the rollback was clear: no one was looking anymore. The pressure for universities to do right by sexual assault survivors was lifted. As of early 2019, it is unclear what the future will hold for campus sexual assault survivors. Will universities continue to make strides to end violence on their campuses? Will they support survivors to ensure they have an equal access to education? In the current political moment, it is unlikely that government actors will be the ones making these decisions. Instead, we turn to student activists and the power they harness through social movements like #MeToo.

#MeToo and the Future of Campus Activism

It is easy to imagine student activism around sexual violence coming to a standstill in this particular historical moment. Instead of the united fight for survivors' rights we might have imagined five years ago, most conversations about Title IX now revolve around the rights of students accused of sexual misconduct. In these discussions, survivors are often forgotten altogether as their right to an education free from gender discrimination is sacrificed to push for unprecedented protections of the accused, under the guise of "due process."[1] But student survivors are not giving up.

Perhaps emboldened by #MeToo—the movement that took hold mere weeks before the DeVos administration began to formally revoke campus survivors' rights—student survivors are speaking out. They are demanding not only recognition for the trauma they have experienced but accountability for their perpetrators and the accommodations necessary to minimize the interruption a sexual assault can cause to an education. They might not always be successful in their pursuits, but they are not backing down. This is a marked changed from when I began studying sexual violence in 2013. At that time, the survivors I spoke with often had never told anyone else about the violence they had endured. Today, most participants in my research have told nearly all of the important people in their lives about their experiences, and many publicly identify as survivors.

In the sections to follow, I tell the stories of two women I have interviewed since #MeToo went viral. They participated in two separate studies I conducted on campus sexual assault, and while their circumstances are quite different from each other, their stories have a few key traits in common. They both live in states where Trump took the majority of votes in the 2016 presidential election and support for the actions of his administration remains high, including the rollback of protections for student survivors. They also both chose to speak out about their experiences with sexism anyway, specifically citing #MeToo in their decision to tell their stories.

Case Study: Chelsea

When I met "Chelsea," she was 31 years old. Her college days were behind her, and she wondered if it was appropriate for her to take up a spot in my study that could be reserved for someone younger and whose experiences were more recent. Despite the time that had passed since her sexual assault, she was nervous to talk about it. Throughout our interview, she rewarded herself with bites of a baked good she had brought along for comfort whenever she made it through an emotionally taxing portion of her story. Once our formal interview was over, I asked Chelsea what had made her want to participate in the study. Her answer was simple: #MeToo.

#MeToo brought to the surface just how much sexual assault and harassment had affected her since puberty. The day we met, Chelsea was angry—not just about her assault but about a decade of poor treatment by men with misogynistic views of women. With the public discourse on sexual harassment now surrounding her, it was impossible to ignore.

> Over the last ten years, I'm kind of rolling along, picking up all of these experiences of street harassment and sexual harassment at work and mansplaining and groping and cat-calling and thinking about rape and [victim blaming] and all those men [who did those things]. And now we get to a point where maybe . . . I started thinking about how that's all related and I've grown into this like—I honestly describe it as a simmering rage that's always in me.

For years, this rage Chelsea described had bubbled out at what seemed like random times. In the #MeToo moment, it had a space, a purpose, and an explanation. She recounted multiple conversations in which she had confronted men who had doubted her or blamed her for the abuse she had experienced. Using #MeToo, she had a framework to address her concerns and tie them to something undeniably larger than her. It allowed for exploration of her undergraduate sexual trauma and legitimized the anger that persisted into her thirties.

Case Study: Megan

Women encountering sexual maltreatment since the #MeToo moment also invoke the movement in finding their voices and demanding action—often quite quickly. This was certainly the case for "Megan," a 20-year-old college senior I interviewed a year after #MeToo went viral. Megan had experienced race- and gender-based harassment and threats from the repairman for her apartment complex. In the immediate aftermath of the encounter, Megan was shocked to her core. She did not have the language to understand what had happened to her and was unsure of how seriously she should take it, but all of that changed when she recounted the episode to her neighbor who directly connected her experience to #MeToo. In her words:

> [Immediately afterward,] I sort of start to explain what happened to [my neighbor] and he's like, "Oh my god. That's unacceptable. You need to call the landlord now and have this man fired. This is what the #MeToo movement is all about, like you really just need to advocate for yourself in this situation." And I was thinking, "Oh, like it's not a big deal." Like I was trying to sweep it under the rug. . . . [But after what my neighbor said,] I called my landlord.

In the weeks to follow, Megan did advocate for herself. She reported what had happened to her landlord and the police. She also sought resources from her campus's victim advocacy center, which connected her to even more resources, including a counselor, and assisted with academic adjustments to help her succeed in school and with temporary housing to help her feel safe. While Megan hardly found justice—both her landlord and the police largely brushed aside her concerns—she did find empowerment, which not only minimized the effect of the harassment on her academics but also led her to fight for her rights as a woman of color in other arenas in her life.

When I asked Megan about the impact that victim advocacy had had on her life, she told me in detail about the way she had previously felt diminished at work by the men around her who regularly questioned her authority or made inappropriate comments about her. After finding empowerment through the resources offered to her by the campus victim advocates, though, Megan confronted her coworkers—and did so successfully. Even just her ability to stand up for herself made Megan feel more powerful:

> I learned extremely valuable lessons about empowered communication and self-advocacy [that have] already bled into my confidence and efficiency in the workplace, where I have already been grappling with some sexist undertones from my colleagues and superiors. . . . I'm definitely feeling more control in my life where I felt like I was being squashed by men in the last two years.

For Megan, #MeToo was the vehicle through which she found her own feminist empowerment. She came to recognize that she did not need to tolerate sexism in any form, even if others might try to cast it as "not a big deal." She found her voice, and when she used it, she discovered that sometimes other people listened.

Concluding Thoughts on #MeToo and Ending College Sexual Violence

Chelsea's and Megan's stories are inspiring, but they are incomplete. While #MeToo has accomplished a lot for women on an individual level—and many of them use those personal achievements to bring a feminist perspective to their experiences of college sexual violence—there has yet to be a #MeToo reckoning at an institutional level that will shape colleges and universities for years to come. #MeToo has hardly brought justice to survivors of campus sexual violence, and it certainly has not ended sexual violence in the college context. To do so will require picking up where feminists, activists, and the Obama administration left off and radically changing the way universities regard women on campus.

Research on college sexual violence—especially from a structural perspective—is still a developing field, but scholars have identified many of the causes of the violence that occurs on campus and have ideas about how to eliminate them.

Central to the most compelling research is taking on high-status, hyper-masculine organizations like fraternities and men's athletic teams, as well as eliminating gender inequality more broadly. Scholars who study the sources of sexual violence have publicly called on universities to ban fraternities (Wade, 2017b), and some campuses, such as Middlebury College, have done so (Schonfeld, 2014). In general, there is compelling evidence that promoting gender equality—and, more explicitly, feminism—on campus is good for student survivors (Boyle et al., 2017). However, most scholars and activists recognize that gender revolution, while an admirable and essential goal, is a long-term endeavor.

There are a few practical methods of preventing and appropriately responding to sexual violence at universities that any college can implement in the interim while also working toward creating a more gender-egalitarian campus. While historically college campuses have placed the burden of sexual assault prevention on women (Bedera & Nordmeyer, 2015), bystander intervention is an empirically validated approach that views the prevention of sexual violence as the responsibility of the entire campus community (Cares et al., 2015; for a review, see DeGue et al., 2014). According to this paradigm, people can stop sexual violence occurring in social contexts like parties or dorms through being aware of their surroundings and actively interfering when they observe someone using violence or coercion. These interventions can be small or large, ranging from physically standing between an aggressor and a potential victim, to pretending to spill a drink on the aggressor to create a diversion that will allow the potential victim to escape, to calling the police (McMahon & Banyard, 2012).

There are also innovations in prevention programming targeting women. "Flip the Script" is a prevention program developed by feminist researchers who have found that teaching women tactics to resist unwanted sexual advances while simultaneously providing education on feminism and challenging broader patriarchal norms reduced sexual victimization significantly among program participants (Senn et al., 2015; Senn & Forrest, 2016). Furthermore, the program boosted college women's confidence and decreased their fear of types of sexual assault that are particularly unlikely (such as stranger rape). As a result, women in Flip the Script felt more comfortable doing everyday things that can cause women stress, such as walking home from class after dark. Both bystander intervention programs and Flip the Script help college women to bear less of the burden of ineffective sexual assault prevention while also encouraging students to rethink the patriarchal structures that have placed that inappropriate burden on the shoulders of women in the first place. In short, even effective short-term solutions have a hidden curriculum of making campuses more gender-egalitarian.

It is also crucial that universities use a trauma-informed and survivor-centered approach when responding to sexual violence that occurs. Universities' unwillingness to hold perpetrators of sexual assault accountable for their actions can be just as traumatizing for survivors as the sexual assault itself (Smith & Freyd, 2013), exacerbating the toll that campus sexual violence takes on survivors and women throughout the campus community who feel undervalued by their universities. Despite the popular notion that universities have no choice but to dissatisfy (or retraumatize) survivors seeking their assistance, there is compelling evidence that universities can provide effective support for survivors that can foster healing, so long as they validate survivors' experiences through their words and actions (Ahrens et al., 2009). There has been a temptation on college campuses to put all administrative energy toward sexual violence prevention, but these efforts will have only limited success so long as universities send a mixed message that, despite a preference for a violence-free campus, sexual violence that occurs will not be taken seriously.

Regardless of the approach a campus takes, it is crucial that it centers the voices of student survivors. In the #MeToo moment, they are speaking up, and we should listen. The most successful reforms to university policy and practice have come from ideas proposed by student survivors, and that should come as no surprise. There is no one with more expertise about the impact of college sexual violence than its victims.

Note

1. Due process concerns do have a place in discussions of Title IX, but the DeVos administration's conception of due process is wholly inappropriate and potentially illegal. For a discussion of appropriate due process protections for those accused of campus sexual misconduct, see Triplett (2012).

References

20 U.S.C. Sec. 1681, Title IX (1972).

Adams-Curtis, L. E., & Forbes, G. B. (2004). College women's experiences of sexual coercion: A review of cultural, perpetrator, victim, and situational variables. *Trauma, Violence & Abuse, 5*(2), 91–122.

Ahrens, C. E., Cabra, G., & Abeling, S. (2009). Healing or hurtful: Sexual assault survivors' interpretations of social reactions from support providers. *Psychology of Women Quarterly, 33*(1), 81–94.

Armstrong, E., Hamilton, L., & Sweeney, S. (2006). Sexual assault on campus: A multilevel, integrative approach to party rape. *Social Problems, 52,* 483–499.

Axinn, W. G., Bardos, M. E., & West, B. T. (2018). General population estimates of the association between college experience and the odds of forced intercourse. *Social Science Research, 70,* 131–143.

Badke, L. K., Porter, K. B., Garrick, J. R., Armstrong, E. A., & Levitsky, S. L. (2016). *Compliance or rhetoric? Are campus sexual misconduct policies fulfilling Title IX legal obligations?* Association for the Study of Higher Education Annual Conference, Columbus, Ohio.

Baker, M. R., Frazier, P. A., Greer, C., Paulsen, J. A., Howard, K., Meredith, L. N., Anders, S. L., & Shallcross, S. L. (2016). Sexual victimization history predicts academic performance in college women. *Journal of Counseling Psychology, 63*(6), 685–692.

Bedera, N., & Nordmeyer, K. (2015). "Never go out alone": An analysis of college rape prevention tips. *Sexuality & Culture, 19*(3), 533–542.

Boyle, K. M., Barr, A., & Clay-Warner, J. (2017). The effect of feminist mobilization and women's status on universities' reporting of rape. *Journal of School Violence, 16*(3), 317–330.

Brownmiller, S. (1975). *Against our will: Men, women, and rape.* Fawcett Books.

Cantor, D., Fisher, B., Chibnall, S., Harps, S., Townsend, R., Thomas, G., Lee, H., Kranz, V., Herbison, R., & Madden, K. (2019). *Report on the AAU campus climate survey of sexual assault and sexual misconduct.* Association of American Universities. https://www.aau.edu/sites/default/files/AAU-Files/Key-Issues/Campus-Safety/FULL_2019_Campus_Climate_Survey.pdf

Cares, A. C., Banyard, V. L., Moynihan, M. M., Williams, L. M., Potter, S. J., & Stapleton, J. G. (2015). Changing attitudes about being a bystander to violence: Translating an in-person sexual violence prevention program to a new campus. *Violence against Women, 2*(12), 165–187.

DeGue, S., Valle, L. A., Holt, M. K., Massetti, G. M., Matjasko, J. L., & Tharp, A. T. (2014). A systematic review of primary prevention strategies for sexual violence perpetration. *Aggression & Violent Behavior, 19*(4), 346–362.

Department of Education. (2018). Nondiscrimination on the basis of sex in education programs or activities receiving federal financial assistance. *Federal Register, 83*(230), 61462–61499.

Dick, K., & Ziering, A. (2016). *The hunting ground: The inside story of sexual assault on American college campuses.* Hot Books.

Foubert, J. D., Newberry, J. T. & Tatum, J. (2007). Behavior differences seven months later: Effects of a rape prevention program. *NASPA Journal, 44*(4), 728–749.

Franklin, C., Bouffard, L. A., & Pratt, T. C. (2012). Sexual assault on college campus: Fraternity affiliation, male peer support, and low self-control. *Criminal Justice and Behavior, 39*(11), 1457–1480.

Jordan, C. E., Combs, J. L., & Smith, G. T. (2014). An exploration of sexual victimization and academic performance among college women. *Trauma, Violence & Abuse, 15*(3), 191–200.

Koss, M. P., & Gidycz, C. A. (1985). Sexual experiences survey: Reliability and validity. *Journal of Consulting and Clinical Psychology, 53*(3), 422–423.

Koss, M. P., & Oros, C. J. (1982). Sexual experiences survey: A research instrument investigating sexual aggression and victimization. *Journal of Consulting and Clinical Psychology, 50*(3), 455–457.

Krebs, C. P., Lindquist, C. H., Warner, T. D., Fisher, B. S., & Martin, S. L. (2007). *The Campus Sexual Assault (CSA) study.* U.S. Department of Justice.

Martin, P. Y. (2016). The rape prone culture of academic contexts: Fraternities and athletics. *Gender & Society, 30*(1), 30–43.

McMahon, S., & Banyard, V. L. (2012). Where can I help? A conceptual framework for the prevention of sexual violence through bystander intervention. *Trauma, Violence & Abuse, 13*(1), 3–14.

Musu-Gillette, L., Ke Wang, A. Z., Khan, J., & Oudekerk, B. (2016). *Indicators of school crime and safety: 2016.* U.S. Department of Education and U.S. Department of Justice.

New York Radical Feminists. (1974). *Rape: The first sourcebook for women* (N. Connell & C. Wilson, Eds.). Times Minor.

Sanday, P. R. (2007). *Fraternity gang rape: Sex, brotherhood, and privilege on campus.* New York University Press.

Schonfeld, Z. (2014, March 10). Inside the colleges that killed frats for good. *Newsweek.* https://www.newsweek.com/inside-colleges-killed-frats-good-231346

Senn, C. Y., Eliasziw, M., Barata, P. C., Thurston, W. E., Newby-Clark, I. R., Radtke, H. L., & Hobden, K. L. (2015). Efficacy of a sexual assault resistance program for university women. *New England Journal of Medicine, 372* 2326–2335.

Senn, C. Y., & Forrest, A. (2016). "And then one night when I went to class . . .": The impact of sexual assault bystander intervention workshops incorporated in academic courses. *Psychology of Violence, 6*(4), 607–618.

Smith, C. P., & Freyd, J. J. (2013). Dangerous safe havens: Institutional betrayal exacerbates sexual trauma. *Journal of Traumatic Stress, 26,* 119–124.

Smith, C. P., & Freyd, J. J. (2014). Institutional betrayal. *American Psychologist, 69,* 575–587.

Smith, C. P., & Freyd, J. J. (2017). Insult, then injury: Interpersonal and institutional betrayal linked to health and dissociation. *Journal of Aggression, Maltreatment & Trauma, 26*(10), 1117–1131.

Triplett, M. R. (2012). Sexual assault on college campuses: Seeking the appropriate balance between due process and victim protection. *Duke Law Journal, 62*(2), 487–527.

Wade, L. (2017a). *American hookup: The new culture of sex on campus.* W. W. Norton.

Wade, L. (2017b, May 19). Why colleges should get rid of fraternities for good. *Time Magazine.* https://time.com/4784875/fraternities-timothy-piazza/

Young, B. R., Desmarais, S. L., Baldwin, J. A., & Chandler, R. (2016). Sexual coercion practices among undergraduate male recreational athletes, intercollegiate athletes, and non-athletes. *Violence against Women, 23*(7), 795–812.

II. Political and Religious Institutions

3. "Pestminster" Politics: Local and International Dimensions of the #MeToo Movement

Amina Zarrugh

In 1991, the American public witnessed vociferous debates about sexual harassment unfold in the Senate confirmation hearings for Clarence Thomas's nomination to the Supreme Court. The allegations of sexual harassment by Thomas remained unknown until a private FBI report with the accuser, Anita Hill, were leaked to the press. Hill had worked for Thomas in the Department of Education and the Equal Employment Opportunity Commission, where he was her supervisor in both working environments. Hill alleged that Thomas had repeatedly pursued her romantically and discussed in explicit detail sexual acts that he had viewed in pornographic films involving sexual intercourse between women and animals, in addition to rape scenes. The exacting details of these sexually explicit comments by Thomas were requested of Hill during her questioning by members of the Senate Judiciary Committee in a hearing process that lasted—uninterrupted—for approximately eight hours (Viebeck, 2018). Hill agreed to and passed a polygraph test, and her credibility was corroborated by Angela Wright and Rose Jourdain, who claimed to have knowledge that Thomas had made sexual comments to other women in his working environment (Shin & Casey, 2017).

Thomas, in defense of the allegations against him, denied the accusations that he had sexually pursued Hill or initiated conversations with her that related to sex in any way. He referred to the entire process as a "circus" and a "national disgrace," adding,

And from my standpoint, as a black American, it is a high-tech lynching for uppity blacks who in any way deign to think for themselves, to do for themselves, to have different ideas, and it is a message that unless you kowtow to an old order, this is what will happen to you. You will be lynched, destroyed, caricatured by a committee of the U.S. Senate rather than hung from a tree. (Committee on the Judiciary, 1991, pp. 157–158)

The explicit imagery of racial violence in the hearing process influenced the debate on whether Hill, who is also African American, had made convincing allegations or whether racial discrimination was the impetus for the hearing and the FBI investigation that followed from the accusations (Jordan, 1992).

As the credibility of both Hill and Thomas were carefully weighed in the public and media, the hearings inaugurated a national conversation about what defines sexual harassment, what constitutes reliable evidence, and what characterizes private and public matters. A preeminent site for the development of law, the arena of politics faces special scrutiny as it relates to matters of sexual ethics. A central dimension of politics is the circulation of power across social groups, such as between men and women, among racial and ethnic groups, and between social classes, among others. The salience of social group belonging was made especially clear during the Hill and Thomas hearings, where gender and race dynamics occupied a central place in how the hearings were conducted, mediated, and consumed. Power inequality across such social groups of belonging, which is an enduring feature of political institutions, is an essential and key aspect of sexual abuse.

In this chapter, I address the history of sexual abuse in politics, focusing specifically on how gender and sexuality have been mobilized during political conquest and governance globally. I then provide an overview of how feminist political philosophers, political scientists, and sociologists have analyzed the role of gender and sexuality within state institutions in order to make legible how sexual abuse unfolds through the everyday workings of politics. Last, I consider two cases of sexual abuse in politics brought to light by the #MeToo movement, which has reintroduced a national (and, ultimately, international) conversation and debate regarding sexual abuse in politics that remained far from finished following the Anita Hill and Clarence Thomas hearings in the early 1990s.

History of Sexual Abuse in Politics

In his study of politics and state formation, sociologist Max Weber (1946) defined the state as "a human community that (successfully) claims *the monopoly of the legitimate use of physical force* within a given territory" (p. 78). Among the significant features that social scientists and theorists could identify as most important to defining the state, Weber emphasized territory and violence. The latter specifically invites us to consider how violence—whether physical, emotional, psychological, or sexual—occupies a central place in the development of states and the organization of politics.

One mode of violence enacted by states has been sexual violence, often in pursuit of expanding colonization or imperial influence (McClintock, 1995; Nagel, 2003; Smith, 2005). Sexual violence has been utilized as a political tool of war for centuries and connects to the state's capacity for violence as well as to gendered notions of nationalism (MacKinnon, 2007a; Nagel, 1998; Yuval-Davis, 1997). Indeed, the nation is often personified in the form of a woman around whom men must mobilize and militarize to protect her "honor" and "sanctity" (Nagel, 1998). In this way, nationalism and politics cannot be disconnected from what Nagel refers to as "ethnosexual connections," or the significance of race and sex to the development of a political community. The social and political systems of patriarchy, which includes historically strict familial control over marital arrangements and family formation, often place undue burden on women to maintain the cultural boundaries of the nation (Yuval-Davis, 1997). Accordingly, their intimate relationships and reproductive capacities are politicized in numerous ways and render them vulnerable to particular forms of sexual violence and degradation, especially during periods of conflict.

With regard to the United States, Andrea Smith (2005) has argued that violence enacted during the colonial period and its extension in the form of contemporary state violence has impacted indigenous women in particular. In contrast to scholars who claim that patriarchy is the central source of violence against women, Smith maintained that it is the intersection of race and empire that illuminates the violence endured by indigenous women in particular:

> Rape as "nothing more or less" than a tool of patriarchal control undergirds the philosophy of the white-dominated women's antiviolence movement. . . . If sexual violence is not simply a tool of patriarchy but also a tool of colonialism and racism, then entire communities of color are the victims of sexual violence. (pp. 7–8)

From this perspective, state violence, and the political projects it advances, occurs at the intersection of race, gender, and colonial or imperial control.

By approaching questions of state violence from intersectional perspectives, we can observe how and why indigenous and Black women, specifically, in the United States have been especially vulnerable to violence (Collins, 1998; Crenshaw, 1991). Within indigenous communities, women during and since the colonial period have endured sexual violence and faced gender-specific adverse health conditions, including miscarriages and fetal abnormalities in pregnancy, caused by systemic environmental racism, including the location of hazardous materials close to or on reservation land (Smith, 2005). In a similar vein, Black women endured sexual abuse by plantation owners during the period of the trans-Atlantic slave trade and in the present day are still disproportionately likely to experience sexual harassment and abuse owing in part to centuries-long racist tropes and institutionalized expectations about Black women's sexual voracity and inviolability (Crenshaw, 1992).

In addition to these repressive forms of violence, states have historically developed policies to control women's bodily autonomy by policing reproduction (Yuval-Davis, 1997). In the United States during the early twentieth century, the eugenics movement—deemed a socially "progressive" movement to help rid society of those individuals regarded as "feebleminded," as a public health measure—was advanced by prominent political figures and social scientists who developed tenuous alliances with proponents of birth control, such as Margaret Sanger (Roberts, 1997). Many working-class white members of society were forcibly sterilized without their consent in order to inhibit their reproduction in accordance with the Supreme Court ruling of *Buck v. Bell*, which nationally legalized sterilization. However, many eugenicists took particular interest in curbing the fertility of Black women. This approach, according to Roberts (1997), rendered birth control "a means of controlling a population rather than a means of increasing women's reproductive autonomy. Birth control in America was defined from the movement's inception in terms of race and could never be properly understood apart from race again" (p. 80). More permanent fertility control measures were circulated in neighborhoods densely populated by Black Americans, and some states in the mid-twentieth century proposed legislation limiting economic welfare payments to mothers who did not curtail their fertility through medical interventions. Policy controversies related to the sterilization and circumscription of fertility among women of color continued in the 1980s among Latinas who alleged that they were sterilized without their consent in Los Angeles County hospitals and, more recently, in debates about consent in the testing, side effects, and administration of Depo-Provera in the United States and globally (Kline, 2010; Stern, 2005). It is important to underscore that these efforts to constrain women's autonomy were political at national and local levels and were articulated in terms of public health measures.

With regard to formal politics, the incorporation of women as legitimate political actors—whether as voters, legislators, or judges—has been accompanied by systemic gender inequality and, in many cases, sexual harassment and abuse. Historically, the incorporation of women into formal politics as voters has been a recurring source of political contention among women activists. Activists on behalf of the abolition of slavery attempted to articulate an analogy between racial oppression and sex-based oppression to demand that the end of slavery be accompanied by political emancipation for both Black Americans and women (Buechler, 1990). Many activists viewed the proposal of the Thirteenth Amendment as "the perfect opportunity to broaden democracy and extend justice by enfranchising black men and women as well as white women" (p. 21). Women activists were ultimately not successful in this bid, and women continued to mobilize, famously in New York State in what became the Seneca Falls Convention in 1848, at which time women wrote and circulated a "Declaration of Sentiments and Principles" that articulated their grievances concerning systemic institutional sexism (p. 138). Women in the United States did not acquire the right to vote—a paradigmatic characteristic of full citizenship—until a women-led movement for suffrage in the early twentieth century led to the promulgation of the Nineteenth Amendment in 1920; women of color struggled to exercise that right in the decades that followed through a series of disenfranchisement methods such as literacy tests, poll taxes, intimidation, and, in some cases, violence.

Gender Politics and the State

In a *Harper's New Monthly Magazine* in January 1884, an exchange between Thomas Jefferson and George Washington was circulated in which Washington compared the House of Representatives to a teacup and the Senate to a tea saucer. The notion was that the Senate's function was

> to let ideas from the House cool off by requiring time in the process of reflection. The House, being the governing body closest to the people (the Senators were then elected by state legislators), would be more apt to reflect upon the passions of the electorate, sometime with good results, sometimes not. (Elliott, 2018, para. 6)

This analogy, whether an authentic statement of Washington or not, communicates the strong ambivalence to direct democracy that is embedded not only in the U.S. structure of political governance but in political systems around the world. The bicameral legislative system in the United States in particular is designed to prevent rapid, dramatic change so as to ensure the stability of the political system. This conservative aspect of political structures can also extend to issues of gender inequality as it concerns accessing political rights and serving in representative roles as well as to how institutions of the state can become sources of sexual violence and abuse (Carroll & Walters, 2016).

Scholarship on states and citizenship in political science and sociology long presumed the construction of an abstract citizen with abstract rights. In scholarship on the "liberal state," MacKinnon (1989) argued that scholars have not scrutinized "the content and limitations of these notions in terms of gender" (p. 160).

According to feminist scholars of states, the social and economic inequalities based on gender are characterized by power and, thus, are political limitations on citizenship. Founded on the primordial patriarchal systems that preceded them, states organize gender relations in ways that privilege male perspectives within the law. According to MacKinnon, "Law, as words in power, writes society in state form and writes the state onto society" (p. 163). Law itself is represented as possessing the masculine values of rationality, objectivity, and neutrality, which obscures its ongoing gendered effects.

MacKinnon (1989, 2007b) has offered several examples of how the state effectively operates as a male state to legitimate male power over women, particularly in the realm of sexual relations. She focused specifically on the political resistance globally to recognizing sexual violence within the context of marriage. The framework regarding marriage embedded within the state in the United States came from inherited legal frameworks that understood women as "legal appendages to men—objects of male power (vis-à-vis their husbands and fathers) whose capacities were legally conscribed to sexual chattel of their spouses" (Goodwin & Lindsay, 2019, p. 2343). Accordingly, nonconsensual sex within marriage was never recognized as rape, which attests to the prevailing assumption within the law that sex was a man's unequivocal right within the context of marriage, regardless of a woman's agency and expressions to the contrary. It was not until the early 1990s that the majority of U.S. states recognized rape as a criminal act within marriage (MacKinnon, 2007b).

As MacKinnon's analyses (1989, 2007a, 2007b) have made clear, the state and law have been organized historically to preserve and protect men's interests within the family and society more generally. Connell (1987) referred to the organization of gender relations within institutions, such as the institution of the family or workplace, as a "gender regime," and the state is no exception. In fact, the state is uniquely positioned to enforce gender regimes through the threat of violence, which is regarded as legitimate. In this way, states as the purview of politics are particularly prone to gender-based violence and abuse. It is important to note that this gender-based violence is not exclusively exerted upon women by men. Connell emphasized that contemporary states do not impose patriarchal arrangements exclusively upon women but also on men who do not conform to what she terms "hegemonic masculinity," or the socially predominant and valued form of masculinity. The violence directed toward men who do not conform to society's preeminent models of masculinity is evinced in the anti-sodomy laws in several states used to confer punishment onto same-sex individuals accused and convicted of sodomy. Connell also offered the case of the disproportionate impact of mass incarceration on men of color in the United States as another example of how race and gender intersect to influence who is more vulnerable to violence in the form of policing, conviction, and incarceration. The criminal legal system is profoundly influenced by politics, and the likelihood of sexual violence and abuse is particularly acute behind bars for both men and women (Wolff et al., 2006).

As a key arbiter of political matters, the media is a social institution closely linked to the state and an important site for conversations about social and political constructions of gender. Sociologists, political scientists, and communication scholars have recently linked the rising sexual objectification of women in media with sexist attitudes toward and sexual harassment of female political candidates (Conroy et al., 2015; Heflick & Goldenburg, 2009; Heldman & Wade, 2011). An early predecessor of what was to come, Geraldine Ferraro, who was the Democratic running mate of Walter F. Mondale in 1984, was introduced by journalist Tom Brokaw as "the first woman to be nominated for vice-president . . . size 6!" (Carlin & Winfrey, 2009, p. 329). In their study of old and new media coverage of vice presidential candidates, Conroy and colleagues (2015) found that coverage of women vice presidential candidates is far more negative and sexist than that of their male counterparts. In what they defined as hard sexism, which refers to "overly gendered insults," (p. 574) Conroy et al. noted that female candidates were four times more likely to experience this form of sexism than male vice presidential candidates and that the coverage was often misogynistic, especially in the case of Alaska governor Sarah Palin, who ran on the 2008 presidential ticket with former senator John McCain:

> Palin was the first vice presidential contender to have a blow-up doll created in her likeness . . . the first to have a pornographic film made with her likeness (titled "Nailin' Paylin"), the first to have her face Photoshopped on the body of a gun-toting, bikini-wearing woman who received millions of views in a matter of days, and the first to have a reputable news service (*Reuters*) publish photos taken between her legs. (p. 583)

This type of coverage and the modes of harassment that follow extend beyond the United States. In their analysis of Australia, the United Kingdom, and Canada, which all share a Westminster system of governance, Collier and Raney (2018) noted that "women's collective experiences of violence in politics are not isolated events but rather, the result of historically entrenched patriarchal institutional rules and norms in politics" (p. 433). Thus, while cultural attitudes contribute in significant ways to the misogyny and sexism that women politicians face, there are also important institutional dimensions that facilitate and perpetuate harassment and sexual violence toward women in politics. More specifically, the adversarial nature of parliamentary systems creates the protected and privileged space for the exchange of insults, vitriolic speech, and harassment as part of the everyday workings of debate and defense of legislation. Collier and Raney pointed out that this institutional arrangement privileges male norms of behavior as quintessentially neutral and protects perpetrators of speech that normally would constitute harassment from any reprisal or accountability. For instance, the first Australian female prime minister, Julia Gillard, offered a critique of misogyny and sexism in Parliament in 2012 and responded to gender-specific insults she had endured in parliamentary debates, such as opponents "calling her 'barren' and incompetent, 'a lying cow,' and a 'bitch,' among other epithets rarely if ever used to describe male heads of state" (p. 442). The accountability for such speech, despite its profoundly gendered quality, has historically been limited due to parliamentary privilege and emphasis on free speech.

Thus, existing research finds that not only are political institutions gendered and historically organized in ways that privilege men, but, more pointedly, those institutions have rendered legal the sexual abuse of and misconduct toward women, which is evinced in numerous legal frameworks ranging from the lack of recognition of spousal rape globally to current discourses and debates in political arenas that continue to mobilize misogynistic and sexist language as quintessentially protected political speech.

Case Studies

The well-documented sexist remarks and sexual abuse that women have endured in politics emerged as a key site of contestation in the #MeToo social mobilizations. Catalyzed by activist Tarana Burke in 2006, the "me too" phrase garnered broader attention when it was employed in October 2017 by actress Alyssa Milano in a tweet (Zacharek, Dockterman, & Edwards, 2017). Following responses from thousands of women to her tweet, it became clear that systemic sexual abuse was not limited to Hollywood actresses and actors, nor was it specific to any type of workplace; sexual abuse could be found in any setting in which a range of power dynamics were unequal between perpetrators and survivors.

The institution of politics, which is especially defined by power hierarchies, quickly surfaced in the appeals of survivors. Survivors implicated politicians in acts of sexual harassment and assault in tweets, blog posts, and articles, such as Senator Al Franken, who was accused of stalking and harassing multiple women. Survivors also appealed to politicians to develop and revise policies to redress harassment and assault by political officeholders (Sabur, 2018). In many cases, survivors and politicians were one and the same, as many political figures such as Ayanna Pressley, the first Black woman elected to Congress from Massachusetts, and Kirsten Gillibrand, a U.S. senator from New York, shared their experiences of sexual violence and harassment, which had sometimes been experienced in their roles as public servants.

It is important to note that the #MeToo movement more generally emerged in the post-2016 presidential election political environment, which was characterized by allegations against Donald Trump of sexual assault and harassment and the release of an *Access Hollywood* video filmed in 2005 that featured Trump claiming to kiss women and "grab them by the pussy" without their consent (Bullock, 2016). In January 2017, women across the United States and around the world mobilized collectively in the Women's March, which has continued to organize in subsequent years. Directly responding to Trump's claims that his fame and power entitled him to erode women's agency and bodily autonomy, women protesters rallied to reiterate the significance of advancing and protecting women's rights in several aspects of social life, including fertility, marriage, the workplace, and immigration. According to the Women's March mission statement, the purpose of the protest turned social movement is "to harness the political power of diverse women and their communities to create transformative social change" (Women's March, 2019). Thus, politics is at the heart of the mobilization as both a mode of engagement and as a structure requiring dramatic systemic change.

In the case studies that follow, I outline how the #MeToo movement has empowered individuals to come forward to report sexual abuse in politics. Given the movement's breadth and scope, I consider how the notion of #MeToo not only has been raised explicitly by survivors but also has influenced the contemporary social and cultural climate in ways that have led to more women coming forward in contentious political moments and have inspired women to consider past sexual relations from new perspectives. In the first case, I examine how #MeToo has been explicitly invoked by survivors of sexual harassment and violence in the United Kingdom, where the hashtag rapidly circulated following its popularization in the United States. In the British case, #MeToo implicated Westminster politicians at multiple levels. In the second case, I consider how the social climate produced by #MeToo affected the reception of Christine Blasey Ford's allegations in July 2018 of attempted rape at the hands of then U.S. Supreme Court nominee Brett Kavanaugh when they were teenagers. As each of these cases demonstrates, the #MeToo movement has had varying levels of impact that have been international in scope. The discussions introduced by #MeToo empower women to directly make claims against former abusers while, in the process, transforming the social and political climate in ways that influence how people interpret sexual harassment and abuse.

Case 1: #MeToo at Westminster

As the #MeToo hashtag enveloped Twitter in October 2017, it was quickly circulated around the world in the same terms or in translated language, such as "#YoTambien" in Spanish-speaking societies, as well as in vernacular specific to other regions and cultures; in France, the hashtag became "#BalanceTonPorc," which translates to "snitch out your pig" (Fox & Diehm, 2017, para. 6). According to social media analytics, the #MeToo hashtag spread around the globe rapidly, and in less than a month it had been invoked millions of times in over 85 countries (Powell, 2017). The countries where the hashtag was cited with the greatest frequency included the "United States, United Kingdom, India, France, and Canada" (para. 16). In the United Kingdom, survivors drew on the #MeToo movement begun in the United States and quickly identified politics as a key source of sexual abuse, with some survivors citing Westminster politicians as harassers or abusers. Later, women developed the #LabourToo website to make party leaders aware of their claims and to demand that leaders advance policy changes (Krook, 2018).

The accusations involving British members of Parliament unleashed a broader collection of #MeToo moments of harassment and abuse that illustrated how sexual abuse at Westminster has been institutionalized over the course of several decades and does not merely represent a handful of isolated incidents. As the revelations unfolded, cabinet ministers and members of Parliament (MPs) were accused of regular sexual harassment and degradation of colleagues and employees and, in a few cases, of sexual violence and assault. In what came to be called the "dirty dossier," the names and accusations of all politicians alleged to have engaged in sexual harassment and abuse were listed in a WhatsApp group message that was later shared, in redacted forms, online (Krook, 2018).

Among the accusations featured in the dossier were that specific cabinet members were "handsy" at parties and generally "inappropriate" with male and female staff (Rampen, 2018, para. 6). Some of the emblematic cases appearing in the dossier included the case of Trade Minister Mark Garnier, who referred to his secretary as "sugar tits" and requested that she buy sex toys; Garnier did not deny the claims but stated that he did not regard them as constituting harassment (Lowe, 2017, para. 13). As another example of how sexualized language and objectification characterized everyday British politics, British diplomat David Davis received attention for attending a conference in 2005 alongside women bearing form-fitting pink shirts that read "It's DD for me," insinuating a bra cup size for his initials (Moore, 2017, para. 3). In another case, Stephen Crabb, a former cabinet minister, allegedly sent sexually explicit text messages to a 19-year-old woman who had sought a job with his office (Groves, 2017). One of the more contentious accusations was against former prime minister Theresa May's deputy, Damian Green, who was accused by journalist Kate Maltby of touching her knee and sending her inappropriate text messages (Lowe, 2017).

It is also important to note that the claims were not exclusively made by women against men; allegations surfaced that government whip Chris Pincher had made unwanted sexual advances toward aspiring Tory activist Alex Story, who stated that Pincher had "started untucking the back of my shirt, massaging my neck, and whispered, 'You'll go far in the Conservative Party'" (Serhan, 2017; Story, 2017, para. 7). Story (2017) alleged that this incident, which occurred before Pincher was a member of the British Parliament, subtly implied to him that his acceptance of the sexual overtures would help him advance his political career. This allegation against Pincher was accompanied by another allegation of an unwanted sexual advance toward Tom Blenkinsop, a former Labour MP (Groves, 2017).

The extensive allegations against Westminster politicians that surfaced were anticipated by *The Sun*, a tabloid newspaper published in the UK and Ireland, which featured a front-page headline article on October 26 titled "Be Afraid . . . Be Very Afraid" (Serhan, 2017). Indeed, it became a common refrain in the British press to call Westminster "Pestminster" for the politicians the press deemed to be "sex pests" in light of the scandal (Rampen, 2018). This scandal itself was preceded by what Rampen (2017) called a "Westminster Weinstein" moment in 2013 when several women reported to senior Liberal Democrats their experiences of sexual harassment and assault by Christopher John Rennard, who, as of November 2020, remains in the House of Lords (para. 8). The outcome of women and men coming forward in 2017, however, was dramatically different, as several men who appeared in the dossier were pressured to resign and leave their political posts. Notable among such politicians was the case of Defense Secretary Michael Fallon, who resigned in response to an incident in 2002 in which he touched a journalist's knee at dinner. While the journalist, Julia Hartley-Brewer, accepted an apology and insisted that she was no longer "distressed" by the incident, Fallon's anticipation of further allegations led him to resign (Lowe, 2017, para. 10).

The case of Fallon, in particular, has raised questions about how the #MeToo movement is affecting Westminster. Critics suggest that the Fallon case is a significant example of how #MeToo has gone too far, as Hartley-Brewer herself does not express umbrage at the act of Fallon touching her knee (Lowe, 2017). Additional criticism emerged concerning the dossier's contents, because while some politicians were cited in the dossier because of their unpopular but legal sexual predilections, others featured were simply engaged in consensual relations with colleagues (Rampen, 2017; Groves, 2017). These critiques have inaugurated a backlash against the #MeToo movement in Britain with claims that all sexual relations will now be subjected to undue scrutiny and that the movement inhibits expressions of affection and sexual interest (Rubin, 2017).

Despite such critiques and the well-established concerns about some of the cases featured in the dossier, there is considerable evidence that sexual degradation, harassment, and abuse is an institutionalized feature of British politics. Recent attention has been paid to the affairs of politicians outside the halls of Westminster in community-based engagements. *Financial Times* investigative journalists recently attended the Presidents Club Charity Dinner, a men-only black-tie event for influential politicians, financial elites, and celebrities in Britain hosted annually to raise funds to support charitable causes (Marriage, 2018). The event has long been rumored to feature scantily clad women hostesses, but the scope of the sexual objectification and harassment was only recently made known when the *Financial Times* journalists decided to focus and report specifically on the issue.

In the course of attending the event, journalists observed how the Presidents Club Charity Dinner facilitated sexual harassment and degradation of women, ranging from the interactions between the 350 men in attendance and the 130 female hostesses, to the specific items being auctioned in support of charity. Auction items included trips to a strip club and a plastic surgery package titled "A Chance to Enhance," the description of which read, "The award winning 111 Harley Street plastic surgery clinic will take years off your life or *add spice to your wife* [emphasis added]" (Marriage, 2018, para. 21). With regard to the hostesses, the strict requirements were that they be "tall, thin, and pretty" and "bring 'BLACK, sexy shoes,' black underwear, and do their hair and make-up as they would to go to a 'smart sexy place'" (Marriage, 2018, para. 27). The hostess agency, Artista, provided the short dresses that invited men to sexually harass and grope the hostesses, which the journalists observed repeatedly over the course of the six-hour event. While the event brochure outlined an anti–sexual harassment policy to which all attendees were expected to adhere, elite men drew hostesses into their laps and invited them to their rooms and after-parties, where they later propositioned them for sex.

The hostesses were warned by the hosting agency that the men might get "annoying" from time to time; if the men were "too annoying," the hostesses could reach out to the agency founder. However, at the same time, agency representatives were enforcing hostess engagement with the men by "prodding less active hostesses to interact with dinner guests" and monitoring bathroom time for hostesses to ensure that they were not shirking their time on the floor with the male dinner guests (Marriage, 2018, para. 46). Upon publication of the investigative piece by the *Financial Times,* the Artista hosting agency and former trustees of the event collectively denied systemic sexual harassment at the annual Presidents Club Charity Dinner. Thus, while this event is held outside the purview of formal politics, the engagement of political elites in this space speaks to the systemic dynamics of gender inequality and sexual harassment that characterize elite institutions like politics.

Among the many reasons that sexual harassment and abuse persist in politics as an institution includes the role of masculinity, the structure of employment in parliaments, and the party system (Krook, 2018). As a predominantly masculine-dominated institution, politics gives way to sexual harassment because it is a norm of politics. As Devanny and Haddon (2015) documented in interviews with women civil servants in British politics going back to 1979, women attested to how institutional sexism had long been "the norm" in civil service and, as a result, some women had left to work in other settings (p. 28). In addition to the corrosive work environment fostered by masculinity, the structure of employment in Westminster is designed such that MPs are "considered self-employed" and directly hire their staff and assistants (Krook, 2018, p. 68). As a result, the staff members of MPs, many of whom are young people who aspire to a future career in politics themselves, are extremely vulnerable and institutionally have no recourse to report instances of sexual harassment, abuse, or violence. Even when allegations of sexual misconduct are made, often to senior political party members, very little accountability follows, or survivors are counseled not to formally report the incident, as was the case when activist Bex Bailey reported to a senior staff member that she had been raped at a party function by a high-ranking party member (Lowe, 2017).

The reticence of senior party members to acknowledge and formally report sexual harassment and violence follows from the critical function that sexual scandals actually play in the workings of politics. Party reputation is of paramount importance, and senior party members, particularly in the whips' office system, regularly utilize sexual scandals to keep their party members in line; as Savage and Helm (2017) wrote, "Whips hold information and use it against individuals only if and when they need to do so, to maintain MPs' loyalty along party lines" (para. 13). Katie Perrior, a former head of communication for Prime Minister Theresa May, affirmed that instances of sexual harassment and abuse are, according to Moore (2017), "used to enforce party discipline," and accordingly "complicity with such abuse of power is built into this system" (para. 9).

In response to the extensive fallout at Westminster from the #MeToo claims and the scrutiny paid to events such as the Presidents Club Charity Dinner, many initiatives have been proposed by Theresa May's office. Namely, the former prime minister has insisted on the dedication of more resources to the issue of sexual harassment and abuse and proposed new codes of procedure to report such cases (Lowe, 2017; Savage & Helm, 2017). In cross-party talks, the prime minister recommended new systems to report sexual misconduct alongside a cultural change in how Westminster and the larger public engages these issues (Serhan, 2017).

Case 2: #MeToo and the U.S. Supreme Court

On the U.S. political scene, women politicians mobilized, like their British counterparts, to highlight how sexual harassment and abuse pervaded multiple levels of politics, from municipal and state levels to the federal level. A little over a week after the #MeToo hashtag went viral, House Intelligence Committee member Representative Jackie Speir, a Democrat from California, shared a video on YouTube detailing her experience of being forcibly kissed by a congressional chief of staff when she was a staffer. She called for women to share their #MeToo stories related to Capitol Hill under the hashtag #metooCongress (Rhodan, 2017). In a similar gesture, women engaged in politics in California advanced the #WeSaidEnough hashtag alongside a letter published in the *Los Angeles Times* that emphasized the sexism, harassment, and assault that female politicians, staff, and lobbyists had endured from California's political elite. Motivated by messages exchanged with Adama Iwu, who leads government relations for Visa and had previously been sexually harassed, more than 140 women directly or indirectly involved in politics signed the letter. As was the case in Westminster, many women cited existing complaint protocol as inadequate to deal effectively with allegations of sexual misconduct (Mason, 2017). From within this context emerged one of the most publicized cases of sexual violence since the #MeToo movement began: the allegation that a nominee for the U.S. Supreme Court, Brett Kavanaugh, had sexually assaulted a researcher and professor at Palo Alto University, Dr. Christine Blasey Ford, at a house party when they were teenagers.

Ford, who expressed strong reticence to come forward, considered sharing her story when Kavanaugh was shortlisted by the president for the new opening on the U.S. Supreme Court. Accordingly, Ford filed a tip in early July 2018 with the *Washington Post* concerning her experience of assault by Kavanaugh and reached out to her congressional representative, Anna G. Eshoo, to make her office aware of her concerns. Through Representative Eshoo's office, Ford authored a letter in late July to Senator Dianne Feinstein detailing the attack and requesting that her identity remain confidential (Brown, 2018). Feinstein, the ranking Democrat on the Senate Judiciary Committee, eventually circulated the letter to the FBI. Throughout August, reporters looked into the then-anonymous allegations and sought to discover the identity of the accuser. During their investigations, journalists began making inquiries with Ford and her work colleagues and started appearing on her college campus and at her home. Ford decided to move forward publicly due to concerns that her story was being misrepresented.

In the piece published by the *Washington Post* detailing Dr. Ford's allegation, she outlined how she was attacked by Judge Kavanaugh and his friend Mark Judge, on a summer evening in Montgomery County, Maryland (Brown, 2018). Ford, who was 14 or 15 years old at the time, stopped at an impromptu gathering at a home after she had been swimming at the Columbia Country Club. The home hosted a small party of teenagers where alcohol was present, and most attendees had drunk about one beer, including herself. Upon making her way upstairs, she said that she was attacked from behind by two clearly inebriated boys—Kavanaugh and

Judge—who pushed her onto a bed in a room where music was playing. Kavanaugh climbed on top of Ford and began groping her and attempted to remove her clothing, which was difficult given the swimsuit she was still sporting underneath. As Ford attempted to escape, Kavanaugh and Judge laughed and Kavanaugh placed his hand on her mouth to prevent anyone from hearing her appeals for help. Ford was able to finally escape from the room when Judge jumped on top of them and all three youths tumbled off the bed. Ford ran to a bathroom on the second floor of the home and waited until she heard Kavanaugh and Judge go down the stairway to make her final escape down the stairs and out of the house. Upon coming forward publicly with her story in the *Washington Post,* the Senate Judiciary Committee began debating whether Ford should testify to the committee about her experience.

Anticipating Dr. Ford's testimony, which would parallel the testimony against Judge Clarence Thomas in 1991, now Professor Anita Hill authored an op-ed in the *New York Times* outlining how the Senate Judiciary Committee should manage the testimony of Dr. Ford differently than it had her own nearly thirty years before, especially, she stated, in light of the cultural changes wrought by the #MeToo movement. Demanding that the procedures for the testimony be "guided by experts" in the field of sexual violence, Hill (2018) proposed that the committee should "refrain from pitting the public interest in confronting sexual harassment against the need for a fair confirmation hearing," because a fair hearing and eliminating sexual misconduct were not contradictory goals (para. 6). She also suggested that a "neutral investigative body with experience in sexual misconduct cases" should investigate the alleged incident and that the hearings that followed should transpire over an adequate period of time to allow for full examination of the testimony and facts of the investigation (para. 7).

Despite Hill's (2018) sage, deeply informed proposals, the Senate Judiciary Committee nevertheless rushed to host testimony of both Dr. Ford and Judge Kavanaugh in the absence of any formal investigation of her allegation. At the advice of her lawyer, Ford took a polygraph test prior to her testimony, which indicated that she had not offered any deceptive responses (a probability of deception less than 0.02) to questions regarding the allegations (Donegan, 2018; Hutzler, 2018). At the testimony itself, Ford appeared prepared, poised, and intellectually rigorous in her opening statement and in her responses to questions, which were posed by a sex crimes prosecutor in lieu of Republican senators. Ford attested that the incident and the laughter from Kavanaugh and Judge as she was assaulted was "indelible in the hippocampus" and that the ongoing trauma and impact of the sexual assault had continued to impact her in the decades since, which had led her to share details of the incident with her therapist and husband (Burke et al., 2018; Jennings & Thebault, 2018). Specifically, the incident was relayed by Ford during a couple's therapy session after she and her husband had disagreements about a home remodel:

> I insisted on a second front door, an idea that he and others disagreed with and could not understand. In explaining why I wanted to have a second front door, I described the assault in detail. I recall saying that the boy who assaulted me could someday be on the U.S. Supreme Court. (Jennings & Thebault, 2018, para. 10)

Notes from her therapist indicated that Ford had reported as early as 2012 enduring a sexual assault as a teenager by students who later became "highly respected and high-ranking members of society in Washington" (Brown, 2018, para. 7). Ford's accusations were later accompanied by allegations from two other women, Deborah Ramirez and Julie Swetnick, who alleged having knowledge of Kavanaugh's drinking and sexual aggression while he was in high school or college (Stahlberg & Fandos, 2018).

In response to this testimony, Kavanaugh emphatically and angrily denied the claims of sexually assaulting Ford or of ever drinking to excess. Kavanaugh cited his high school planner to indicate that he had not attended any house party on the alleged night of the sexual assault. Senators confronted him about his drinking habits and sexual innuendos, including a "Devil's Triangle" (a colloquial reference to a sexual act between two men and one woman), that appeared in his high school yearbook, which he ultimately denied were sexual references but instead claimed were drinking games (Harrison, 2018, para. 1). In response to questions and in his opening statement, Judge Kavanaugh alleged that Democratic senators were engaged in a political conspiracy to deny him the seat on U.S. Supreme Court. Yet evidence surfaced that Kavanaugh did have a reputation for drinking excessively. Judge, the other individual alleged to have participated in the assault, claimed to have no memory of the assault before Ford's name was released but had authored a memoir about his own battle with alcoholism in which he referred to a childhood friend with whom he used to drink regularly as "Bart O'Kavanaugh" (Brown, 2018).

Ultimately, the Senate Judiciary Committee did not allow time for a full investigation, and just over a week after the testimonies, Judge Kavanaugh was confirmed to the U.S. Supreme Court by a vote of 50 to 48 on October 6, 2018 (Garrand, 2019). Despite his confirmation, it is clear that Ford's testimony and her courage to come forward inspired considerable mobilization around sexual harassment and violence and support. Amid the testimony itself, women began calling into C-Span, a network that regularly broadcasts proceedings of the federal government and other programming related to public affairs, to share their stories of sexual harassment and abuse (Stahlberg & Fandos, 2018). Women on Twitter also created the hashtag #WhyIDidntReport to detail why many survivors of sexual abuse do not come forward to report their experiences to law enforcement or others, and the public raised GoFundMe donations to financially support Dr. Ford amid death threats that required her family to travel with hired security and move away from their home (Edwards 2018; Richards 2018). In the days following Ford's testimony, journalist Connie Chung authored an open letter to Ford to share her own experience of sexual assault at the hands of a family physician when she was in her twenties. She affirmed in her experience that though she could not remember every particular, she recalled in detail the abuse she endured: "I am writing you because I know that exact dates, exact years are insignificant. We remember exactly what happened to us and who did it to us. We remember the truth forever" (Chung, 2018, para. 20).

In a similar gesture, leaders of the #MeToo movement, including founder Tarana Burke, issued a statement of support to Ford in the form of a "love letter" that emphasized that her courage and her testimony were heard and believed and constituted a powerful act of heroism, even if it did not prevent Kavanaugh from serving on the Supreme Court. Two sections of the letter read,

> We witnessed you show up for duty not as a superhero, but as a fully human woman. You showed us that the new hero—the kind of heroism called for in this moment—is a woman facing the patriarchy with no weapons other than her voice, her body, and the truth.

> Our generation has found in you what those before us found in Professor Anita Hill: a heroism based not on greed, ego, violence, and self-serving nationalism but truth, vulnerability, and the courage to sacrifice one's own safety for the greater good. When you stood there in front of us, Dr. Ford, we found a heroism that we could not only believe in, but become. (Burke et al., 2018, paras. 9–10)

The outpouring of support, financial and emotional, to Dr. Ford demonstrates how the ongoing efforts of the #MeToo movement have fostered a different cultural climate for survivors of sexual violence. However, as the #MeToo letter to Ford attests, the specter of Anita Hill's testimony in the early 1990s continues to loom large, and the similar outcome demonstrates the limits of change as well.

Ongoing Debates and Policy Implications

The cultural and political debates introduced by #MeToo have continued to occupy public discourse in the United States and around the world since the hashtag grew in popularity in 2017. In surveys conducted by Pew Research in 2018, however, U.S. respondents regarded in very partisan ways the notion that women are often not believed when they report incidents of sexual violence: roughly 60 percent of respondents who leaned Democrat and only 28 percent of respondents who leaned Republican stated that women not being believed was a major problem as it related to sexual harassment and assault in the workplace today (Graf, 2018). These findings demonstrate another dimension of the #MeToo movement's relationship to politics, which is that the movement has been received very differently across partisan lines.

In fact, a key ongoing debate surrounding the #MeToo movement has surfaced in some of the backlash that the movement has faced in relation to the political cases of #MeToo claims, including that of Judge Brett Kavanaugh's nomination. The contention that women can make false claims against men has been a common point of debate and critique of the #MeToo movement and has surfaced in a range of online rebuttals and hashtags, such as #HimToo. In its inception, #HimToo was a simple hashtag that implied that a male individual was also taking part in an activity. However, the hashtag has been appropriated in several ways, including to support Tim Kaine as Hillary Clinton's running mate in the 2016 election, as a pairing with #LockHerUp to implicate former President Barack Obama alongside Hillary Clinton for crimes, and to highlight male survivors of sexual violence, given the #MeToo movement's initial focus on female survivors. The #HimToo hashtag was elevated during the Kavanaugh hearings to greater acclaim and attention as it spread inaccurate and unsubstantiated information concerning the prevalence of false allegations (Ellis, 2018). False reports regarding sexual violence can only be estimated, but estimates range from as little as 2 percent of claims to approximately 10 percent of claims, which is comparable to false reports of any other crime (National Sexual Violence Resource Center, 2012).

The ambivalence and debates regarding the #MeToo movement notwithstanding, legal scholars find that there is potential for #MeToo to move from a social movement to a legal movement. Namely, #MeToo emphasizes the severity of sexual harassment and abuse, demonstrating its devastating and protracted effects on an individual emotionally and psychologically as well as in terms of one's employment experiences. In contrast, existing law views sexual harassment specifically as a "relatively trivial harm" produced by "sexual desire" (Hébert, 2018, pp. 325, 327). Thus, #MeToo is poised to make an important intervention in underscoring the significance of sexual harassment because of the power dynamics involved, which influences why many women do not come forward to report sexual abuse in the workplace or to law enforcement (Hébert, 2018).

From the perspective of MacKinnon (2018), whose legal scholarship contributed to the establishment of sexual harassment law, the #MeToo movement has shifted the culture around believing victims enough to make changes that the law historically has not. In particular, MacKinnon has seen the #MeToo movement as having the potential to transform some of the greatest obstacles to reporting sexual harassment:

> Institutional or statutory changes could include prohibitions or limits on various forms of secrecy and non-transparency that hide the extent of sexual abuse and enforce survivor isolation, such as forced arbitration, silencing nondisclosure agreements even in cases of physical attacks and multiple perpetration, and confidential settlements. (para. 11)

In all types of workplaces, including politics, nondisclosure agreements and settlements have been a key mode of silencing survivors and, accordingly, insulating perpetrators to continue to abuse.

With regard to sexual abuse among politicians, policy changes inspired by the #MeToo movement are currently in development across several states. In the United States, congressional leaders have voted to require all House offices to develop and implement anti-harassment and antidiscrimination policies. Each office "must outline a process to prevent, investigate and correct office harassment and discrimination occurring in a timely manner," and "the reporting process must include a path for reporting harassment to more than just an immediate supervisor" (Tully-McManus, 2019, para. 5). While each office will develop its own policy, each policy is required to define "hostile work environment sexual harassment" (para. 4). These revisions replace previous practices that exacted a mandatory mediation between survivor and employer and a 30-day waiting period before a survivor could initiate the next steps of the reporting process.

These changes attempt to redress the structural conditions of abuse in political institutions that were a key grievance in both Westminster and Capitol Hill, particularly between staffers and members of Parliament. Such changes are tangible examples of how the publicity of sexual abuse introduced by the #MeToo movement has empowered survivors to come forward in ways that have exerted pressure on key institutions to acknowledge and address sexual harassment and violence as systemic and significant. As the love letter to Dr. Ford stated, "You showed a world of discounted people what courage looks like" (Burke et al., 2018, para. 14). In many ways, the #MeToo movement has collectively shown not only discounted people but also powerholders that sexual violence will not be silently endured and accepted without consequence.

References

Brown, E. (2018, September 16). California professor, writer of confidential Brett Kavanaugh letter, speaks out about her allegation of sexual assault. *Washington Post.* https://www.washingtonpost.com/investigations/california-professor

-writer-of-confidential-brett-kavanaugh-letter-speaks-out-about-her-allegation
-of-sexual-assault/2018/09/16/46982194-b846–11e8–94eb-3bd52dfe917b_story
.html?utm_term=.b655cd753cee

Buechler, S. M. (1990). *Women's movements in the United States: Woman suffrage, equal rights, and beyond.* Rutgers University Press.

Bullock, P. (2016, October 8). Transcript: Donald Trump's taped comments about women. *New York Times.* https://www.nytimes.com/2016/10/08/us/donald -trump-tape-transcript.html

Burke, T., de Cadenet, A., Doyle, G., Ross, T. E., and Ferrera, A. (2018). *A love letter to Dr. Christine Blasey Ford.* MeToo Movement. https://metoomvmt.org/a-love -letter-to-dr-christine-blasey-ford/

Carlin, D. B., & Winfrey, K. L. (2009). Have you come a long way, baby? Hillary Clinton, Sarah Palin, and sexism in 2008 campaign coverage. *Communication Studies, 60*(4), 326–343.

Carroll, S. J., & Walters, S. D. (2016). Ask a feminist: A conversation with Susan J. Carroll on gender and electoral politics. *Signs: Journal of Women in Culture and Society.* http://signsjournal.org/ask-a-feminist-carroll-walters/

Chung, C. (2018, October 3). Dear Christine Blasey Ford, I, too, was sexually assaulted—and it's seared into my memory forever. *Washington Post.* https:// www.washingtonpost.com/opinions/dear-christine-blasey-ford-i-too-was -sexually-assaulted—and-its-seared-into-my-memory-forever/2018/10/03 /2449ed3c-c68a-11e8–9b1c-a90f1daae309_story.html?utm_term =.22e3be5790d4

Collier, C. N., & Raney, T. (2018). Understanding sexism and sexual harassment in politics: A comparison of Westminster Parliaments in Australia, the United Kingdom, and Canada. *Social Politics: International Studies in Gender, State and Society, 25*(3), 432–455.

Collins, P. H. (1998). *Fighting words: Black women and the search for justice.* University of Minnesota Press.

Committee on the Judiciary. (1991, October 11, 12, 13). *First session on the nomination of Clarence Thomas to be Associate Justice of the Supreme Court of the United States. Hearings before the Committee on the Judiciary, United States Senate,* 102nd Cong., Part 4 of 4 Parts. https://www.govinfo.gov/content/pkg /GPO-CHRG-THOMAS/pdf/GPO-CHRG-THOMAS-4.pdf

Connell, R. W. (1987). *Gender and power: Society, the person, and sexual politics.* Stanford University Press.

Conroy, M., Oliver, S., Breckenridge-Jackson, I., & Heldman, C. (2015). From Ferraro to Palin: Sexism in coverage of vice presidential candidates in old and new media. *Politics, Groups, and Identities, 3*(4), 573–591.

Crenshaw, K. (1991). Mapping the margins: Intersectionality, identity politics, and violence against women of color. *Stanford Law Review, 43*(6), 1241–1299.

Crenshaw, K. (1992). Race, gender, and sexual harassment. *Southern California Law Review 65*, 1467–1476.

Devanny, J., & Haddon, C. (2015). *Women and Whitehall: Gender and the civil service since 1979.* Institute for Government. https://www.instituteforgovernment. org.uk/publications/women-and-whitehall

Donegan, M. (2018, September 20). What #MeToo hasn't changed for Christine Blasey Ford. *New Yorker.* https://www.newyorker.com/culture/cultural-comment /what-metoo-hasnt-changed-for-christine-blasey-ford

Edwards, H. S. (2018, December 11). Why Americans are still grappling with Christine Blasey Ford's legacy. *Time.* http://time.com/5476021/christine-blasey-ford-legacy/

Elliott, Jim. (2018, September 22). A saucer of tea. *Sidney Herald.* https://www. sidneyherald.com/opinion/columnists/a-saucer-of-tea/article_bccf71e4-be83 -11e8-9b16-bbd09c98cc05.html

Ellis, E. G. (2018, September 27). *How #HimToo became the anti-#MeToo of the Kavanaugh hearings.* Wired. https://www.wired.com/story/brett-kavanaugh -hearings-himtoo-metoo-christine-blasey-ford/

Fox, K., & Diehm, J. (2017, November 9). *#MeToo's global moment: The anatomy of a viral campaign.* CNN. https://www.cnn.com/2017/11/09/world/metoo-hashtag -global-movement/index.html

Garrand, D. (2019, April 17). *Time names Christine Blasey Ford and Brett Kavanaugh on 100 most influential people list.* CBS News. https://www.cbsnews.com /news/time-magazine-christine-blasey-ford-brett-kavanaugh-time-100-most -influential-people-2019/

Goodwin, M., & Lindsay, M. (2019). American courts and the sex blind spot: Legitimacy and representation. *Fordham Law Review, 87*(6), 2337–2384.

Graff, N. (2018, April 4). *Sexual harassment at work in the era of #MeToo.* Pew Research Center. https://www.pewsocialtrends.org/2018/04/04/sexual-harassment -at-work-in-the-era-of-metoo/

Groves, J. (2017, November 6). Amber Rudd goes to war on her own MPs: Home Secretary wants sex pests kicked out of Parliament despite fears that by-elections could bring the government down. *Daily Mail.* https://www.dailymail .co.uk/news/article-5052631/Amber-Rudd-wants-sex-pests-MPs-kicked -Parliament.html

Harrison, S. (2018, September 30). *The debate over "Devil's Triangle" shows Wikipedia at its best.* Slate. https://slate.com/technology/2018/09/kavanaugh-wikipedia -devils-triangle.html

Hébert, L. C. (2018). Is MeToo only a social movement or a legal movement too? *Employee Rights and Employment Policy Journal, 22*, 321–336.

Heflick, N. A., & Goldenberg, J. L. (2009). Objectifying Sarah Palin: Evidence that objectification causes women to be perceived as less competent and less fully human. *Journal of Experimental Social Psychology, 45*(3), 598–601.

Heldman, C., & Wade, L. (2011). Sexualizing Sarah Palin: The social and political context of the sexual objectification of female candidates. *Sex Roles, 65,* 156–164.

Hill, A. (2018, September 18). Anita Hill: How to get the Kavanaugh hearings right. *New York Times.* https://www.nytimes.com/2018/09/18/opinion/anita-hill-brett -kavanaugh-clarence-thomas.html

Hutzler, A. (2018, September 27). Brett Kavanaugh once praised polygraph tests, despite Republicans now using them to question Christine Blasey Ford. *Newsweek.* https://www.newsweek.com/brett-kavanaugh-polygraph-christine-blasey -ford-1142439

Jennings, N., & Thebault, R. (2018, September 26). "Seared into my memory": Christine Blasey Ford's opening statement to the Senate, annotated. *Washington Post.* https://www.washingtonpost.com/politics/2018/09/26/seared-into -my-memory-christine-blasey-fords-opening-statement-senate-annotated/

Jordan, E. C. (1992). Race, gender, and social class in the Thomas sexual harassment hearings: The hidden fault lines in political discourse. *Harvard Women's Law Journal, 15,* 1–24.

Kline, W. (2010). *Bodies of knowledge: Sexuality, reproduction, and women's health in the Second Wave.* University of Chicago Press.

Krook, M. L. (2018). Westminster too: On sexual harassment in British politics. *Political Quarterly, 89*(1), 65–72.

Lowe, J. (2017, November 1). #MeToo sexual assault and harassment scandal in British Parliament causes Defense minister to resign. *Newsweek.* https://www. newsweek.com/metoo-politics-britain-parliament-698906

MacKinnon, C. A. (1989). *Toward a feminist theory of state.* Harvard University Press.

MacKinnon, C. A. (2007a). *Are women human? And other international dialogues.* Harvard University Press.

MacKinnon, C. A. (2007b). *Women's lives, men's laws.* Belknap Press of Harvard University Press.

MacKinnon, C. A. (2018, February 4). #MeToo has done what the law could not. *New York Times.* https://www.nytimes.com/2018/02/04/opinion/metoo-law -legal-system.html

Marriage, M. (2018, January 23). Men only: Inside the charity fundraiser where hostesses are put on show. *Financial Times.* https://www.ft.com/content /075d679e-0033–11e8–9650–9c0ad2d7c5b5

Mason, M. (2017, October 17). Female lawmakers, staffers, and lobbyists speak out on "pervasive" harassment in California's capital. *Los Angeles Times.* https://www. latimes.com/politics/la-pol-ca-women-harassment-capitol-20171017-story.html

McClintock, A. (1995). *Imperial leather: Race, gender and sexuality in the colonial conquest.* Routledge.

Moore, S. (2017, October 30). Complicity in the sexual abuse of women is built in to the heart of our politics. *The Guardian*. https://www.theguardian.com /commentisfree/2017/oct/30/complicity-sexual-abuse-women-built-heart-politics

Nagel, J. (1998). Masculinity and nationalism: Gender and sexuality in the making of nations. *Ethnic and Racial Studies, 21*(2), 242–269.

Nagel, J. (2003). *Race, ethnicity, and sexuality: Intimate intersections, forbidden frontiers.* Oxford University Press.

National Sexual Violence Resource Center. (2012). *False reporting: overview.* https:// www.nsvrc.org/sites/default/files/Publications_NSVRC_Overview_False -Reporting.pdf

Powell, C. (2017, December 15). How #MeToo has spread like wildfire around the world. *Newsweek*. https://www.newsweek.com/how-metoo-has-spread-wildfire -around-world-749171

Rampen, J. (2017, November 3). A week in Pestminster: How the sexual harassment scandal unfolded. *New Statesman America*. https://www.newstatesman.com /politics/staggers/2017/11/week-pestminster-how-sexual-harassment-scandal -unfolded

Rampen, J. (2018, January 25). *Britain's #MeToo moment is taking down some of the most powerful men in the country.* Slate. https://slate.com/news-and-politics /2018/01/britains-metoo-movement-is-uncovering-a-culture-of-rampant -sexism-and-harassment-in-londons-corridors-of-power.html

Rhodan, M. (2017, October 27). This congresswoman wants women on Capitol Hill to say #MeToo. *Time*. http://time.com/5000282/this-congresswoman-wants -women-on-capitol-hill-to-say-metoo/

Richards, K. (2018, September 27). Brett Kavanaugh hearing: GoFundMe campaign for Christine Blasey Ford skyrockets on day of testimony. *The Independent*. https://www.independent.co.uk/news/world/americas/christine-ford-gofundme -campaign-brett-kavanaugh-hearing-amount-donate-a8558676.html

Roberts, D. (1997). *Killing the Black body: Race, reproduction, and the meaning of liberty.* Penguin Random House.

Rubin, G. (2017, November 1). Weinstein, Westminster, and me too: How on Earth do we navigate sexual relations now? *The Telegraph*. https://www.telegraph.co .uk/men/thinking-man/weinstein-westminster-earth-do-navigate-sexual -relations-now/

Sabur, R. (2018, December 13). "Me Too" victory in US Congress as politicians change sexual harassment rules. *The Telegraph*. https://www.telegraph.co.uk /news/2018/12/13/metoo-victory-us-congress-politicians-change-sexual -harassment/

Savage, M., & Helm, T. (2017, November 4). Why a tide of sexual allegations has swept through Westminster. *The Guardian*. https://www.theguardian.com /politics/2017/nov/04/sexual-allegations-westminster-scandal

Serhan, Y. (2017, November 8). A "warped and degrading" culture in Westminster. *The Atlantic*. https://www.theatlantic.com/international/archive/2017/11/the-uks-sexual-harassment-scandal/545066

Shin, A., & Casey, L. (2017, November 22). Anita Hill and her 1991 congressional defenders to Joe Biden: You were part of the problem. *Washington Post*. https://www.washingtonpost.com/lifestyle/magazine/anita-hill-and-her-1991-congressional-defenders-to-joe-biden-you-were-part-of-the-problem/2017/11/21/2303ba8a-ce69-11e7-a1a3-0d1e45a6de3d_story.html?noredirect=on&utm_term=.83210ee2d8d4

Smith, A. (2005). *Conquest: Sexual violence and the American Indian genocide*. South End Press.

Stahlberg, S. G., & Fandos, N. (2018, September 27). Brett Kavanaugh and Christine Blasey Ford duel with tears and fury. *New York Times*. https://www.nytimes.com/2018/09/27/us/politics/brett-kavanaugh-confirmation-hearings.html

Stern, A. M. (2005). Sterilized in the name of public health: Race, immigration, and reproductive control in modern California. *American Journal of Public Health, 95*(7), 1128–1138.

Story, A. (2017, November 4). Alex Story tells of "awkward moment with Tory whip." *Daily Mail*. https://www.dailymail.co.uk/news/article-5050563/ALEX-STORY-tells-awkward-moment-Tory-whip.html

Tully-McManus, K. (2019, February 7). House offices on timeline to implement anti-harassment policies. *Roll Call*. https://www.rollcall.com/news/congress/house-offices-on-timeline-to-implement-anti-harassment-policies

Viebeck, E. (2018, September 27). Here's what happened when Anita Hill testified against Clarence Thomas in 1991. *Chicago Tribune*. https://www.chicagotribune.com/nation-world/ct-anita-hill-clarence-thomas-20180927-story.html

Weber, M. (1946). *From Max Weber: Essays in sociology* (M. Weber, H. H. Gerth, & C. W. Mills, Eds.). Oxford University Press.

Wolff, N., Blitz, C. L., Shi, J., Bachman, R., & Siegel, J. A. (2006). Sexual violence inside prisons: Rates of victimization. *Journal of Urban Health, 83*(5), 835–848.

Women's March. (2019). *Mission and principles*. https://womensmarch.com/mission-and-principles

Yuval-Davis, N. (1997). *Gender and nation*. SAGE Publications.

Zacharek, S., Dockterman, E., & Edwards, H. S. (2017, December 18). The silence breakers. *Time Magazine*. http://time.com/time-person-of-the-year-2017-silence-breakers/

4. Sexual Abuse in Religious Institutions

Jason D. Spraitz and Kendra N. Bowen

The early 1980s case of sexually abusive priest Gilbert Gauthe was the first to receive prominent attention in the United States (DePalma, 2002), and follow-up stories and recollections of his victim-survivors and others involved detail how the institution of the church contributed to the ongoing systemic abuse. In addition, the treatment of victims and whistleblowers mirrors the known trials and tribulations that #MeToo survivors face.

In a *New York Times* story from 2002, Anthony DePalma detailed what survivors suffered through in the aftermath of their abuse. For example, telling their stories in the early 1980s "made them pariahs to some in this intensely Catholic community" (para. 8) that was a part of the Roman Catholic diocese of Lafayette in Louisiana. As one victim explained, "I was condemned in my own community—my brother's boss, who was a deacon at church, fired him and wouldn't talk to me" (para. 14). A clinical psychologist who treated several victims noted that they "suffer from anxiety, mood swings and loss of self-esteem . . . [and] struggle with issues like authority, intimacy and trust." It has been reported that former classmates have "referred to the victims as Gauthe's whores" (para. 26).

Though the Catholic Church is the most recognized religious institution dealing with child sexual abuse allegations, it is not the only one (Harper & Perkins, 2018). Although sexual abuse of minor children by clergy first gained attention via the Gauthe case in Louisiana in 1983, the history of sexual abuse within the Catholic Church did not gain widespread notoriety until 2002, when the *Boston Globe* exposed decades of abuse and corruption in the Archdiocese of Boston.

Following that, researchers from John Jay College of Criminal Justice conducted a national study of abuse within the church, and in subsequent years, additional researchers have studied various aspects of clergy sexual abuse.

While clergy sexual abuse was not initially tied to the #MeToo movement, recent disclosures and grand jury decisions have inextricably linked survivors with each other. In addition, behavioral trends displayed by individual priests, diocesan leaders, and decision makers are similar to those displayed by other sexual abusers.

This chapter addresses what is known of sexual abuse in religious communities and how allegations of abuse are handled. Further, we examine the #ChurchToo hashtag and its disclosures, analyze barriers to reporting, and describe protocols and policy implications.

Magnitude of the Problem

Data on religious institutions and child sexual abuse are scarce (Keenan, 2012), but the research that has been conducted on the topic has mainly focused on the Catholic Church. In the United States, the *Nature and Scope of Sexual Abuse of Minors by Catholic Priests and Deacons in the United States, 1950–2002* (John Jay College of Criminal Justice, 2004; Terry & Smith 2006), commissioned by the U.S. Conference of Catholic Bishops, found that approximately 4 percent of clergy had sexually victimized minors in the time period under examination. Since the publication of this report, thousands of additional victims have come forward. However, research suggests that offending within the church peaked in the 1980s and has been declining since (Terry et al., 2011).

Research in other countries is similar. In 1996, the Catholic Archdiocese of Melbourne, Australia, created the *Melbourne Response,* an ongoing initiative to assist victims of abuse at the hands of church officials. An independent commissioner, Peter O'Callaghan, a respected counsel in Victoria, was appointed to head this response. He found more than 300 confirmed cases of clergy child sexual abuse (Cummins et al., 2012; Harper & Perkins, 2018; Family and Community Development Committee, 2013). O'Callaghan told the Family and Community Development Committee,

> There is very little fakery in respect of sexual abuse. At the time of my appointment, because money was involved, I had the perception that there may be a number of bogus applicants, and that has not occurred at all. I have no doubt as to the veracity of the complaints which have been made. People do not, for obvious reasons, simulate or make up that they have been sexually abused. (Family and Community Development Committee, 2013, p. 401)

These findings were from one archdiocese in Australia. Further, Cardinal George Pell, who founded this initiative, was himself sentenced to six years in prison in March 2019 after being convicted of child sex changes (Albeck-Ripka & Cave, 2019; James, 2019). This, in addition to older allegations against Pell, has made several church officials and experts in the field question the *Melbourne Response,* suggesting the church should end self-investigation and controversial compensation schemes (Henriques-Gomes, 2019; James, 2019).

In 2010, the German government set up a confidential telephone line for victims to report claims of sexual abuse. During an 18-month period, more than 4,000 people called to report victimization of child sexual abuse; many alleged abuses were by Catholic or Protestant institutional offenders (Spröber et al., 2014). In Ireland, the *Commission of Investigation Report into the Catholic Archdiocese of Dublin* reported that 172 named priests and 11 unnamed priests had been accused of child sexual abuse (Murphy et al., 2009). The commission investigated complaints made against a representative sample of 46 priests by more than 320 abuse victims.

The largest study conducted in the United States on clergy sexual abuse was commissioned by the United States Conference of Catholic Bishops. Unlike other countries, the U.S. government has been silent on child sexual abuse in religious institutions, despite calls from the Catholic Whistleblowers organization and at least 25 other organizations (Hamilton, 2017). In response, states have created their own laws to combat this type of institutional abuse. For example, on July 1, 2019, Virginia became the 28th state to require priests, ministers, rabbis, and other clergy officials to report suspected abuse to local law enforcement. However, exceptions exist, such as anything said during confession or while a minister is counseling a parishioner (Fizer, 2019). Additionally, states have extended statutes of limitation for sexually violent crimes, both criminally and in civil court. Washington recently extended the statute of limitations for some sexual assault cases while removing it altogether for more serious crimes against children. California removed its statute of limitations on most felony sex crimes (Quinlan, 2019). According to the Rape, Abuse and Incest National Network (RAINN, n.d.), seven states do not have a statute of limitations for felony-level sex crimes: Kentucky, Maryland, North Carolina, South Carolina, Virginia, West Virginia, and Wyoming.

Mishandling of Cases by Catholic Institutions

In August 2018, the findings of a yearslong Pennsylvania grand jury investigation into clergy sexual abuse within six Roman Catholic dioceses across the commonwealth were released as the *40th Statewide Investigating Grand Jury Report*

1. The report documented allegations of abuse from the Dioceses of Harrisburg, Allentown, Pittsburgh, Greensburg, Erie, and Scranton. For context, these six dioceses cover 54 of the 67 counties in Pennsylvania. The grand jury reviewed approximately 500,000 pages of diocesan documentation, which contained "credible allegations against over three hundred predator priests" (*40th Statewide Investigating Grand Jury Report 1* [hereafter cited as *Grand Jury Report*], 2018, p. 1). Jury members were able to identify more than 1,000 child victims, though they noted, "We believe that the real number—of children whose records were lost, or who were afraid to come forward—is in the thousands" (p. 1). The grand jury reported that most victims were boys and that many were prepubescent, which aligns with findings from the John Jay College *Nature and Scope* study (2004). Terry and Freilich (2012) noted that about 80 percent of known victims from 1950 to 2002 were boys; young boys between the ages of 11 and 14 made up 40 percent of known victims.

In addition, the grand jury report detailed extensive use of sexual grooming tactics by abusive clergy as well as the justification and neutralization of illegal behavior by accused clerics and diocesan leaders. Prior research by Spraitz and colleagues has extensively detailed the use of neutralization techniques by priests and others (Spraitz & Bowen, 2016; Spraitz & Bowen, 2018; Spraitz et al., 2016; Spraitz et al., 2017) and has identified sexual grooming patterns that abusive priests use (Spraitz & Bowen, 2019; Spraitz et al., 2018). Numerous studies on grooming have identified factors that offenders look for when selecting victims. These include physical attractiveness (Elliott et al., 1995), psychological or emotional vulnerabilities (Elliott et al., 1995; Finkelhor, 1994; Olson et al.; Williams et al., 2013), and negative family situations (Elliott et al., 1995; Lang & Frenzel, 1988; Olson et al., 2007; Terry & Freilich, 2012). Winters and Jeglic (2017) detailed that once a potential victim is selected by an offender, the offender will figure out a way to gain access to the victim, will begin emotionally manipulating the victim, and gradually will establish trust in order to increase physical contact and desensitize the victim against physical touch.

In terms of sexual grooming tactics used by Catholic priests specifically, Spraitz et al. (2018) identified eight strategies used by abusive priests in one Illinois diocese. The identification of these tactics was supported in follow-up research by Spraitz and Bowen (2019) of abusive clerics from a Catholic institution in Minnesota. Sexually abusive priests groom their victims using one or more of the following techniques: (1) providing them with alcohol, drugs, or tobacco; (2) gifting other items to them; (3) secluding them via overnight outings or trips; (4) desensitizing them to physical touch; (5) feigning friendship or mentorship; (6) playing favorites or pitting potential victims against each other; (7) developing a relationship with the family of a potential victim, which is akin to social grooming; and (8) taking advantage of the respect and reverence bestowed upon a priest in order to avoid detection or downplay suspicion (Spraitz et al., 2018; Spraitz & Bowen, 2019).

The 2018 grand jury report also outlined how systemic the abuse was to the institution as a whole. The grand jury wrote that all the victims "were brushed aside . . . by church leaders who preferred to protect the abusers and their institution above all" (*Grand Jury Report*, 2018, p. 1). This sentiment is not unique among Catholic dioceses. While examining documents from the Archdiocese of Milwaukee, Spraitz et al. (2016) found that in response to a report of a priest molesting a young boy on a fishing trip, an unknown diocesan administrator wrote, "I would try to keep the lid on the thing, so no police record would be made. . . . Parents will not be informed" (p. 277). This behavior is not even unique to Pennsylvania dioceses. In 2016, the 37th Statewide Investigating Grand Jury in Pennsylvania reported on its investigation into the Altoona–Johnstown diocese. Findings suggested that a former bishop felt no legal obligation to report any allegations or accusations of sexual misconduct by priests to civil authorities (Smith, 2016). As the 40th Grand Jury wrote, "The pattern was pretty much the same. The main thing was not to help children, but to avoid 'scandal'" (*Grand Jury Report*, 2018, p. 2).

In research documenting abuse at a Benedictine abbey in Minnesota, Spraitz et al. (2017) found that scandal avoidance was an oft-used practice. One abbot admitted a knowing failure to disclose misconduct, which was due in part to "the effect that such an announcement would have on the capital campaign and enrollment" at a church (p. 200). Additionally, a memo from an abbey chancellor to several other administrators detailed the importance of keeping allegations against another clergyman quiet: "There would be some serious disruption to parish life if [the accused] were immediately removed. We are all aware that the parish is about to celebrate its 100th anniversary and to kick off a major capital fund drive" (p. 200). These examples suggest that diocesan administrators knew the deleterious effect public disclosure of sexual abuse by priests would have on their ability to raise funds from parish communities.

The final, and perhaps most important, item that the 40th Statewide Investigating Grand Jury in Pennsylvania provided was a summary of informal rules that dioceses had followed when in receipt of an abuse allegation. The grand jury categorized this as a "playbook." As such, it helped solidify the notion that clergy sexual abuse was a systemic institutional ill. There were seven practices that the grand jury identified. First, dioceses used euphemisms when describing sexual assaults. "Never say 'rape'; say 'inappropriate contact' or 'boundary issues'" (*Grand Jury Report*, 2018, p. 3). Second, they conducted sham investigations. The dioceses did not use trained personnel to conduct investigations into abuse; rather, they had untrained clergy members ask superficial questions before reaching prede-termined outcomes. Third, they sent accused clerics to church-run treatment centers for psychiatric evaluation. This has been seen in evaluations of Wisconsin and Minnesota offenders too; Spraitz and colleagues (2017) noted that the evaluation would occur almost immediately before the priest was transferred to another church. Frawley-O'Dea (2004) also provided a succinct outline of this institutional response.

Fourth, and related to transfers, dioceses would not say why a priest had been removed. Essentially, they would lie to parishioners by reporting that he was on "sick leave, or suffering" some type of mental breakdown (*Grand Jury Report*, 2018, p. 3). Fifth, even if the sexually abusive conduct was known in the parish community, dioceses would follow through with the transfer because it was likely that the parishioners at the receiving institution would not know about the illegal conduct. Remember, much of the documentation that we have on sexual abuse by Catholic clergy is from a time before knowledge of this type of institutional abuse was widespread. It was seemingly less difficult to engage in this type of coverup.

Sixth, the church continued to pay housing and living expenses of abusive clergy. Research conducted by Spraitz et al. (2018) and Spraitz and Bowen (2019) suggested that a lot of sexual grooming occurred in a priest's living quarters or at other diocesan-owned property, like cabins and lake houses. Seventh, the grand jury found that dioceses throughout Pennsylvania did not treat child sexual abuse by clergy as a crime; rather, it was something they treated as a personnel matter to be dealt with internally (*Grand Jury Report*, 2018).

Other Religious Institutional Research on Child Sexual Abuse

The highly publicized abuse within the Catholic Church demonstrates how factors such as religious beliefs and religious institutions can hinder victim disclosure and allow abuse to continue (see, for example, Collins et al., 2014; Dale & Alpert, 2007). Yet, research on other religious denominations remains sparse. Additionally, we realize that the discussion that follows is not exhaustive in terms of religious denominations and clerics reviewed. For many religions, extensive research of this type has not been conducted yet. Thus, we do not discuss Muslim imams, Hindu gurus, or Buddhist monks below; for further examination of responses to sexual abuse within other religions, see Rashid and Barron (2019).

Jewish Communities

Although research has been conducted on the Orthodox Jewish community and child sexual abuse, considerably less is known about religious officials committing child sexual abuse. Katzenstein and Fontes (2017) found that there are five factors that influence the lack of reporting in Orthodox communities. First, the concept of *mesira* prohibits members from reporting criminal actions to secular authorities and speaking unfavorably about other Jewish community members. Second, community members have a long history of intimidating victims, making them and others in the community fearful to report. Friedman (2013) quoted a survivor from the Orthodox community as saying,

> What they have done to me since is a lot worse than even the original abuse. They cut me off in the most complete way I can imagine. What's even worse, I don't think it's only about me. They've made an example of me for the rest of the community to make sure that nobody else speaks out about abuse. (p. 1)

A former district attorney from Brooklyn described one Orthodox community in Brooklyn as using "Mafia-like" intimidation against child sexual abuse victims and their families (Edelman, 2014).

The third factor that Katzenstein and Fontes (2017) suggested deters victims from reporting is the stigma and shame brought upon the family. The fourth factor is the reliance on rabbinical courts to serve as governing authorities in the community. Rabbinical courts typically do not inform civil legal authorities when members break the law (Otterman & Rivera, 2012). The last factor is the role that gender plays in the community. Boys and girls are usually educated separately, and there is a lack of sex education. Katzenstein and Fontes (2017) noted that men are often viewed as the ultimate authority, and profound respect for elders within the community contributes to the likelihood of non-reporting by the victim and those who know about the victimization (see Blackler, 2012).

Jehovah's Witnesses

Goodstein (2002) described sexual abuse policies within the Jehovah's Witnesses denomination, finding that its sexual misconduct policies are focused on biblical standards. Allegations of sexual misconduct are heard by a male panel of elders, and cases can be substantiated when the child has two witnesses to verify the allegation or the offender admits guilt (McClellan & Milroy, 2016). Even then, the congregation is told of the discipline but not of the reason for it. A report in Australia that examined more than six decades of information about sexual misconduct by Jehovah's Witnesses found that over 1,000 members had been accused of child sexual abuse, though none of the accused were reported to law enforcement officials (Schmidt, 2016). The Royal Commission into Institutional Responses to Child Sexual Abuse in Australia found the following policies (in addition to the ones stated above) or lack thereof problematic: the organization does not have a policy of reporting child sexual abuse to outside organizations, such as law enforcement; males are the only decision-making authority; the organization has a policy and practice of shunning members who wish to leave the organization; and the organization has ineffective policies in place to manage the risk of child sexual abuse within the organization (McClellan & Milroy, 2016).

Dozens of claims have been filed in the United States alleging that Jehovah's Witnesses church officials have mismanaged cases of sexual misconduct or simply covered them up (Volz, 2018). One survivor said, "They had used the Bible to victim-shame me for what I had done, and they never did anything to him [the accused]. He got married, and he remained within the congregation—a child molester living among them" (Chuck, 2018, para. 10).

The Church of Jesus Christ of Latter-day Saints

There have been allegations that the Church of Jesus Christ of Latter-day Saints refuses access to information about accusations of sexual abuse within the church (Mountain West News Bureau, 2018), so academic research conducted on the church is scant. In a study conducted more than 20 years ago, 71 Mormon women who were survivors of child sexual abuse were interviewed. Of those, 61 participants talked to church leaders about the abuse, and 49 of those 61 described negative reactions or outcomes, including feelings of judgment, not being believed, or the church providing protection for the accused (Gerdes et al., 1996).

Several lawsuits have claimed that the Mormon church, historically an insular religious community, turns a "blind eye" to child sexual abuse or blatantly protects the image of the church. Some accusations have stemmed from the Indian Student Placement Program, which the church operated from the 1940s until 2000, where Navajo children were placed with Mormon foster families. At least nine lawsuits have been settled related to this program and accusations of child sexual abuse (Mountain West News Bureau, 2018)

More recent allegations concern operations of its sexual abuse hotline for church leaders created in 1995. Though church officials contend the hotline advises bishops about reporting laws, others suggest it is used to cover up accusations of sexual abuse and protect the church from potential lawsuits (Collman, 2019). Details about the number of people who call the hotline or what percentage of cases are referred to law enforcement from the hotline are not disclosed (Meier, 2019). Confidential settlements allow the church to shield information from the public. Because of this, the scope of the problem is unknown (Terry, 2013).

Given #MeToo and #ChurchToo, attention has focused on the church and the responsibility it has for its victims. In the fall of 2018, the Church of Jesus Christ of Latter-day Saints established a website, ChurchofJesusChrist.org, that provides help and resources to victims of abuse, an outlet to report such abuse, prevention and protection tips, and information on how others can help victims (West, 2018).

Protestant Denominations

Protestant denominations have autonomous organization structures and numerous reporting systems, making it difficult to estimate child sexual abuse. Denney et al. (2018) noted that despite the large number of congregations and members—there are an estimated 314,000 Protestant congregations in the United States serving nearly 60 million congregants—research on sexual abuse is lacking. Jenkins (1996) estimated that approximately 10 percent of Protestant clergy are connected to sexual misconduct with children and adults. Two of the three insurance companies for various Protestant religious organizations disclosed that over a five-year period, one company paid approximately $4 million for child sexual abuse and sexual misconduct settlements, while the other company reported paying approximately $7.8 million over a 15-year span (Moyer, 2007). Further, Denney et al. (2018) noted that the three insurance companies that provide coverage for Protestant churches disclosed 7,095 instances of sexual abuse in those churches from 1987 to 2007. Nearly $90 million in insurance claims was paid out.

A discontinued website, Reformation.com, cataloged newspaper articles about Protestant ministers and sexual misconduct. A list of 838 ministers who had allegations against them was compiled as of 2010 (Terry, 2013). Using news articles from 1999 to 2014, Denney et al. (2018) recorded a sample of 326 individual cases of sexual abuse in Protestant churches. Their analysis of the 326 cases revealed 454 alleged offenses of sexual misconduct in 41 states. Nearly 80 percent of the 454 offenses were contact offenses, such as sexual assault and rape. Non-contact offenses included sexual harassment and possession of child pornography. Further analysis revealed that nearly 40 percent of the abuse occurred at the church, while one-third of all offenses occurred at the offender's home and nearly 13 percent of abuse occurred off-site, typically in the offender's car. More than 10 percent of alleged abuse occurred at a church-sponsored activity, such as a camping trip or mission trip. These locations are not unique to abusers from Protestant denominations; they are also seen in research on sexual abuse in other types of religious organizations.

Denney et al. (2018) were able to distinguish the role that each offender played within the church. Approximately 35 percent of offenders were pastors, and more than 31 percent were youth ministers. The remaining one-third of offenders were listed as associate pastors, music ministers, Sunday school teachers, deacons, camp workers, church members, volunteers, and pastor's wife. Knowing the offender's role plays a critical part in increasing awareness of how opportunity and access contribute to sexual abuse in church settings; again, this is not unique to Protestant denominations.

From February to June 2019, the *Houston Chronicle* released a six-part investigative series on the Southern Baptist church. It found that sexual abuse allegations had been known since 1998. Reporters from the *Houston Chronicle* and the *San Antonio Express-News* uncovered evidence that more than 250 employees and volunteers within Southern Baptist churches were charged with sex related crimes between 2008 and 2018 (Downen et al., 2019). In total, approximately 380 alleged perpetrators, 220 of whom have been convicted or taken plea deals, had over 700 victims.

Like in many of the other church institutions, several former presidents and prominent leaders in the religious organization have been accused of covering up the scandals. In response to the allegations within the church, the Southern Baptist Convention hosted a three-day Caring Well conference in North Texas that included over 1,600 church officials, victim advocates, attorneys, therapists, and survivors (Crary, 2019c; Perry, 2019). However, the commission's president said the conference was "not intended to produce new policies or recommendations"; rather, its goal was "to provide churches with expert advice on how to prevent abuse and support abuse survivors" (Crary, 2019c, para. 12). The denomination has made resources and training available to its churches; however, these are voluntary. As of August 2019, Perry (2019) found that less than 2 percent of its churches have taken advantage of them.

Case Study: #ChurchToo

Religious institutions were thrust into the #MeToo discussion in November 2017 after Hannah Paasch and Emily Joy started #ChurchToo on Twitter. Paasch and Joy encouraged other Twitter users to share their stories of sexual abuse and sexism within the church, particularly those in evangelical faiths. Overnight, the tweets went viral, and Joy and Paasch were inundated with notifications on their phones (Andrews, 2018a).

According to Andrews (2018a), "purity culture" is a main reason that sexual abuse within evangelical churches has remained hidden for so long. Essentially, evangelicals believe sex before marriage is taboo, because sexual purity is the foundation of traditional family units and traditional gender roles. Andrews wrote that this culture "places an incredibly high value on virginity—female virginity, in particular" (para. 17). Further, women and girls are considered "sexual gatekeepers," while boys and men are treated as "slaves to their unquenchable desires" (para. 17). Similarly, in a review of the memoir *Pure,* Dubick (2018, para. 4) wrote, "Boys are taught that their minds are a gateway to sin, women are taught that their bodies are [a gateway to sin]," and girls are responsible for both their own purity as well as that of the boys around them. Anderson noted, "Men are told that they will be driven totally by their desire for sex and women are the ones that have to stop them" (2018a, para. 21). Often, evangelical girls and women who are victimized are told they were not convincing enough when they said "no" or that they did not fight hard enough.

Joy's story of abuse was similar to many others in that her abuser was in a position of power and groomed her. She was 16 when the abuse started; her abuser, a youth leader at her evangelical church, was a man in his early 30s. Her tweets detailed how her abuser feigned friendship and mentorship but soon began giving dating advice and eventually pursued a romantic relationship. A thread of tweets posted by Joy (2017) discussed what happened:

> So I fancied myself in love with him. He encouraged me not to tell my parents or anyone else (obviously). Eventually I was able to tell one friend. And technically, "nothing happened." I say "technically" because the emails. There were so many emails. And gmail chats. And secret texts. I deleted them all years ago but you can imagine what was in them. Talking about how badly he wanted to marry me, how badly he wanted to kiss me. Reminder that I was 16 and he was … 31? 32? And he was in a position of power. A "leader." That was ten years ago so he's got to be in his early 40s now.

The abuse ended when Joy's parents found out and notified the church. Similar to what we know of the Catholic response to allegations of abuse, Joy's church made her abuser leave the youth group, and he eventually moved on to other churches. Joy (2017) tweeted, "But no one ever found out why except a select few." And, in keeping with purity culture, Joy's parents seemingly held her responsible for her own victimization. She tweeted, "My parents made *me* call *him* and apologize *to him* (and confiscated my social media passwords and grounded me from driving and generally treated me like the Jezebel in this situation)."

Sexually abusive acts that gave rise to the #ChurchToo hashtag also have contributed to previously unseen levels of movement from one church to another by younger churchgoers. According to the 2019 Sexual Misconduct and Churchgoers Study, 10 percent of Protestants between the ages of 18 and 34 who attend church have switched churches because of inadequate responses to sexual misconduct (Shellnut, 2019). Comparatively, just 5 percent of all 1,815 respondents reported doing the same. Additionally, 9 percent of those under 35 reported not feeling safe from misconduct.

Barriers to Reporting

Despite the accumulation of knowledge about abuse incidents in religious institutions, we likely know of only a small fraction of offenses, because victims endure several barriers to reporting the abuse they have suffered. As detailed in the case study above, purity culture presents a big barrier to reporting. As Andrews explained, "This culture of purity has created an environment in which . . . people simply believe that sexual assault or misconduct cannot happen within it" (2018a, para. 25) or that if somebody is following "God's plan," sexual assault will not occur. Because of this, if victims come forward, they will likely be stigmatized and the assault will be treated as a sin committed by the abused instead of a crime committed by the abuser. Attorney Boz Tchividjian, grandson of evangelical preacher Billy Graham, noted that victims are often blamed and accused of seducing the person who abused them (Christian Post, 2014).

This response is akin to one of the main techniques of neutralization, "condemnation of condemners," coined by Sykes and Matza (1957). Simply, this neutralization technique allows the accused to reject the allegations by placing undue blame on the victim or attacking the victim or whomever is speaking out on behalf of the victim. In their study of neutralization behaviors displayed by accused priests from Milwaukee, Spraitz and Bowen (2016) uncovered multiple examples of priests condemning their accusers. One alleged abuser continually attacked the credibility of the victim:

> When discussing the charge that he assaulted altar boys in the rectory, he wrote, "[M]y accuser is far sicker than I even imagined." Continuing in a letter to an administrator in 1993, Priest 5 then discusses a proposed meeting with his accuser that was suggested by a psychologist; the priest states his reluctance to meet and writes of the victim, "I am convinced more than ever of his illness." Nearly one decade later, Priest 5 wrote several letters to Pope John Paul II. In one of those letters, the priest characterized his accuser as a "six-time criminal" who led a "non-exemplary life." (p. 2530)

Attacking the credibility and competency of known victims deters those who have not come forward from reporting their abuse. Yet, it is not always the accused who attacks the victim. For example, in Emily Joy's disclosure discussed above, it was her parents that made her apologize to her abuser and punished her for her own victimization. Such reactions contribute to feelings of stigma and shame, thus deterring victims from disclosing their abuse.

The concept of reverential fear and religious duress also can help explain why victims do not report their victimizations. Benkert and Doyle (2009, p. 224) explained reverential fear as something "induced not from an unjust force from without but from the reverence one has for an authority figure." Meanwhile, they defined religious duress as caused by surrogates of an omnipotent supreme being. It is reasonable to believe that priests, deacons, pastors, youth ministers, and Sunday school teachers, among others, are all considered Christlike surrogates within their respective churches. Spraitz and Bowen (2019) saw this concept in their research of one Minnesota religious institution; "victims' feelings about the monks' status likely influenced them to stay silent about the abuse. . . . The notion that 'he was a priest' and that abusive behavior should not be questioned was seen" (p. 717).

This feeling experienced by some victims ties in with the existence of dysfunctional power dynamics within religious institutions. Mainly, men are in charge and women are seen as subservient (Moslener, 2018), a relationship that helps explain barriers to reporting in evangelical churches. However, empirical research of sexual abuse within the Catholic Church suggests that most victims in that specific institution were boys (Terry & Freilich, 2012). Thus, there may be a lack of generalizability across religious denominations. Nevertheless, each of the concepts discussed assist with understanding why victims of institutional sexual abuse in religious settings do not come forward or do so reluctantly.

Responses

Religious organizations have made several attempts to implement policies and protocols intended to prevent further sexual abuse. The effectiveness of these measures remains questionable. Specific public responses that have been taken are discussed below.

Charter for the Protection of Children and Young People

The United States Conference of Catholic Bishops adopted the *Charter for the Protection of Children and Young People* in June 2002. Essentially, the charter implemented a zero-tolerance policy for sexual abuse and misconduct in Catholic institutions. Pope John Paul II said, "There is no place in the priesthood or religious life for those who would harm the young" (United States Conference of Catholic Bishops, 2011, p. 6).

Passage of the charter led to immediate action in some dioceses. For example, the Archdiocese of Milwaukee identified and removed from active ministry a half dozen priests in 2002 (Spraitz & Bowen, 2016). Furthermore,

> in early 2004, Archbishop Dolan conducted an audit of priests' personnel files to ensure the discovery of all allegations of sexual abuse; in July 2004, the names of the 45 priests who would be restricted under Article V of the *Charter* were published. . . . On July 1, 2013, personnel files for 42 of the 45 listed priests were made publicly available by the Archdiocese of Milwaukee. (p. 2519)

Nearly two decades after the passage of the charter, abuse cases continue to be reported. In its *2018 Annual Report*, released in May 2019, the U.S. Conference of Catholic Bishops noted that during the current reporting period (July 1, 2017, to June 30, 2018), 1,385 victim-survivors of clergy sexual abuse alleged 1,455 acts of abuse; victim-survivors came from 126 different Catholic dioceses. These figures represented an increase in both the number of victim-survivors coming forward and abuse incidents reported compared with the year prior, which saw 652 victim-survivors alleging 693 incidents. Authors of the 2018 report also noted that 785 allegations were received from five dioceses in New York State as part of its Independent Reconciliation and Compensation program. These statistics show that abuse continues to occur and suggest that many victim-survivors have not come forward yet and maybe never will.

Statute of Limitations Laws

Several U.S. states, including California, Delaware, Hawaii, and Minnesota, have created "lookback windows" that allow victims of sexual abuse to file lawsuits against institutions that hold some culpability for the abuse that occurred (Crary, 2019a). In addition, more than 20 states also are exploring the possibility of opening these windows to allow more survivors to come forward.

Several entities, such as the Catholic Church, the Boy Scouts of America, and representatives from the insurance industry, are lobbying against any changes to statutes of limitations (Crary, 2019a). The New York Catholic Conference, a representative of bishops in the state of New York, believes opening up reporting windows would "force institutions to defend alleged" decades-old conduct (Crary, 2019a, para. 16). Cardinal Dolan, the archbishop of New York, has argued that the church is fulfilling its obligation to victims and cites numbers from a compensation program that has helped over 1,000 victim-survivors since 2016; this program has paid more than $200 million during that time. Additionally, opponents of amending statutes of limitations worry that these laws will lead to more dioceses declaring bankruptcy.

Despite these objections, New Jersey recently became the latest state to open a filing window for survivors of sexual abuse when Governor Phil Murphy signed legislation opening a two-year window beginning December 2019. The window applies to "sexual abuse victims of any age" and gives them the opportunity to "bring lawsuits for sexual abuse in cases that were previously barred by the statute of limitations" (Anderson & Associates, 2019, para. 3). Also, under the law, "child sexual abuse survivors will be able to file sexual abuse lawsuits until age 55, or seven years from the date they discover the cause of their injuries, whichever is later" (para. 3). Jeff Anderson, an attorney who represents survivors of sexual abuse, argues that the law "helps survivors take back the power that was stolen from them when they were abused" (para. 3).

Church Culture

As the works cited in this chapter suggest, a shift in church culture may help reduce sexual misconduct. Churches should focus their policies on increased reporting as well as on holding accountable officials who do nothing when victims come forward or who attempt to silence and cover up these individuals' accounts. For example, Pope Francis has mandated each diocese have a reporting office by June 2020 to encourage reporting (Tornielli, 2019). However, not much is known about these reporting centers. Additionally, new policies released by the Catholic Church to curtail the sexual abuse scandal do not detail specific consequences or punishments if these polices are not upheld by church officials (Green, 2019). The lack of specificity may promote a culture of silence within churches. Policies to encourage reporting should include appointing laypersons or neutral outsiders to work with the church to encourage victims to come forward to them instead of to the church officials. Policies regarding accountability should be clear and stipulate negative ramifications for officials who do not abide by them. These steps would help increase transparency and confidence in the church.

Case Study: Willow Creek Community Church

In early August 2018, the #ChurchToo movement achieved a very significant victory when pastor Heather Larson and the board of elders at Willow Creek Community Church, a suburban Chicago megachurch with approximately 25,000 members, publicly resigned and apologized to victims of sexual abuse (Andrews, 2018b). Their resignations were in response to sexual assault and sexual harassment allegations made against founding pastor Bill Hybels. Although many accusations had first been levied in early 2018, the church had been investigating him internally for nearly four years. Still, in April 2018, Larson and the board of elders stood by Hybels when he denied the allegations, and he was allowed to retire six months early on his own terms.

The release of a *New York Times* story about Hybels seemingly caused the multiple pastors and the board of elders to rethink their support. In the story, Hybels was accused of emotional abuse, of physical abuse, and of demanding that his executive assistant perform sexual acts on him (Goldstein, 2018). The abuse began in 1986 with a back rub in which Hybels unhooked the victim's bra; the abuse continued for two years. Hybels not only sexually assaulted the victim but sexually harassed her too. In a postscript to a note praising the work the victim was doing, Hybels wrote, "Plus, you are a knockout!" The victim was determined to maintain her silence; she says that she did not want to hurt the church.

After learning of these allegations, one of the lead pastors at Willow Creek vomited before services began (Andrews, 2018b), and another resigned immediately following services (Goldstein, 2018). Days later, Larson and the board resigned. As Andrews (2018b) noted, when #ChurchToo first began in November 2017, it did not seem possible that it would have a profound impact in evangelical circles. It did not even seem possible when Andrews wrote about #ChurchToo in May

2018—at least, the author did not think so: "While the church was finally being forced to deal with something that was a long time coming, these all-powerful men were only starting to see consequences. And it still seemed that something like what happened this week at Willow Creek was impossible" (para. 9).

Conclusion

Child sexual abuse has occurred in all religious denominations, although most research has focused on abuse within the Catholic Church. The #MeToo and #ChurchToo movements have increased awareness and news media attention on the issue. These movements also have given victims of all ages a broader platform for society to hear their stories. Research into institutional sexual abuse, the #MeToo movement, and #ChurchToo are making a positive difference, but there is still more to do. In addition, most denominations have yet to invite external voices to be part of the process or to oversee changes. This type of transparency is necessary to increase societal faith in religious institutions, since many of the largest religious denominations in the United States have seen decreased membership due to the spillover effect of abuse cases (Crary, 2019b). Perhaps because of this, the #MeToo and #ChurchToo movements continue to make larger impacts than ever before on religious institutional responses to sexual abuse.

References

Albeck-Ripka, L., & Cave, D. (2019, March 12). Cardinal George Pell of Australia sentenced to six years in prison. *New York Times.* https://www.nytimes.com /2019/03/12/world/australia/george-pell-sentence.html

Anderson & Associates. (2019, May 13). *Childhood sexual abuse survivors given more time to seek justice, healing: Two-year window allows survivors of any age to file lawsuits.* https://www.andersonadvocates.com/Home/Details/2386

Andrews, B. (2018a, May 25). As a teen, Emily Joy was abused by a church youth leader: Now she's leading a movement to change Evangelical America. *Mother Jones.* https://www.motherjones.com/crime-justice/2018/05/evangelical-church -metoo-movement-abuse/

Andrews, B. (2018b, August 10). The #ChurchToo movement just scored a major victory for victims of sexual abuse. *Mother Jones.* https://www.motherjones.com /crime-justice/2018/08/the-churchtoo-movement-just-scored-a-historic -victory-for-victims-of-sexual-abuse-willowcreek-community-church-bill-hybels/

Benkert, M., & Doyle, T. P. (2009). Clericalism, religious duress and its psychological impact on victims of clergy sexual abuse. *Pastoral Psychology, 58*(3), 223–238. https://doi.org/10.1007/s11089–008–0188–0

Blackler, Z. (2012, May 16). Brooklyn's Orthodox Jews rally behind accused in child abuse case. *The Guardian.* https://www.theguardian.com/world/2012/may/16 /orthodox-sex-abuse-scandal-new-york

Christian Post. (2014, June 23). *Boz Tchividjian says churches cause damage by failing to take sex abuse seriously* [Video file]. YouTube. https://www.youtube.com /watch?v=Kq21m-0vEmA

Chuck, E. (2018, October 7). *Jehovah's Witnesses "use the Bible to victim-shame," sex abuse survivor says.* NBC News. https://www.nbcnews.com/news/us -news/jehovah-s-witnesses-use-bible-victim-shame-sex-abuse-survivor -n916326

Collins, C., O'Neill, M., Fontes, L. A., & Ossege, J. (2014). Catholicism and childhood sexual abuse: Women's coping and psychotherapy. *Journal of Child Sexual Abuse, 23,* 519–537. https://doi.org/10.1080/10538712.2014.918071

Collman, A. (2019, May 3). The Mormon church has been accused of using their sexual abuse hotline to quiet victims and stave off potential lawsuits. *Business Insider.* https://www.businessinsider.com/mormon-church-accused-of -silencing-sexual-assault-claims-2019-5

Crary, D. (2019a, January 23). States consider easing statute of limitations on child sex-abuse cases. *PBS NewsHour.* https://www.pbs.org/newshour/nation/states -consider-easing-of-limitations-on-child-sex-abuse-cases

Crary, D. (2019b, March 3). 3 of U.S.'s biggest religious denominations in turmoil over sex abuse, LGBT policy. *PBS NewsHour.* https://www.pbs.org/newshour /nation/3-big-us-churches-in-turmoil-over-sex-abuse-lgbt-policy

Crary, D. (2019c, October 1). Southern Baptists ready to put spotlight on sex-abuse crisis. *National Catholic Reporter.* https://www.ncronline.org/news /accountability/southern-baptists-ready-put-spotlight-sex-abuse-crisis

Cummins, P., Scott, D., & Scales, B. (2012). *Report of the Protecting Victoria's Vulnerable Children inquiry.* State of Victoria Government, Melbourne, Australia.

Dale, K. A., & Alpert, J. L. (2007). Hiding behind the cloth: Child sexual abuse and the Catholic Church. *Journal of Child Sexual Abuse, 16*(3), 59–74. https://doi .org/10.1300/J070v16n03_04

Denney, A. S., Kerley, K. R., & Gross, N. G. (2018). Child sexual abuse in Protestant Christian congregations: A descriptive analysis of offense and offender characteristics. *Religions, 9*(27), 1–13. https://doi.org/10.3390/rel9010027

DePalma, A. (2002, March 19). Church scandal resurrects old hurts in Louisiana bayou. *New York Times.* https://www.nytimes.com/2002/03/19/us/church -scandal-resurrects-old-hurts-in-louisiana-bayou.html

Downen, R., Olsen, L., & Tedesco, J. (2019, February 10). Abuse of faith. *Houston Chronicle.* https://www.houstonchronicle.com/news/investigations/article /Southern-Baptist-sexual-abuse-spreads-as-leaders-13588038.php

Dubick, S. (2018, October 16). *How evangelical purity culture can lead to a lifetime of sexual shame*. Vice. https://www.vice.com/en_us/article/pa98x8/purity -culture-linday-kay-klein-pure-review

Edelman, S. (2014, August 10). Brooklyn DA exposes hidden Orthodox sex cases. *New York Post*. https://nypost.com/2014/08/10/brooklyn-da-exposes-hidden -orthodox-sex-cases-kept-secret/

Elliott, M., Browne, K., & Kilcoyne, J. (1995). Child sexual abuse prevention: What offenders tell us. *Child Abuse & Neglect, 19*, 579–594.

Family and Community Development Committee. (2013). *Betrayal of trust: Inquiry into the handling of child abuse by religious and other non-government organisations*. Parliament of Victoria, Melbourne, Australia.

Finkelhor, D. (1994). Current information on the scope and nature of child sexual abuse. *The Future of Children, 4*(2), 31–53. https://doi.org/10.2307/1602522

Fizer, C. (2019, March 27). *Governor signs bill requiring clergy to report child abuse*. AP News. https://www.apnews.com/a8cb464319be471fa12f92a20b5cb3c1

40th Statewide Investigating Grand Jury Report 1. (2018). DocumentCloud.org . https://www.documentcloud.org/documents/4756977–40th-Statewide -Investigating-Grand-Jury-Interim.html

Frawley-O'Dea, M. G. (2004). The history and consequences of the sexual-abuse crisis in the Catholic Church. *Studies in Gender and Sexuality, 5*(1), 11–30.

Friedman, A. (2013). Breaking the code of silence. *Jerusalem Report, 24*, 6.

Gerdes, K. E., Beck, M. N., Cowan-Hancock, S., & Wilkinson-Sparks, T. (1996). Adult survivors of childhood sexual abuse: The case of Mormon women. *Affilia, 11*(1), 39–60.

Goldstein, L. (2018, August 5). He's a superstar pastor. She worked for him and says he groped her repeatedly. *New York Times*. https://www.nytimes.com/2018/08 /05/us/bill-hybels-willow-creek-pat-baranowski.html?action=click&module =Intentional&pgtype=Article

Goodstein, L. (2002, August 11). Ousted members say Jehovah's Witnesses' policy on abuse hides offenses. *New York Times*. https://www.nytimes.com/2002/08/11/us /ousted-members-say-jehovah-s-witnesses-policy-on-abuse-hides-offenses.html

Green, E. (2019, May 12). Pope Francis stops hiding from the church's sexual abuse epidemic. *The Atlantic*. https://www.theatlantic.com/politics/archive/2019/05 /catholic-church-sex-abusepope-francis/589243/

Hamilton, M. A. (2017). The barriers to a national inquiry into child sexual abuse in the United States. *Child Abuse & Neglect, 74*, 107–110. https://doi.org/10.1016 /j.chiabu.2017.10.004

Harper, C. A., & Perkins, C. (2018). Reporting child sexual abuse within religious settings: Challenges and future directions. *Child Abuse Review, 27*, 30–41.

Henriques-Gomes, L. (2019, March 4). Q&A: Church leaders say George Pell's Melbourne Response should be scrapped. *The Guardian*. https://www.theguardian

.com/australia-news/2019/mar/05/qa-church-leader-says-george-pells-melbourne-response-should-be-scrapped

James, M. (2019, March 12). George Pell, once Australia's most senior Catholic, given 6 years for child sex abuse. *USA Today.* https://www.usatoday.com/story/news/world/2019/03/12/catholic-church-george-pell-six-years-child-sex-case/3146864002/

Jenkins, P. (1996). *Pedophiles and priests: Anatomy of a contemporary crisis.* Oxford University Press.

John Jay College of Criminal Justice. (2004). *The nature and scope of sexual abuse of minors by Catholic priests and deacons in the United States, 1950–2002.* United States Conference of Catholic Bishops.

Joy, E. [@emilyjoypoetry]. (2017, November 20). *So I fancied myself in love with him. He encouraged me not to tell my parents or anyone else (obviously)* [Tweet]. Twitter. https://twitter.com/emilyjoypoetry/status/932789883508314112

Katzenstein, D., & Fontes, L. A. (2017). Twice silenced: The underreporting of child sexual abuse in Orthodox Jewish communities. *Journal of Child Sexual Abuse, 26*(6), 752–767. https://doi.org/10.1080/10538712.2017.1336505

Keenan, M. (2012). *Child sexual abuse and the Catholic Church: Gender, power, and organizational culture.* Oxford University Press.

Lang, R., & Frenzel, R. (1988). How sex offenders lure children. *Annals of Sex Research, 1,* 303–317.

McClellan, P., & Milroy, H. (2016). *Report of Case Study No. 29: The response of the Jehovah's Witnesses and Watchtower Bible and Tract Society of Australia Ltd. to allegations of child sexual abuse.* Royal Commission into Institutional Responses to Child Sexual Abuse.

Meier, B. (2019, May 3). *The Mormon church has been accused of using a victims' hotline to hide claims of sexual abuse.* Vice News. https://news.vice.com/en_us/article/d3n73w/duty-to-report-the-mormon-church-has-been-accused-of-using-a-victims-hotline-to-hide-sexual-abuse-claims

Moslener, S. (2018, June 12). *Sexual purity, #ChurchToo, and the crisis of male evangelical leadership.* Religion & Politics. https://religionandpolitics.org/2018/06/12/sexual-purity-churchtoo-and-the-crisis-of-male-evangelical-leadership/

Mountain West News Bureau. (2018, October 1). *Claims of sexual abuse continue to haunt LDS Church.* Wyoming Public Media. https://www.wyomingpublicmedia.org/post/claims-sexual-abuse-continue-haunt-lds-church#stream/0

Moyer, W. (2007, August 27). *Child sex abuse by Protestant clergy difficult to document.* StopBaptistPredators.org. http://stopbaptistpredators.org/article07/child_sex_abuse_by_protestant_clergy.html

Murphy, Y., Mangan, I., & O'Neill, H. (2009). *Commission of Investigation Report into the Catholic Archdiocese of Dublin.* Irish Department of Justice and Equality.

Olson, L. N., Daggs, J. L., Ellevold, B. L., & Rogers, T. K. K. (2007). Entrapping the innocent: Toward a theory of child sexual predators' luring communication. *Communication Theory, 17*(3), 231–251. https://doi.org/10.1111/j.1468–2885.2007.00294.x

Otterman, S., & Rivera, R. (2012, May 9). Ultra-Orthodox shun their own for reporting child sexual abuse. *New York Times.* https://www.nytimes.com/2012/05/10/nyregion/ultra-orthodox-jews-shun-their-own-for-reporting-child-sexual-abuse.html?_r=3

Perry, A. (2019, October 7). SBC president: We failed to heed victims' voices. *Christianity Today.* https://www.christianitytoday.com/news/2019/october/southern-baptist-president-greear-caring-well.html

Quinlan, C. (2019, April 20). *Washington state passes law extending statute of limitations for victims of sexual violence.* ThinkProgress. https://thinkprogress.org/washington-state-passes-law-extending-statute-of-limitations-for-victims-of-sexual-violence-49d88db6a08e/

RAINN. (n.d.). *State by state guidelines on statutes of limitations.* https://www.rainn.org/state-state-guide-statutes-limitations

Rashid, F., & Barron, I. (2019). Why the focus of clerical child sexual abuse has largely remained on the Catholic Church amongst other non-Catholic Christian denominations and religions. *Journal of Child Sexual Abuse.* Advanced online publication. https://doi.org/10.1080/10538712.2018.1563261

Schmidt, S. (2016, November 28). Australian Jehovah's Witnesses protected over a thousand members accused of child abuse, report says. *Washington Post.* https://www.washingtonpost.com/news/morning-mix/wp/2016/11/28/australian-jehovahs-witnesses-protected-over-a-thousand-members-accused-of-child-abuse-report-says/?utm_term=.6a25ab80f4fa

Shellnut, K. (2019, May 21). 1 in 10 young Protestants have left a church over abuse. *Christianity Today.* https://www.christianitytoday.com/news/2019/may/lifeway-protestant-abuse-survey-young-christians-leave-chur.html

Smith, P. (2016, March 1). Grand jury: Altoona diocese concealed sex abuse of hundreds of children by priests. *Pittsburgh Post-Gazette.* https://www.post-gazette.com/news/state/2016/03/01/Staggering-abuse-cover-up-in-Altoona-Johnstown-diocese-grand-jury-says/stories/201603010091

Spraitz, J. D., & Bowen, K. N. (2016). Techniques of neutralization and persistent sexual abuse by clergy: A content analysis of priest personnel files from the Archdiocese of Milwaukee. *Journal of Interpersonal Violence, 31*(15), 2515–2538.

Spraitz, J. D., & Bowen, K. N. (2018). Denial of responsibility and failure to act: Examining persistent sexual abuse in the Archdiocese of Milwaukee. *Family & Intimate Partner Violence Quarterly, 11*(1), 59–67. (Reprinted from "Denial of responsibility and failure to act: Examining persistent sexual abuse in the Archdiocese of Milwaukee," 2014, *Sexual Assault Report,* 18[2], 17–32.)

Spraitz, J. D., & Bowen, K. N. (2019). Examination of a nascent taxonomy of priest sexual grooming. *Sexual Abuse, 31*(6), 707–728. https://doi.org/10.1177/1079063218809095

Spraitz, J. D., Bowen, K. N., & Arthurs, S. (2017). Neutralisation and sexual abuse: A study of monks from one Benedictine abbey. *Journal of Sexual Aggression, 23*(2), 195–206.

Spraitz, J. D., Bowen, K. N., & Bowers, J. H. (2016). Neutralizations and a history of "keeping the lid" on it: How church leaders handled and explained sexual abuse in one diocese. *Journal of Crime and Justice, 39*(2), 264–281. https://doi.org/10.1080/0735648x.2014.995204

Spraitz, J. D., Bowen, K. N., & Strange, L. (2018). Introducing a behavioral taxonomy of priest sexual grooming. *International Journal for Crime, Justice and Social Democracy, 7*(1), 30–43.

Spröber, N., Schneider, T., Rassenhofer, M., Seitz, A., Liebhardt, H., König, L., & Fegert, J. M. (2014). Child sexual abuse in religiously affiliated and secular institutions: A retrospective descriptive analysis of data provided by victims in a government-sponsored reappraisal program in Germany. *BMC Public Health, 14*, 1–12. https://doi.org/10.1186/1471-2458-14-282

Sykes, G. M., & Matza, D. (1957). Techniques of neutralization: A theory of delinquency. *American Sociological Review, 22*(6), 664–670.

Terry, K. J. (2013). *Sexual offenses and offenders: Theory, practice and policy* (2nd ed.). Cengage.

Terry, K. J., & Freilich, J. D. (2012). Understanding child sexual abuse by Catholic priests from a situational perspective. *Journal of Child Sexual Abuse, 21*(4), 437–455. https://doi.org/10.1080/10538712.2012.693579

Terry, K. & Smith, M. L. (2006). *The nature and scope of sexual abuse of minors by Catholic Priests and Deacons in the United States, 1950–2002: Supplementary Data Analysis*. United States Conference of Catholic Bishops.

Terry, K. J., Smith, M. L., Schuth, K., Kelly, J. R., Vollman, B., & Massey, C. (2011). *The causes and context of sexual abuse of minors by Catholic priests in the United States, 1950–2010*. United States Conference of Catholic Bishops.

Tornielli, A. (2019, May 9). *New norms for the whole church against those who abuse or cover up*. Vatican News. https://www.vaticannews.va/en/pope/news/2019-05/pope-francis-motu-proprio-sex-abuse-clergy-religious-church.html

United States Conference of Catholic Bishops. (2011). *Charter for the protection of children and young people*. http://www.usccb.org

United States Conference of Catholic Bishops. (2019). *2018 annual report: Findings and recommendations*. http://www.usccb.org

Volz, M. (2018, September 27). *Jury: Jehovah's Witnesses ordered by jury to pay $35M to abuse survivor*. Associated Press. https://apnews.com/article/d0be64f0546e4d8ca878d9e8449f52c7

West, C. (2018, October 25). *New church website provides hope and healing for victims of abuse.* LDS.org Church News. https://www.lds.org/church/news/new-church-website-provides-hope-and-healing-for-victims-of-abuse?lang=eng

Williams, R., Elliott, I. A., & Beech, A. R. (2013). Identifying sexual grooming themes used by Internet sex offenders. *Deviant Behavior, 34*(2), 135–152. https://doi.org/10.1080/01639625.2012.707550

Winters, G. M., & Jeglic, E. L. (2017). Stages of sexual grooming: Recognizing potentially predatory behaviors of child molesters. *Deviant Behavior, 38*(6), 724–733.

III. Custodial Institutions

5.   #MeToo in the U.S. Foster Care System

Reneè Lamphere

At year-end 2016, more than 437,000 children were in the U.S. foster care system (Wulfhorst, 2018). Most youth in the foster care system enter it because of abuse, neglect, drug use, incarceration, or abandonment on the part of their parents or caregivers (Katz et al., 2017). They are removed from their homes to protect them from continued parental maltreatment (Euser et al., 2013). In an ideal world, a foster care home would be a place where a child's safety and healing is prioritized, and for some children, being put in a foster care home does create a stable environment in which they can thrive. Unfortunately, a number of youth may experience abuse and maltreatment after entering the child welfare system, long after being separated from their primary caregiver (Breno & Galupo, 2007; Buehler et al., 2006; Katz et al., 2017; Tittle et al., 2008). While abuse can come in many forms, the substantiated allegations of sexual abuse in foster care far outnumber allegations of any other type of abuse (such as physical abuse or emotional abuse) (Breno & Galupo, 2007).

As discussed throughout this book, the #MeToo movement has shed light on sexual abuse in the United States and across the world; it is similarly having an impact on the foster care system. In this chapter, I will explore the prevalence and impact of child sexual abuse on youth in the foster care system. After discussing the scope of the problem, I will provide case studies that demonstrate the impact of #MeToo on the foster care system. Finally, I will discuss future directions, focusing on those individuals in the justice system who advocate for the well-being of youth in the foster care system.

Literature Review

Foster Care Placement Instability

Children in the foster care system are considered a vulnerable population due to the serious and complex problems they face behaviorally, physically, mentally, and developmentally (Dowdell et al., 2009; Maliszewski & Brown, 2014). According to Dowdell et al. (2009), the majority of youth in foster care are dealing with issues such as "coping difficulties, school difficulties and failure, learning disorders, attention disorders, depression, and aggressive behaviors" (p. 174). Youth who exhibit these behaviors are at a higher risk for foster care instability, often being moved from placement to placement (James, 2004; Katz et al., 2017; Leathers, 2006).

According to DiGiuseppe and Christakis (2003), the average length of stay in foster care is approximately two years. Further, more than 50 percent of foster care youth will end up in more than one placement, with an additional 20 percent experiencing three or more placements in less than a one-year time period. For many children, frequent instability only exacerbates their problems, which ultimately puts them more at risk for continued instability; this situation becomes a cycle of instability that is nearly impossible to escape. Children from unstable foster care homes exhibit more behavioral problems when compared with youth in stable foster care placement (that is, a placement within 45 days of entry into the system lasting more than 24 months). Those in stable foster care tend to be young with no prior history in the child welfare system and report better overall wellbeing when compared with those with placement instability (Dowdell et al., 2009).

It is important to examine placement instability when discussing sexual abuse in foster care, as these two concepts are inextricably tied. An example of this can be seen in research by Dowdell and colleagues (2009), which sampled 155 girls in foster care between the ages of 4 and 17. The girls in this sample had been previously evaluated for various behavioral problems, aggression, and sexually abusive behaviors. Researchers found that all 155 girls had an extensive history of abuse, with 68 percent reporting sexual abuse by one or more individuals. Of those who were sexually abused, almost all were subjected to multiple assaults, some lasting years or longer. Not surprisingly, another variable that was very common in the sample was foster care placement instability. By the age of 16, more than 90 percent of the girls had two or more changes in caregivers, and approximately 65 percent experienced nine or more changes in their living situation. Similar results were found by Breno and Galupo (2007), who reviewed the sexual abuse history of 84 women who successfully aged out of the child welfare system. The placement history of the girls who were sexually abused was distinct, with abused girls changing foster care placements more than twice as often as youths without a sexual abuse history.

Foster Care Youth and Childhood Sexual Abuse

Childhood sexual abuse (CSA) is defined as "every form of sexual interaction with a child between 0 and 17 years of age against the will of the child or without the possibility for the child to refuse the interaction" (Euser et al., 2013, p. 221). Further, these interactions involve acts with or without physical contact, for example, "penetration, molestation with genital contact, child prostitution, involvement in pornography, or voyeurism" (p. 221). Meta-analyses of research on CSA find it to be a global problem, with self-report incident rates of approximately 125 per 1,000 children worldwide (Stoltenborgh, 2011). In the United States, it is estimated that about 1 in 10 children will experience CSA prior to age 18 (Griffiths, Murphy, & Harper, 2016).

Looking specifically at CSA and foster care youth, early research by Benedict and colleagues (1996) on the prevalence of sexual abuse in a sample of foster care youth found that of all abuse incidents reported, sexual abuse was the most prevalent form of abuse, making up approximately 49 percent of all reports. Other, more recent research has yielded similar results. High rates of sexual abuse were found among youth in a therapeutic foster home setting, and a sample of foster care youth from North Carolina found that over 50 percent of the sample were exposed to sexual abuse (Dorsey et al., 2012). In general, youth from the foster care system are more likely than those youth who are not in the system to report sexual abuse (Coleman-Cowger et al., 2011).

Euser and colleagues (2013) explored some of the reasons why youth in foster care may be at greater risk for CSA. First, as discussed, children who are removed from the home are more likely to exhibit emotional and behavioral problems, making them vulnerable to further maltreatment while in foster care. Further, the nonbiological relationship between foster care youth and their foster caregivers may increase the risk for CSA. For example, research by van Ijzendoorn et al. (2009) found that children from stepfamilies were at an increased risk of CSA when compared with children in biological families. Also, particularly for youth who find themselves in residential group homes, the mixed-gender composition of these facilities coupled with insufficient monitoring by staff leaves these individuals at increased risk of sexual abuse by their peers (Euser et al., 2013).

There are many potential negative consequences for CSA survivors. One such consequence is the development of mental health disorders, depression in particular (Dowdell et al., 2009; Edmond et al., 2006). Other types of mental health problems such as eating disorders, anxiety, post-traumatic stress disorders, and substance use disorders also affect foster care youth (Breno & Galupo, 2007; Edmond et al., 2006). CSA survivors are at an increased risk of reoccurring victimization, and research shows that they are more likely to put their own children at risk of abuse and neglect when they become parents (Euser et al., 2013; Trickett et al., 2011).

Another important reason to understand the impact of CSA on foster care children is because of the correlation between CSA and high-risk sexual behaviors among youth in foster care (Gonzalez-Blanks & Yates, 2016; Hall et al., 2018; Maliszewski & Brown, 2014). Risky sexual behaviors such as having sex without contraception, having unprotected sex, or having sex at a younger age are disproportionately high among foster care youth, especially when compared with youth not in foster care (Courtney et al., 2014). In addition, while limited, the research on former foster care youth demonstrates that the presence of sexually risky behaviors remains elevated throughout their transition to adulthood, with particularly high rates among the approximately 10 percent of foster care youth who age out of the system (Ahrens et al., 2012; Ahrens et al., 2013). Additionally, the experiences that foster care youth have with CSA can affect their romantic relationships later in life. These youth are more likely to engage in insecure attachment patterns with their romantic partners (such as distrust, dependency), leaving the youth more likely to engage in multiple, brief relationships, which is a catalyst for risky sexual behaviors (Cicchetti & Toth, 2005; Senn & Carey, 2010). It is especially important to look at the long-term effects of CSA and sexual risk-taking on foster care youth, as these behaviors put them at a higher risk to become victims of human trafficking (Goldenberg et al., 2015).

Foster Care Youth and Human Trafficking

The topic of human trafficking has received considerable attention in recent years, both publicly and in academic research. It is estimated that anywhere from 100,000 to 300,000 youth annually are at risk of sexual exploitation and human trafficking (Landers et al., 2017). Through this research, a growing awareness has arisen that many of these children enter into human trafficking via the child welfare system (Hallett, 2016; Landers et al., 2017). Research by the National Foster Youth Institute (NFYI) (2019) revealed that in 2013, 60 percent of the child sex trafficking victims recovered through FBI raids were from foster care or group homes. In 2017, one in seven children reported missing was likely a victim of sex trafficking, and of those children, 88 percent had been in the care of the child welfare system before they went missing (Wulfhorst, 2018). According to the NFYI (2019), children in foster care, many of whom are lacking love and stability in their home lives, are particularly vulnerable to exploitation by sex traffickers. Unfortunately, many girls who end up leaving the foster care system this way are trafficked into prostitution, where they are routinely subject to sexual, physical, and emotional violence.

In looking further at the human trafficking of foster care children, it is important to examine the manner in which these children are becoming known to traffickers.

Victims are often sought from many different angles, which makes combating human trafficking particularly hard. While some children are found at bus stops, shopping malls, and street corners, they are also often found on social media or in chat rooms (Wulfhorst, 2018). The traffickers may even turn to the foster care children themselves to exploit others like them. It is not uncommon for a trafficker to spark a relationship with one foster care child, exploit that relationship, and then send that child back into group homes to lure other children to leave (Landers et al., 2017; Walker, 2013). While foster care children across the United States are being affected by sex trafficking, foster children in large cities like New York and Los Angeles are especially susceptible to becoming trafficked (NFYI, 2019).

There are many reasons why people who exploit children would be attracted to children in foster care homes. First, exploiters are attracted to children with vulnerabilities, and many foster care youths have these vulnerabilities, such as a history of trauma and CSA, lack of family and social support, and inadequate parent/guardian supervision (Landers et al., 2017). Further, children with trauma histories are more likely to develop stronger bonds with their exploiters, making it more difficult to identify their own exploitation. Exploiters know that these children are seeking out familial relationships, and they gain advantage with them by offering to satisfy those unfulfilled needs. Also, youth in foster care with a history of CSA are more likely to run away, which increases their risk of human trafficking. While not all runaways find themselves on the street, research has found that one-third of those who go to the streets are approached by an exploiter within 48 hours of running away (Spangenberg, 2001). This is all complicated by the fact that the human trafficking industry is hidden in nature. Systemic and individual level factors make many human trafficking victims reluctant to self-disclose their victimization; therefore, it is difficult to estimate the true impact of human trafficking on youth in foster care (Fedina, 2014; Landers et al., 2017).

#MeToo Stories in the Foster Care System

In October 2017, actress Alyssa Milano sent a tweet encouraging women who had been sexually abused or harassed to write "me too" as their status on social media platforms in order to bring light to the magnitude of the problem (Garcia, 2017). In addition to the millions of posts that were made, #MeToo emerged as a movement for people to tell their stories of sexual abuse and hold offenders accountable for their actions. As the #MeToo movement progresses, more factions of people are telling their stories, including stories of CSA. For example, in January 2018, more than 150 women came forward to give statements of sexual abuse they had suffered at the hands of Lawrence Nassar, the former USA Gymnastics and Michigan State University doctor (Correa, 2018). Nassar, who had already been given a 60-year federal sentence for child pornography charges, received 40 to 175 years in state prison for sexual abuse against the women who came forward, some testifying to being as young as six when they were sexually abused. At sentencing, Judge Rosemarie Aquilina stated, "I just signed your death warrant" as Nassar was escorted out of the courtroom (Cacciola & Mather, 2018). While Correa (2018) argued that this was the #MeToo moment for women's gymnastics, other coaches have come forward about a "culture of abuse" in professional childhood sports, citing Jerry Sandusky and the Penn State scandal, among others. The conviction of Nassar is certainly a step in the right direction, but he is far from the sole perpetrator, and more needs to be done for young people who are survivors of CSA.

Bostick (2018) argues that child sexual abuse has not been given the recognition it should in the #MeToo movement, as the focus has been mainly on adult victims and sexual abuse in the workplace. A subsidiary movement known as #MeTooK12 has recently emerged with a focus on sexual misconduct in the school system. While a positive development, even #MeTooK12 leaves many children who experience CSA out of the conversation, such as youth in the foster care system.

To help bring foster care youth into the #MeToo movement and the national conversation about sexual abuse, the Winter 2019 issue of *Represent*, a magazine for youth in foster care, was dedicated completely to #MeToo. The issue featured stories dealing with sexual trafficking, with not being believed when victims did come forward, and with foster parents who harbor sexual predators, among other concerns (Vitzthum, 2019). One story in this special issue came from an anonymous author who, at the time of her writing, had been in the foster care system for two years (Anonymous, 2019). A male friend of her foster mother moved into the home. The author knew it was against the rules to have someone live in a foster care home who had not gone through a criminal background check, but she trusted her foster mother and did not say anything to her case worker. The male friend started to slowly break the rules her foster care mother had established for her, such as giving her snacks in her room, giving her money, and taking her on elaborate shopping trips. After some time, she stopped getting a friendly feeling from him and, looking back on it, realized that the man was grooming her for a sexual relationship. When she told her foster mother about the situation, the foster mother admitted that she knew the male friend had a "liking for little girls" and that he was a known predator but believed that the author was to blame for "enticing" him sexually. The foster mother continues to allow the man into her home, despite knowing what he did to the author. At the time of the writing, the author was months from aging out of the system and felt that was the only way she would ever truly be safe from abuse.

Marreka Beckett's #MeToo foster care story (2019) is interesting as it does not examine abuse within the system but instead focuses on how the foster care system helped end her abuse. Beckett grew up in Jamaica, where she experienced abuse and violence at the hands of her biological parents, their significant others, and an aunt. At age 14 she came to the United States with her grandmother, and at that time she tried to speak up about the abuse she had endured, but her grandmother did not believe her. She began acting out and fighting with her grandmother, who threatened to have her deported back to Jamaica. A friend told her about a man named "Bob" who could help her get money and get out of her grandmother's home. Bob ended up abusing Beckett physically, emotionally, and sexually. He took her from state to state, selling her for sex to other men. In an attempt to escape abuse, Beckett found herself entangled in sexual exploitation and human trafficking. This lasted for three months, until witnesses saw Bob beating Beckett in public and the police got involved. Beckett was returned to her grandmother's house, where she was physically abused by an older cousin. She called the police, and Child Protective Services became involved and removed her from the home. She was placed into Gateways, a residential foster care home for girls who have been sexually trafficked. Through intensive counseling and programming, Beckett learned valuable life lessons, such as how to manage her emotions and how to make safe, responsible decisions. Beckett says, "They taught me that I don't need a man to make me happy and that I could aspire to more. I got off all drugs, even cigarettes. I learned to love myself." At the time of this writing Beckett was in foster care and was working toward her high school equivalency degree, working, and writing for *Represent* magazine. On telling her #MeToo story and the impact it will have, Beckett said, "I advocate for girls who don't have a voice. Even when I'm hard on myself, I can still be kind to other girls. I can let them know they're not alone, that it's not their fault, and to keep telling the truth."

Guardians Ad Litem: Voices for Abused Foster Care Youth

Many children enter the foster care system because of abuse or neglect by their biological parents or caregivers. Most of these cases are identified and initiated by various third parties, such as teachers, medical professionals, social workers, and criminal justice agents, who have observed firsthand abuse or neglect of a child (Bonner & Sheriff, 2013). The family court system is complex and can be hostile at times, complicating the view of what is in the best interest of a child. Recognizing this, in 1974 Congress enacted the Child Abuse Prevention and Treatment Act, requiring states to assign guardians ad litem (GALs) to represent children in juvenile dependency cases (Gleiss, 2010; Harhut, 2000). GALs are individuals appointed by the court to serve as neutral, independent investigators on behalf of the court (Bonmil et al., 2011). After a thorough investigation, they will file a report with the court, making recommendations regarding the specific parenting issues presented in a case. GALs can recommend testing, counseling, and other social services that would benefit a family (Alfano, 2012).

While GALs are typically appointed in dependency cases, some states allow them in cases involving adoption, child custody, visitation, child support, and paternity (Bonner & Sheriff, 2013; Mabry, 2013). GALs' duty is to inform the court about what they believe to be in the best interest of children (Mabry, 2013). In fact, while known as GALs or as court-appointed special advocates in most states, in Maryland these individuals are referred to as "Child's Best Interest Attorney[s]" (Bonner & Sheriff, 2013, p. 515). In many states, GALs are lawyers or mental health professionals (Bonmil et al., 2011); however, in some states, these are non-attorney volunteers who have been trained specifically to advocate for children (Bonner & Sheriff, 2013).

While GALs have distinct responsibilities different from those of a child's attorney, there is debate over what exactly GALs' responsibilities should be. For example, while GALs and attorneys both take a child's wishes into consideration, a GAL must take an independent position, even if that is contrary to the child's wishes (Mabry, 2013). From an attorney's perspective, the child's wishes are the determining factor; for GALs, they are among many relevant factors. There is also considerable debate over the content of what can be included in a GAL's court report. These reports might contain hearsay regarding information previously provided by the involved parties or opinions on party credibility (Dore, 2016). There has been a push for reform to improve the quality of GALs and their reports. The most common approach has been the implementation of evaluation standards, such as those in Washington State, which require GALs to have documentation to substantiate the claims in their reports.

Being a GAL can be difficult at times. Bonmil et al. (2011) note that some GALs go into hostile litigation situations thinking that everyone involved will cooperate in the best interest of a child only to find themselves "thrust into the reality of a war zone" (p. 88). GALs' court reports generally influence child custody decisions, and loss of custody can impact families substantially (such as in the areas of financial support, distribution of property, and the like). This can cause already fragile individuals to act out against GALs in anger. As discussed by Bonmil and colleagues, "Even trained and seasoned GALs can be blindsided when they find that their involvement with a troubled family results in their becoming a target of intimidation and retaliation" (p. 88). In addition to potential harassment from family members, there have been circumstances where GALs have been "threatened with lawsuits alleging malpractice, defamation, or negligence" (p. 90). To safeguard GALs' ability to advocate for the best interest of a child, most jurisdictions provide some form of immunity for GALs. This immunity typically extends to "claims arising out of performance of court-appointed duties, including testifying, writing reports and formulating recommendations" (p. 91). The GAL practice as it stands today is operating as an imperfect model, and there is a need for further exploration regarding the legal issues that GALs face.

While challenging, even sad at times, GALs recognize that the task they perform is important. This is illustrated in the 2017 Florida Guardian Ad Litem report called *Making the Impossible, Possible*, which examined the personal stories of GAL advocates. One GAL, reflecting on her responsibilities, stated that GALs "are hope, strength, and safety for a young person, who sometimes does not have anybody else to provide this for them." In another story, a 24-year-old single woman took in her five nieces and nephews but was unable to afford a pair of cleats for her oldest nephew to play football. By working with local community members, the GAL was able to get the child the cleats he needed. As noted by the caregiver, "That gesture by his GAL volunteer led to better behavior and improved grades once the child started to play football." From investigation and court report writing to helping with the fulfillment of basic needs, GALs provide valuable work to the populations they serve. It is important for the courts to recognize the role these individuals play in the system and to "strive to protect the legitimacy and integrity of the GAL process" (Bonmil et al., 2011, p. 97).

Policy Implications and Conclusions

Dowdell et al. (2009) discussed potential implications for those who work with foster care youth who may have experienced CSA and offered advice for dealing with these populations. For instance, when those in the clinical setting, such as nurses and doctors, encounter a child from the foster care system, they should conduct a thorough physical health assessment and make sure care has not been fragmented due to instability. Likewise, those who interact with foster care children should also work closely with social services to ensure the basic needs of the youth are met. Finally, children, particularly girls from the foster care system, should be assessed by youth services practitioners for their exposure to violence and abusive behaviors, for high-risk behaviors they might engage in, and for number of foster care placements. The plan of care for these individuals should focus on identifying key problems and coordinating interventions with all parties involved with that particular child. Perhaps taking a multidimensional treatment foster care approach would help in this regard. Foster parents are considered part of the treatment team; as such, they are recruited, are specifically trained, and are in daily contact with the rest of the treatment team (Crime Solutions, 2011). Intense recruitment and background screening of foster parents coupled with daily contact may help identify potentially abusive parents and situations before sexual violence occurs. Additionally, research suggests that by supporting caregiver (that is, foster parent) health and emotional wellness and by helping these individuals learn how to navigate the system (such as school help, legal advice, medical/mental health, and so on), the likelihood of a positive outcome for both the child and caregiver increases (Dowdell, 2004; Dowdell et al., 2009). A multidimensional treatment foster care approach could help this come to fruition.

In looking to tie together #MeToo, CSA, GALs, and the foster care system, Health (2017) discussed the story of Tamika Hedin. Hedin was adopted by her biological aunt and, unfortunately, into a home where she was sexually abused by her adoptive stepfather. As a result of this abuse, she ended up in the foster care system. When she first entered the system, she was introverted and coped with her situation through silence. Her refusal to talk led to further abuse by her peers. Shortly after entering foster care she met her GAL. Her GAL recognized that she was experiencing difficulties adjusting to foster care and introduced her to poetry. Now a published writer and a poet, Hedin reflected upon the impact that her GAL and poetry has had on her life. "[Since then], poetry has been my therapy. Maya [Angelou] made me realize that there is life after trauma. A beautiful, powerful, peaceful existence that we all have to create within and for ourselves. I want to be somebody's Maya." (para. 3). Tamika Hedin's story is a reflection of healing through trauma and of the impact that GALs can have on the lives of youth in the foster care system. Guardians ad litem are well positioned to provide a needed voice for all vulnerable children, including those at risk of child sexual victimization.

References

Ahrens, K., Katon, W., McCarty, C., Richardson, L. P., & Courtney, M. (2012). Association between childhood sexual abuse and transactional sex in youth aging out of foster care. *Child Abuse and Neglect, 36,* 75–80.

Ahrens, K. R., McCarty, C., Simoni, J., Dworsky, A., & Courtney, M. E. (2013). Psychosocial pathways to sexually transmitted infection risk among youth transitioning out of foster care: Evidence from a longitudinal cohort study. *Journal of Adolescent Health, 53,* 478–485.

Alfano, M. (2012). How to try a case without a guardian *ad litem* when you really need one. *New Hampshire Bar Journal, 53*(2), 18–22.

Anonymous. (2019). Choosing predators over girls: When your home isn't safe. *Represent: The Voice of Youth in Care,* no. 135 (Winter). https://www.represent-mag.org/issues/FCYU135/Choosing_Predators_Over_Girls.html?story_id=FCYU-2019-01-27

Beckett, M. M. (2019). Claiming the life I deserve: I was raped and trafficked, but I wasn't silenced. *Represent: The Voice of Youth in Care,* no. 135 (Winter). https://

www.representmag.org/issues/FCYU135/Claiming_the_Life_I_Deserve.html ?story_id=FCYU-2019-01-08

Benedict, M., Zuravin, S., Somerfield, M., & Brandt, D. (1996). The reported health and functioning of children maltreated while in family foster care. *Child Abuse and Neglect, 20*(7), 561–571.

Bonmil, M., Freitas, D., & Freitas, C. (2011). The toll of high conflict on guardian ad litem practice. *American Journal of Family Law, 25*(3), 87–104.

Bonner, M. H., & Sheriff, J. A. (2013). A child needs a champion: Guardian *ad litem* representation for prenatal children. *William & Mary Journal of Women and the Law, 19*, 511–584.

Bostick, D. (2018, March 19). How #MeToo is leaving child victims behind. *The Week.* https://theweek.com/articles/749634/how-metoo-leaving-child-victims -behind

Breno, A. L., & Galupo, M. P. (2007). Sexual abuse histories of young women in the U.S. child welfare system: A focus on trauma-related beliefs and resilience. *Research, Treatment, & Program Innovations for Victims, Survivors, & Offenders, 16*(2), 97–113.

Buehler, C., Rhodes, K., Orme, J., & Cuddeback, G. (2006). The potential for successful family foster care: Conceptualizing competency domains for foster parents. *Child Welfare, 85*(3), 523–558.

Cacciola, S., & Mather, V. (2018, January 24). Larry Nassar sentencing: "I just signed your death warrant." *New York Times.* https://www.nytimes.com/2018 /01/24/sports/larry-nassar-sentencing.html

Cicchetti, D., & Toth, S. L. (2005). Child maltreatment. *Annual Review of Clinical Psychology, 1*, 409–438.

Coleman-Cowger, V. H., Green, B. A., & Clark, T. T. (2011). The impact of mental health issues, substance use, and exposure to victimization on pregnancy rates among a sample of youth with past-year foster care placement. *Youth and Child Services Review, 33*(11), 2207–2212.

Correa, C. (2018, January 25). The #MeToo movement: For U.S. gymnasts, why did justice take so long? *New York Times.* https://www.nytimes.com/2018/01/25/us /the-metoo-moment-for-us-gymnasts-olympics-nassar-justice.html

Courtney, M. E., Charles, P., Okpych, N. J., Napolitano, L., & Halsted, K. (2014). *Findings from the California Youth Transitions to Adulthood Study (CalY-OUTH): Conditions of foster youth at age 17.* Chapin Hall at the University of Chicago.

Crime Solutions. (2011, June 10). *Program profile: Multidimensional treatment foster care—adolescents.* https://www.crimesolutions.gov/ProgramDetails.aspx ?ID=141

DiGiuseppe, D. L., & Christakis, D. A. (2003). Continuity of care for children in foster care. *Pediatrics, 111*, 208–213.

Dore, M. K. 2016. Court-appointed parenting evaluators and guardians ad litem: Practical realities and an argument for abolition. *Family & Intimate Partner Violence Quarterly, 8*(3), 279–285.

Dorsey, S., Burns, B. J., Southerland, D. G., Cox, J. R., Wagner, H. R., & Farmer, E. M. Z. (2012). Prior trauma exposure for youth in treatment foster care. *Journal of Child and Family Studies, 21*(5), 816–824.

Dowdell, E. B. (2004). Grandmother caregivers and caregiver burden. *MCN: The American Journal of Maternal/Child Nursing, 29*(5), 299–304.

Dowdell, E. B., Cavanaugh, D. J., Burgess, A. W., & Prentky, R. A. (2009). Girls in foster care: A vulnerable and high-risk group. *MCN: The American Journal of Maternal Child Nursing, 34*(3), 172–178.

Edmond, T., Auslander, W., Elze, D. E., & Bowland, S. (2006). Signs of resilience in sexually abused adolescent girls in the foster care system. *Journal of Child Sexual Abuse, 15*(1), 1–28.

Euser, S., Alink, L., Tharner, A., van Ijzendoorn, M. H., & Bakermans-Kranenburg, M. J. (2013). The prevalence of child sexual abuse in out-of-home care: A comparison between abuse in residential and in foster care. *Child Maltreatment, 18*(4), 221–231.

Fedina, L. (2014). Use and misuse of research in books on sex trafficking: Implications for interdisciplinary researchers, practitioners, and advocates. *Trauma, Violence, & Abuse, 16*(2), 188–198.

Florida Guardian Ad Litem. (2017). *Making the impossible, possible: Stories of advocacy.* https://guardianadlitem.org/wp-content/uploads/2014/08/GAL-Annual-Report-2017-web.pdf

Garcia, S. E. (2017, October 20). The woman who created #MeToo long before hashtags. *New York Times.* https://www.nytimes.com/2017/10/20/us/me-too-movement-tarana-burke.html

Gleiss, E. (2010). The due process rights of parents to cross-examine guardians *ad litem* in custody disputes: The reality and the ideal. *Minnesota Law Review, 94,* 2103–2135.

Goldenberg, S. M., Silverman, J. G., Engstrom, D., Bojorquez-Chapela, I., Usita, P., Rolon, M. L., & Strathdee, S. A. (2015). Exploring the context of trafficking and adolescent sex industry involvement in Tijuana, Mexico: Consequences for HIV risk and prevention. *Violence against Women, 21*(4), 478–499.

Gonzalez-Blanks, A., & Yates, T. M. (2016). Sexual risk-taking among recently emancipated female foster youth: Sexual trauma and failed family reunification experiences. *Journal of Research on Adolescence, 26*(4), 819–829.

Griffiths, A., Murphy, A. L., & Harper, W. (2016). Child sexual abuse and the impact of rurality on foster care outcomes: An exploratory analysis. *Child Welfare, 95*(1), 57–76.

Hall, K. L., Stinson, J. D., & Moser, M. R. (2018). Impact of childhood adversity and out-of-home placement for male adolescents who have engaged in sexually abusive behavior. *Child Maltreatment, 23*(1), 63–73.

Hallett, S. (2016). "An uncomfortable comfortableness": "Care," child protection and child sexual exploitation. *British Journal of Social Work, 46*, 2137–2152.

Harhut, C. T. (2000). An expanded role for the guardian ad litem. *Juvenile & Family Court Journal, 51*(3), 31–35.

Health, R. (2017, November 6). *Heartbreaking poem about sexual violence in foster system show the power of #MeToo*. Afropunk. https://afropunk.com/2017/11/heartbreaking-poem-sexual-violence-foster-system-shows-power-metoo/

James, S. (2004). Why do foster care placements disrupt? An investigation of reasons for placement change in foster care. *Social Service Review, 78*(4), 601–627.

Katz, C. C., Courtney, M. E., & Novotny, E. (2017). Pre–foster care maltreatment class as a predictor of maltreatment in foster care. *Child & Adolescent Social Work Journal, 34*(1), 35–49.

Landers, M., McGrath, K., Johnson, M. H., Armstrong, M. I., & Dollard, N. (2017). Baseline characteristics of dependent youth who have been commercially sexually exploited: Findings from a specialized treatment program. *Journal of Child Sexual Abuse, 26*(6), 692–709.

Leathers, S. J. (2006). Placement disruption and negative placement outcomes among adolescents in long-term foster care: The role of behavior problems. *Child Abuse and Neglect, 30*(3), 307–324.

Mabry, C. R. (2013). Guardians ad litem: Should the child's best interests advocate give more credence to the child's best wishes in custody cases? *American Journal of Family Law, 27*, 172–188.

Maliszewski, G., & Brown, C. (2014). Familism, substance abuse, and sexual risk among foster care alumni. *Children and Youth Services Review, 36*, 206–212.

National Foster Youth Institute [NFYI]. (2019). *Sex trafficking*. https://www.nfyi.org/issues/sex-trafficking/

Senn, T., & Carey, M. (2010). Child maltreatment and women's adult sexual risk behavior: Childhood sexual abuse as a unique risk factor. *Child Maltreatment, 15*, 324–335.

Spangenberg, M. (2001). *Prostituted youth in New York: An overview*. End Child Prostitution, Child Pornography, and Trafficking of Children (ECPAT). https://d1qky03pi1c9bx.cloudfront.net/00028B1B-B0DB-4FCD-A991–219527535DAB/7922f23e-a266–44f4-aae4–0f525f3dbe7d.pdf

Stoltenborgh, M., van Ijzendoorn, M. H., Euser, E. M., & Bakermans-Kranenburg, M. J. (2011). A global perspective on child sexual abuse: Meta-analysis of prevalence around the world. *Child Maltreatment, 26*, 79–101.

Tittle, G., Poertner, J., & Garnier, P. (2008). Child maltreatment in out of home care: What do we know now? *Urbana, 51*, 61–80.

Trickett, P. K., Noll, J. G., & Putnam, F. W. (2011). The impact of sexual abuse on female development: Lessons from a multigenerational longitudinal study. *Development and Psychopathology, 23,* 453–476.

van Ijzendoorn, M. H., Euser, E. M., Prinzie, P., Juffer, F., & Bakermans-Kranenburg, M. J. (2009). Elevated risk of child maltreatment in families with stepparents but not with adoptive parents. *Child Maltreatment, 14,* 369–374.

Vitzthum, V. (2019). #MeToo: Telling our stories can change the world. *Represent: The Voice of Youth in Care,* no. 135 (Winter). https://www.ycteenmag.org/issues/FCYU135/_MeToo:_Telling_Our_Stories_Can_Change_the_World.html?story_id=FCYU-2019-01-04

Walker, K. (2013). *Ending the commercial sexual exploitation of children: A call for multi-system collaboration in California.* California Child Welfare Council. https://youthlaw.org/publication/ending-commercial-sexual-exploitation-of-children-a-call-for-multi-system-collaboration-in-california/

Wulfhorst, E. (2018, May 3). *Without family, U.S. children in foster care easy prey for human traffickers.* Reuters. https://www.reuters.com/article/us-usa-trafficking-fostercare/without-family-u-s-children-in-foster-care-easy-prey-for-human-traffickers-idUSKBN1I40OM

6. Examining Sexual Violence and Harassment in the U.S. Corrections System through #MeToo

Reneè Lamphere and Matthew Hassett

"Me Too." These two simple words have come to represent the stories of survivors of sexual violence and harassment throughout the United States and the world. Also known as the #MeToo movement, the social media hashtag gained public attention in October 2017 when American actress Alyssa Milano made her now famous Twitter post—though, as the editors of this book note in the introduction, the origin of the Me Too movement can be traced back to Tarana Burke in 2006 (Garcia, 2017; Jaffe, 2018). Burke, creator of the nonprofit organization Just Be Inc., named her organization's campaign "Me Too" as an expression of unity among survivors (Jaffe, 2018).

While the #MeToo movement initially received much attention in the entertainment industry, politics/government, and Wall Street, it has garnered new attention in the criminal justice system (Cornelius, 2018). We are starting to see some of those accused in the #MeToo movement being held legally accountable for their actions. For example, in April 2018, actor Bill Cosby was found guilty of drugging and molesting a Temple University employee in 2004 (Nadolny et al., 2018). Although the Cosby conviction is arguably an outlier, it demonstrates that the momentum of #MeToo is reaching a broad scope of institutions. One aspect of the American criminal justice system that has felt the impact of the #MeToo movement is the corrections system (Cornelius, 2018). Shermer and Sudo (2017) have argued that sexual violence in prison is one of the most pressing issues in American corrections today. This assertion appears to be true given the estimated prevalence of sexual violence in prison. While an exact number will never be known for a variety of reasons, it is estimated that 125,000 to 600,000 prisoners are raped each year in U.S. prisons and jails (Nolan & Telford, 2006; Shermer & Sudo, 2017). Though this number may shock some, for many, it is not shocking at all. Cornelius (2018) argued that part of the reason for the general public's seeming apathy toward sexual violence in prison is because the idea of it has become normalized in mainstream American culture. From casual jokes about "not dropping the soap in the shower" to dramatic depictions of prison sex in television and movies, the public is aware that sexual violence is happening in the corrections system, but "some members of the public are not especially troubled by this picture of prison life—they figure the bad guys have it coming" (p. 2). With the lack of a platform, such as social media, to tell their stories and an often unsympathetic public, incarcerated victims have difficulty making their voices heard. With the momentum of #MeToo motivating survivors throughout the world, a question that needs to be addressed is this: What impact, if any, will the #MeToo movement have on the U.S. corrections system?

The purpose of this chapter is to explore the topic of sexual violence in American corrections, focusing on sexual violence in both prisons and jails. In addition to discussing the manifestation and prevalence of sexual violence in prisons and jails, we will also examine what is being done to combat these incidents, paying attention to the impact of the Prison Rape Elimination Act (PREA) of 2003. Finally, we consider how the #MeToo movement has impacted the corrections system, detailing cases of currently and formerly incarcerated individuals who have come forward to share their stories of victimization.

Sexual Violence in Prisons and Jails

Understanding Sex and Sexuality in a Correctional Setting

Human beings are sexual beings; thus, it is not surprising that matters of sex and sexuality inevitably come up when discussing incarcerated populations. In fact, feminist scholar Alice Ristroph (2006) argued that the experience of modern incarceration is inherently sexual in nature. In backing this assertion, Nielsen (2017) contended that from "the extreme regulation of bodies" to "the utter lack of privacy," the prison experience is an "embodiment" of sex and sexuality for incarcerated individuals (p. 234). Thinking of sexuality in prison as inherent, however, also comes with the risk of thinking that sexual coercion is also intrinsic to the imprisonment experience (Ristroph, 2006). For many years the general attitude toward rape in prison, especially for those outside of prison, was that it was part of the punishment for breaking the law and there was nothing that could be done to prevent it.

Many of the same problems that have historically plagued victims of sexual assault outside of prison also affect incarcerated populations. For example, traditional definitions of rape have been limited in terms of the gender of the perpetrator or victim and of the type of acts that were prohibited (that is, male perpetrators, female victims, forced vaginal sex) (Weiner, 2013). These same perceptions—often misperceptions—about rape are arguably more amplified in the prison environment. Ristroph (2006) has contended that the stereotypical account of prison rape "posits predator and prey: a cruel, sadistic perpetrator who manipulates or violently overpowers a vulnerable victim" (p. 141). While accounts of this nature certainly occur in prison, Ristroph argued that it is a "misleading and radically incomplete" picture of the realities of sexual assault in prison (p. 141). The overemphasis on physical violence may send the wrong message to those who experience abuse. For example, if an act is not overtly violent, some victims may believe their victimization is not real, does not matter, or is even their own fault. If the #MeToo movement has taught us anything, it is that there are survivors and perpetrators of sexual violence who do not conform to our preconceived notions of victim and offender. It is important to recognize these misconceptions in the hope that doing so will give way to a deeper, more meaningful understanding of sexual violence among incarcerated populations.

Inquiry on Sexual Violence in Corrections Prior to PREA

In order to understand the status of sexual victimization in U.S. corrections today, it is important to look at how sexual violence has been studied historically. One of the earliest investigations in the academic literature about prison rape came via a review of American prisons by Fishman (1934), where pressured and forced sexual contact among prisoners was found to be more common than previously thought. Fishman, one of the first people to describe "forced homosexuality" in U.S. prisons and jails, expressed sympathy and a humanitarian concern for the wellbeing of victims, especially young males, whom he felt were the most vulnerable to rape in prison (Fishman, 1934; Struckman-Johnson & Struckman-Johnson, 2013). Sexual violence in prison continued to occur, and by the 1960s, it was declared an "epidemic" among inmates in Philadelphia jails (Struckman-Johnson et al., 2013).

Scacco (1982) wrote the first professional book on prison rape. He advocated for the allowance of masturbation, conjugal visits, and consensual male-male sex as a means to decrease sexual tension and aggression in prisons. In the same year, Cotton and Groth published the first protocol for response to prison rape. The authors felt for the plight of the incarcerated male victim of prison rape and suggested that, much like female victims in the community, incarcerated male victims can also experience the symptoms of rape trauma syndrome. Various researchers (Dumond, 1992, 2000; Eigenberg, 1989; Hensley, 2002; Lockwood, 1980; Struckman-Johnson et al., 1996) have pushed the topic of sexual violence in prison to the forefront of academia. Again, while the populations studied and results of these inquiries have varied, the message was clear: sexual violence victimization was occurring in U.S. prisons and jails, and something should be done to stop it. These pioneers of sexual assault research in corrections were instrumental in harnessing the momentum for the passage of PREA in 2003.

Before moving on, it is important to note that much like research today, most of the early research that was done on sex in prison was shaped by what Ristroph (2006) argued were "normative conceptions of gender, sexuality, coercion, and consent" (p. 143). Some assumed that sexual orientation and sexuality were fixed, especially when compared with more recent studies that offer more flexible definitions of sex and sexuality. Even the most recent studies, however, often make a clear distinction between coerced and consensual sex, but these lines may not be so clear or distinctive for those who are incarcerated. For example, in an environment such as prison, which holds people against their will, can consent ever really be given? Questions such as this need to continue to be considered as we improve and evolve our methods for studying sex and sexuality among incarcerated populations.

Rates and Characteristics of Sexual Victimization in Corrections

Much like sexual assault outside of the correctional setting, the rates of sexual victimization vary, particularly when official reports of victimization are compared with self-reports. The self-reported rates of sexual victimization have varied since this topic was first studied, but estimates range from a low of 1 percent to as high as 40 percent of the total prison population (Wolff et al., 2006; Wolff et al., 2010). Official reports on sexual victimization typically show a smaller but still significant level of victimization when compared with self-report studies. For example, a recent Bureau of Justice Statistics report on sexual victimizations in 2015 found that correctional administrators disclosed 24,661 allegations of sexual victimization in U.S. prisons and jails (Rantala, 2018). Of those official reports by administrators, nearly 6 percent ($n = 1,473$) were substantiated. This equates to a victimization rate of 0.70 per 1,000 inmates in state prisons and 0.80 in U.S. jails.

As stated, higher rates of victimization are seen in self-report measures of victimization. A 2012 study of formerly incarcerated state prisoners by Beck and Johnson found that approximately 1 in 10 respondents recounted one or more incidents of sexual victimization during their most recent period of incarceration (9.6 percent). The rates of victimization reported involving another inmate were 5.4 percent, similar to those incidents involving staff as perpetrators (5.3 percent). Interestingly, inmates were three times more likely to report that the sexual contact with staff was consensual in nature. Among the victims of staff sexual misconduct, four out of five incidents were males reporting sexual activity with female staff.

Reflected within the statistics of incidence presented above, prison rape and victimization are multifaceted issues. It should be noted, however, that complex issues tend to be common within correctional settings. Some have argued that many problems within prisons can potentially be characterized as inmate responses to the "coercive nature" of the prison system itself (Piehl & Useem, 2011). Prison rape/sexual assault has been classified as an epidemic that can threaten the lives of anyone within a prison setting (Gottschalk, 2006). As such, stating that particular "types" of prisoners are the only ones who are at risk would be a fallacy. However, that does not mean that the likelihood of being a perpetrator or victim of prison rape/sexual assault is consistent among all inmates. In contrast, experts within this area have attempted to identify factors that may make somebody a higher risk for involvement.

Since prison rape and sexual assault have been well-recognized issues for quite some time, studies have been conducted that comment on individuals with a greater propensity to become involved. For instance, research has consistently found that female inmates are at a greater risk than males, with some data showing female victimization to be more than four times greater than male victimization (Wolff et al., 2006). Other studies not only have supported this disparity but have produced knowledge on different aspects of the gender link as well. Struckman-Johnson and Struckman-Johnson (2002) found that half of the victimizations of female inmates in their sample were perpetrated by other inmates, and there were many instances of abuse by prison staff. These researchers were able to connect female inmate victimization with personal status and aspects of an offense. Specifically, heterosexual Caucasian inmates who were incarcerated for committing more serious crimes (that is, crimes against persons) were at a greater risk of victimization. Importantly, it was discovered that female inmates had a greater risk of becoming a victim of *sexual aggression* by other inmates and of *sexual exploitation* by prison staff. This conclusion has been supported by further research that has shown that females make up a small portion of prison inmates but are disproportionately more likely to file complaints against staff members (Baker et al., 2013).

One population of inmates who have a particularly high risk of victimization, by both fellow inmates and staff, are LGBTQ inmates (Malkin & DeJong, 2019). An estimated 35–40 percent of all transgender inmates report being sexually assaulted while incarcerated (Beck, 2014; Beck et al., 2013). In a report on formerly incarcerated individuals, similar percentages of victimization were found for bisexual and gay inmates who reported victimization by another inmate, at 34 percent and 39 percent, respectively (Beck & Johnson, 2012). This same report found that among homosexual female inmates, the victimization rate was 13 percent for inmate-on-inmate victimization, while the rate of staff sexual victimization for homosexual inmates doubled that of heterosexual inmates (8 percent vs. 4 percent).

Barriers to Understanding Sexual Violence in Prison and Jails

There are many issues that play into the variance of reported sexual violence in jails and prisons. As stated, one must first consider whether the information gathered is from official reports or self-report measures. Much like sexual violence outside of prison, there is reason to believe that sexual violence is underreported by inmates, meaning official reports may underrepresent the true extent of the problem (Fellner, 2010). Another issue that plays into the variance of rates of sexual assault is that incarcerated inmates and administrators may have different definitions of sexual assault and victimization. For example, an inmate may be verbally coerced into a sexual act, but the absence of physical coercion may mean the inmate does not view the sexual exchange as an assault. This definitional difference can result in inmates failing to report their victimization, which will result in low official counts of sexual assault and the appearance that a facility is safer than it actually is (Fowler et al., 2010). In fact, one of the goals of PREA is to broaden inmate definitions of sexual assault, with the hope that new definitions will encourage victims to seek help and officially report their victimization.

In addition to the above-mentioned barriers, one must also consider specific issues related to research methodology that affect the overall victimization rates, such as issues with measurement, sample size and composition, and the time period being studied (Wolff et al., 2010). The values and assumptions of the people who are conducting the research must also be considered. As argued by Ristroph (2006), research on prison sex is shaped by the subjective way researchers conceptualize gender and sexuality, as well as coercion and consent. While more recent studies have taken these normative conceptions into consideration, it makes a historical interpretation of the true rates of sexual victimization in prison nearly impossible. It is important to note that the limitations mentioned have not gone unnoticed by scholars, criminal justice officials, and policy makers and were influential in the passage of PREA in 2003.

Policy: The Implementation and Impact of PREA

As with any criminal justice policy, what is perhaps more important than its development and adoption is the way the policy is implemented. That is, many policies may be well intentioned and can be well written, but if they are not appropriately implemented into their settings, then the chance of their having any substantial impact can disappear. PREA serves as a great example of legislation being specifically adopted to address a persistent problem within corrections—rape and sexual assault. The adoption of the legislation was accompanied by great political optics, because it was passed on a bipartisan basis that brought together a Republican president, conservative-minded groups, and civil rights organizations (Corlew,

2006; Gottschalk, 2006; Jenness et al., 2010; Mair et al., 2003). However, arguably the most important aspect of PREA was the degree of success it had with long-term implementation of policies and practices that could produce positive results. The final report of the National Prison Rape Elimination Commission suggested that since the implementation of PREA, the handling of prison rape and sexual assault was, in some ways, moving in a positive direction (Graham & Hastings, 2011).

Some of the overreaching goals of PREA were to create a zero-tolerance environment for prison rape and sexual assault and to promote and provide funding for related research (PREA, 2003). The research aspect of PREA primarily sought to better understand the phenomenon of prison rape, which, as noted above, has been long recognized as a major issue within U.S. correctional systems (Jenness & Smyth, 2011; Kappeler & Potter, 2018; Moster & Jeglic, 2009; Nielsen, 2017). However, besides these empirical investigations that helped experts better understand the problem of prison rape and sexual assault, research into other areas has been important as well.

Most notably, research on the implementation of PREA policies and practices is vital. Such studies can illuminate the degree to which all the positive initiatives included within PREA are taking place where needed. Importantly, legislation that seeks to improve prison conditions can be futile if not supported by stakeholders within the prison system. That is, prison administrators and staff are responsible for turning legislation like PREA into a measurable reality within correctional systems. Understanding the importance of institutional support within a specific prison system, researchers have attempted to measure it quantitatively. For instance, Moster and Jeglic (2009) asked a random sample of 500 wardens from prisons across the United States about their perceptions on PREA implementation. Following the adoption of PREA, this study found that over half of the wardens reported that policies had been enacted that were based on PREA.

Besides obtaining data from a sample of prison administrators across many states, another good measure of the degree of successful implementation of PREA could be to look at specific correctional institutions that have applied for funding under the act. The implementation of PREA in the state of Nebraska serves as a good case study of how federal funds can be strategically used at the state level. With the funding that the federal government provided under the act, the Nebraska Department of Correctional Services (NDCS) was able to identify specific problems that existed within its correctional system (Corlew, 2006). Also, more importantly, the grant funding provided to the NDCS assisted stakeholders with the development and implementation of concrete procedures to address specific issues.

What was undertaken by the NDCS is a great example of criminal justice policy moving from being simply words on paper to practical applications. This was exemplified by the fact that the obtained funds were strategically allocated to specific institutional needs that were identified as problematic. For example, funds were used to improve the department's inmate classification system to make more appropriate housing assignments. This helped minimize victimization risk and improved the inmate misconduct databases, allowing the NDCS to track sexual assault incidents (Corlew, 2006).

#MeToo Stories in the Corrections System

Those who have followed the #MeToo movement know that women across the United States and the world have been empowered to come forward and tell their stories of sexual violence and harassment. The impact of #MeToo can also be seen within the corrections system. As argued by one scholar, "Corrections has had its #MeToo moment, too—but it happened fifteen years ago, with hearings that led to the passage of PREA" (Cornelius, 2018, p. 1). Certainly, the passage of PREA was a huge victory for incarcerated victims of sexual violence, but that does not mean that there is not work left to be done. Though the current #MeToo movement in the corrections system has not garnered as much attention as PREA, individual accounts of incarcerated individuals, particularly formerly incarcerated women, are beginning to make their way forward as a result of #MeToo. It should be noted that while these individual accounts are being told, incarcerated women as a whole have been left out of the #MeToo discussion (Brown, 2018; Endicott, 2018). The reasons for this vary.

First, one must consider that prisons and jails, by their nature, isolate individuals from society. This leaves many incarcerated women in a system where few checks exist to hold individual staff members accountable for their actions, exacerbating problems of sexual assault and harassment (Endicott, 2018). Second, women make up a small percentage of the prison population (approximately 7 percent); thus, issues that affect incarcerated women often garner less attention (Bureau of Justice Statistics, 2018; Endicott, 2018; The Sentencing Project, 2018). Finally, one must consider the characteristics of the individuals who make up the population of incarcerated women. For example, in U.S. jails, the majority of incarcerated women did not have a job prior to arrest, one-third suffer from serious mental illness, and two-thirds are women of color (Vera Institute of Justice, 2016). Most incarcerated women come from marginalized populations that are often already overlooked by society, so it is not very surprising that their inclusion in the #MeToo movement is limited in nature. Despite this limited inclusion, the individual accounts that are emerging are powerful and are adding to the momentum of #MeToo in the correctional setting.

Endicott (2018) chronicled the story of Stacy Rojas, who is non-gender-conforming and was one of several inmates who filed a lawsuit in November 2017 regarding an alleged incident of harassment that occurred two years prior. Rojas and their coplaintiffs contended that in November 2015, while incarcerated at Central California Women's Facility, they were assaulted and berated by male guards. The allegations included a guard stomping on one woman's breast while another cut off a woman's clothing and left her naked in an isolation cell for an extended period of time; all the while they berated the incarcerated victims with graphic sexual insults and suggestions. According to Diana Block, founding member of the California Coalition for Women Prisoners (which is helping Rojas with the lawsuit), the structure of prisons in California is such that an environment is created where people, primarily men, have absolute authority over incarcerated persons. As stated by Block, "All the dynamics of sexism and patriarchy and sexual violence that are very prevalent in the society as a whole are translated directly into the conduct and behavior within prisons with very little protection or surveillance or recourse" (Endicott, 2018, p. 1). Even standard correctional practices, many of which are designed with men in mind, can be traumatizing for incarcerated women. For example, acts like changing clothes, using the bathroom, and submitting to body searches can take on a violating nature for incarcerated females, especially when performed in front of male guards. Rojas, who is no longer incarcerated, discussed the "survivor's guilt" they feel when thinking of the women who are still incarcerated and going through these difficult experiences. While this notion is depressing at times, it has left Rojas determined to speak up with the hope that their story will spark meaningful change for incarcerated women (Endicott, 2018).

Another #MeToo correctional story is from Kim Brown, a criminal justice reform activist who spent 17 years in prison. According to Brown (2018), shortly after her incarceration she began experiencing unwanted sexual attention from male correctional officers. This unwanted harassment soon became a part of her daily life. She stated that it was not abnormal for such unwanted attention to turn into sexual assault for both her and many of the women who were incarcerated with her. As discussed by Brown, many victims fail to come forward because they fear retaliation if they speak up. It was not uncommon for the prison administration to respond to allegations of sexual abuse by transferring the victim out of the facility. For Brown, a transfer might have placed her at a facility farther away from family, which would have made visitation nearly impossible; this gave her an incentive not to speak up. But the #MeToo movement has helped empower Brown to tell her story. As a result, she has partnered with the Women and Justice Project to work toward the transformation of Manhattan's Bayview Correctional Facility in New York. The facility, which once had the highest rate of reported staff sexual abuse in the state, is now being turned into The Women's Building. This facility will offer space and resources for social justice leaders around the world to promote the women's rights movement (Brown, 2018; The Women's Building, 2018). Much like Stacy Rojas, Kim Brown's story gives an important voice to an underrepresented population and shows how the #MeToo movement is helping to empower incarcerated women.

Even though the empowerment of women has been the primary focus of #MeToo, stories of male sexual victimization have also been told as a result of this movement. The late Linkin Park member Chester Bennington, Major League Baseball pitcher R. A. Dickey, former National Hockey League star Theo Fleury, and film director Tyler Perry are among the male celebrities who have recently disclosed that they were sexually abused (Associated Press, 2018). Some male victims of sexual abuse note that, because the origins of #MeToo focused on female victimization, men's stories are not being given a comparable level of public empathy or understanding. In fact, some male victims of sexual assault started sharing their stories via the Twitter hashtag #MenToo. Though not as prevalent as sexual violence among females, the victimization of males is still significant and worthy of discussion. According to the National Sexual Violence Resource Center (2018), in the United States 1 in 71 men will be raped at some point, and 1 in 6 men will experience some form of sexual violence. As previously discussed, the rates of sexual victimization for incarcerated populations vary greatly between studies, but even conservative rates of male victimization in prison suggest that this is a problem of growing concern (Shermer & Sudo, 2017; Wolff et al., 2006).

An example of how the #MeToo movement has impacted incarcerated men can be seen in the writings of Jerry Metcalf, a man who is incarcerated and currently serving a sentence of 40–60 years for second-degree murder. Metcalf (2018) drew similarities between his experiences of inhumane and dehumanizing treatment at the hands of prison guards and the way many Hollywood actresses felt at the hands of their abusers: "In those actress' industry, men run the show, so if a woman wants to follow her dream and become an actress, she has to put up with shit from those powerful men, just like we do" (p. 2). Metcalf recalled many stories he has heard in his years of incarceration of guards and other staff sexually harassing inmates or pressuring them to have sex. He disclosed that he personally experienced these harms.

While #MeToo focuses on victimization, an interesting and maybe unanticipated result of this movement is that it also forces perpetrators (who are primarily male) to look at behaviors and attitudes they hold toward women as a whole and toward sex in general. Metcalf argued that #MeToo is also starting discussions among incarcerated men about their own, often poor, behaviors, beliefs, and attitudes about women and sex. He admitted that when he was younger, he felt it was okay to touch women on the buttocks or to pass women between male friends as if they were sexual objects being traded. While thinking of these things can be a source of shame, for others it also is a source of growth and healing. As summed up by Metcalf, "If any of [those thoughts] lingered inside me, the #MeToo movement has helped wipe them out. . . . The pain I saw in those women's eyes on TV, the fear, the degradation . . . I never want to be responsible for making anyone feel those things" (p. 3).

Conclusion

In the #MeToo era, where so many voices are being heard, how do we ensure that the voices of incarcerated populations are heard as well? Part of the solution needs to be a reframing of the context in which we view sexual assaults in prisons and jails. To put it simply, we need to stop thinking of sexual assault in prisons and jails as a "criminal justice problem" and start thinking of it as a problem that affects us all. Nielsen (2017) argued that "society would receive a net benefit from decreasing violence, enacted upon and by prisoners, both inside and outside of prison" (p. 235). This is especially important because although strides have been made in addressing the prison rape and sexual assault epidemic through policies such as PREA, incidents of victimization are still being uncovered nearly two decades after PREA's passage (Rowell-Cunsolo et al., 2014). The issue has not been "eliminated," as the name of the legislation may imply.

The vast majority of people who are incarcerated will not be incarcerated indefinitely. Approximately 95 percent of all state prisoners will be released from custody at some point (Hughes & Wilson, 2018). Toward the end of an inmate's sentence, a process of "reentry" begins within the prison setting and ends outside of it. Those who return to the community after experiencing sexual violence while incarcerated are "more likely to normalize, accept, and perpetuate disturbing patterns of sexual violence already present" (Nielsen, 2017, p. 235). When framed in this context, reducing sexual violence for incarcerated populations is advantageous for society.

Sexual violence training for correctional officers and jail administrators should be mandatory. These practitioners are the most powerful people in correctional settings due to the lack of power and autonomy of inmates. Several topics could be addressed in these trainings. Appropriate beliefs and attitudes and knowledge about sexual assault are crucial to reducing sexual violence (Cook & Lane, 2017). Therefore, the more facts and information given in training sessions, the better equipped employees are to combat the issue. Additionally, issues regarding consent (or lack thereof) in these settings are critical for employees to understand, and not only consent between inmates but also the ethical and criminal consequences of sexual relationships between officers and inmates. Last, institutions must prioritize responding to individuals who report abuse; this will show that sexual violence is taken seriously within the institution. If employees and the incarcerated know complaints are given concerned attention, it increases the likelihood that victims and bystanders will report activity and possibly help deter future incidents.

Regarding policy, not only should it promote the elimination of sexual violence in our corrections system, but it also should focus on helping victims heal from the trauma experienced. Treatment should be offered in correctional facilities; if the inmate is nearing release, then protocols should be in place to coordinate treatment upon release. Also, information should be provided about long-term resources that can assist healing outside of prison and jail settings. Finally, it is important to delegitimize the misperceptions that the general public has toward sexual assault in prison.

As we watch the #MeToo movement continue to gain momentum in mainstream culture, it will be of interest to see what impact this has on the criminal justice system, especially our incarcerated populations. While PREA was a big step in the right direction, it is certainly not a catch-all for preventing sexual violence in prisons and jails. Completely eliminating sexual assaults in carceral environments, as the PREA name suggests, may be impossible. Continued research is needed on the implementation and effectiveness of PREA moving forward if sexual violence is going to be reduced in incarcerated populations.

References

Associated Press (2017, October 17). *More than 12M "Me Too" Facebook posts, comments, reactions in 24 hours.* CBS News. https://www.cbsnews.com/news/metoo-more-than-12-million-facebook-posts-comments-reactions-24-hours/

Associated Press (2018, April 19). Male victims of sex abuse feel left behind by #MeToo parade. *New York Post.* https://nypost.com/2018/04/19/male-victims-of-sex-abuse-feel-left-behind-by-metoo-parade/

Baker, T., Bedard, L., & Gertz, M. G. (2013). The unique experience of female prisoners. In G. F. Cole & M. G. Gertz (Eds.), *The criminal justice system: Politics and policies* (pp. 482–500). Wadsworth.

Beck, A. J. (2014). *Sexual victimization in prisons and jails reported by inmates, 2011–2012. Supplemental tables: Prevalence of sexual victimization among transgender adult inmates.* NCJ Publication No. 241399. Bureau of Justice Statistics. https://www.bjs.gov/content/pub/pdf/svpjri1112_st.pdf

Beck, A. J., Berzofsky, M., Caspar R., & Krebs, C. (2013). *Sexual victimization in prisons and jails reported by inmates, 2011–2012. National Inmate Survey, 2011–2012.* NCJ Publication No. 241399. Bureau of Justice Statistics. https://www.bjs.gov/content/pub/pdf/svpjri1112.pdf

Beck, A. J. & Johnson, C. (2012). *Sexual victimization reported by former state prisoners, 2008.* NCJ Publication No. 237363. Bureau of Justice Statistics. https://www.bjs.gov/content/pub/pdf/svrfsp08.pdf

Brown, K. (2018, April 11). *Women in prison are still waiting for their Me Too moment.* HuffPost. https://www.huffingtonpost.com/entry/opinion-brown-me-too-women-prisons_us_5ac28e1de4b00fa46f854abf

Bureau of Justice Statistics. (2018). *Prisoners in 2016.* NCJ Publication No. 251149. https://www.bjs.gov/content/pub/pdf/p16.pdf

Cook, C. L., & Lane, J. (2017). Blaming the victim: Perceptions about incarcerated sexual assault victim culpability among a sample of jail correctional officers. *Victims & Offenders, 12*(3), 347–380.

Corlew, K. R. (2006). Congress attempts to shine a light on a dark problem: An in-depth look at the Prison Rape Elimination Act of 2003. *American Journal of Criminal Law, 33*(2), 157–190.

Cornelius, G. (2018). Corrections had its #MeToo moment—fifteen years ago. Let's not forget the lesson. *Corrections Managers' Report, 24*(1), 1–14.

Cotton, D. J., & Groth, A. N. (1982). Inmate rape: Prevention and intervention. *Journal of Prison and Jail Health, 2*(1), 47–57.

Dumond, R. W. (1992). The sexual assault of male inmates in incarcerated settings. *International Journal of Sociology of Law, 20*(2), 135–157.

Dumond, R. W. (2000). Inmate sexual assault: The plague which persists. *Prison Journal, 80*(4), 407–414.

Eigenberg, H. M. (1989). Male rape: An empirical examination of correctional officers' attitudes toward male rape in prison. *Prison Journal, 68*(2), 39–56.

Endicott, M. (2018, August 29). *"No longer human": Women's prisons are a breeding ground for sexual harassment, abuse.* ThinkProgress. https://thinkprogress.org/ sexual-harassment-abuse-womens-prisons-me-too-5231b62c1785/

Fellner, J. (2010). Ensuring progress: Accountability standards recommended by the national prison rape elimination commission. *Pace Law Review, 30*(5), 1625–1645.

Fishman, J. F. (1934). *Sex in prison: Revealing sex conditions in American prisons.* National Library Press.

Fowler, S. K., Blackburn, A. G., Marquart, J. W., & Mullings, J. L. (2010). Inmates' cultural beliefs about sexual violence and their relationship to definitions of sexual assault. *Journal of Offender Rehabilitation, 49*(3), 180–199.

Garcia, S. E. (2017, October 20). The woman who created #MeToo long before hashtags. *New York Times.* https://www.nytimes.com/2017/10/20/us/me-too-movement-tarana-burke.html

Gottschalk, M. (2006). *The prison and the gallows: The politics of mass incarceration in America.* Cambridge University Press.

Graham, T., & Hastings, A. (2011). Vera and the Prison Rape Elimination Act. *Federal Sentencing Reporter, 24*(1), 42–43. https://doi.org/10.1525/fsr.2011.24.1.42

Hensley, C. (2002). *Prison sex: Practice and policy.* Rienner.

Hughes, T. & Wilson, D. J. (2018). *Reentry trends in the U.S. Bureau of Justice Statistics.* Bureau of Justice Statistics. https://www.bjs.gov/content/reentry/reentry.cfm#highlights

Jaffe, S. (2018). The collective power of #MeToo. *Dissent, 65*(2), 80–87.

Jenness, V., Maxson, C. L., Sumner, J. M., & Matsuda, K. N. (2010). Accomplishing the difficult but not impossible: Collecting self-report data on inmate-on-inmate sexual assault in prison. *Criminal Justice Policy Review, 21*(1), 3–30. https://doi.org/10.1177/0887403409341451

Jenness, V., & Smyth, M. (2011). The passage and implementation of the Prison Rape Elimination Act: Legal endogeneity and the uncertain road from symbolic law to instrumental effects. *Stanford Law & Policy Review, 22*(2), 489–527.

Kappeler, V. E., & Potter, G. W. (2018). *The mythology of crime and criminal justice* (5th ed.). Waveland Press.

Lockwood, D. (1980). *Prison sexual violence.* Elsevier.

Mair, J. S., Frattaroli, S., & Teret, S. P. (2003). New hope for victims of prison sexual assault. *Journal of Law, Medicine & Ethics, 31*(4), 602–606.

Malkin, M. L., & DeJong, C. (2019). Protections for transgender inmates under PREA: A comparison of state correctional policies in the United States. *Sexuality Research and Social Policy, 16*, 393–407. https://doi.org/10.1007/s13178-018-0354-9

Metcalf, J. (2018, September 20). *When prisoners say #MeToo.* The Marshall Project. https://www.themarshallproject.org/2018/09/20/when-prisoners-say-metoo

Moster, A. N., & Jeglic, E. L. (2009). Prison warden attitudes toward prison rape and sexual assault: Findings since the Prison Rape Elimination Act (PREA). *Prison Journal, 89*(1), 65–78. https://doi.org/10.1177/0032885508329981

Nadolny, T. L., Roebuck, J., & McCrystal, L. (2018, April 28). How Cosby verdict could signal #MeToo impact on criminal justice system. *Philadelphia Inquirer.* http://www2.philly.com/philly/news/bill-cosby-guilty-sexual-assault-legal-implications-20180428.html

National Sexual Violence Resource Center (2018). *Get statistics.* https://www.nsvrc.org/statistics

Nielsen, M. (2017). Beyond PREA: An interdisciplinary framework for evaluating sexual violence in prisons. *UCLA Law Review, 64*(1), 230–280.

Nolan, P. & Telford, M. (2006). Indifferent no more: People of faith mobilize to end prison rape. *Journal of Legislation, 32*(2), 128–141.

Piehl, A. M., & Useem, B. (2011). Prisons. In J. Q. Wilson & J. Petersilia (Eds.), *Crime and Public Policy* (pp. 532–558). Oxford University Press.

Prison Rape Elimination Act [PREA], 42 U.S.C. §§ 15602–15609 (2003).

Rantala, R. R. (2018). *Sexual victimization reported by adult correctional authorities, 2012-15.* NCJ Publication No. 251146. Bureau of Justice Statistics. https://www.bjs.gov/content/pub/pdf/svraca1215.pdf

Ristroph, A. (2006). Sexual punishments. *Columbia Journal of Gender and Law, 15*(1), 139–184.

Rowell-Cunsolo, T. L., Harrison, R. J., & Haile, R. (2014). Exposure to prison sexual assault among incarcerated Black men. *Journal of African American Studies, 18*(1), 54–62. https://doi.org/10.1007/s12111-013-9253-6

Scacco, A. M. (1982). *Male rape: A case book of sexual aggressions.* AMS Press.

The Sentencing Project (2018, May). *Incarcerated women and girls, 1980–2016.* https://www.sentencingproject.org/wp-content/uploads/2016/02/Incarcerated-Women-and-Girls-1980–2016.pdf?eType=EmailBlastContent&eId=12d509dd-a247–4f77-a4f8–6d0fdbe0cd6e

Shermer, L. O., & Sudo, H. (2017). Fear of rape from behind prison walls. *International Journal of Prisoner Health, 13*(2), 68–80.

Struckman-Johnson, C., & Struckman-Johnson, D. (2002). Sexual coercion reported by women in three midwestern prisons. *Journal of Sex Research, 39*(3), 217–227.

Struckman-Johnson, C., Stuckman-Johnson, D. (2013). Stopping prison rape: The evolution of standards recommended by PREA's national Prison Rape Elimination Commission. *Prison Journal, 93*(3), 335–354.

Struckman-Johnson, C. J., Struckman-Johnson, D. L., Rucker, L., Bumby, K., & Donaldson, S. (1996). Sexual coercion reported by men and women in prison. *Journal of Sex Research, 33*(1), 67–76.

Struckman-Johnson, D., Struckman-Johnson C., Kruse, J. D., Gross, P. M. & Sumners, B. J. (2013). A pre-PREA survey of inmate and correctional staff opinions on how to prevent prison sexual assault. *Prison Journal, 93*(4), 429–452.

Vera Institute of Justice (2016, August). *Overlooked: Women and jails in an era of reform.* https://www.vera.org/publications/overlooked-women-and-jails-report

Weiner, P. (2013). The evolving jurisprudence of the crime of rape in international criminal law. *Boston College Law Review, 54*(3), 1207–1237.

Wolff, N., Blitz, C. L., Shi, J., Bachman, R., & Siegel, J. A. (2006). Sexual violence inside prisons: Rates of victimization. *Journal of Urban Health, 83*(5), 835–848.

Wolff, N., Shi, J., & Bachman, R. (2010). Measuring victimization inside prisons: Questioning the questions. *Journal of Interpersonal Violence, 23*(10), 1343–1362.

The Women's Building (2018). *Our story.* http://womensbuildingnyc.org/the-womens-building/

IV. Media and Cultural Institutions

7. Lights, Camera, Abuse: Exploring #MeToo in Hollywood

Ashley Wellman

Sexual harassment and abuse in Hollywood have been long-standing problems and yet only recently have been exposed as large-scale issues. From famous actors to powerful executives, the nature of the Hollywood industry has created a breeding ground for such behavior and has served as the setting for sexual harassment and abuse for much of its history. Despite whispers, rumors, and "common knowledge" of pervasive abuse, until recently sexual violence within the entertainment industry had become an accepted reality. It would take a movement of high-profile survivors, both male and female, to bring attention to the abuse. Through the reemergence of the #MeToo movement, Hollywood is now one of the most well-documented breeding grounds for sexual violence, and many within the industry are demanding that it no longer be ignored. The #MeToo movement has forced us to recognize that too many victims have been abused or harassed by powerful individuals (Copeland, 2018).

The current chapter explores the creation and progression of the #MeToo movement and exposes the deep, historical roots of abuse in Hollywood. Through case studies of Bill Cosby and Harvey Weinstein, I discuss how such abuse has been allowed to occur and how, for so long, perpetrators have not been held accountable. The emergence of male survivors and the work of the Time's Up coalition provide hope that change is possible. New initiatives, changing guidelines, harsher penalties, and strong survivors speaking out against sexual violence are the start of shifting a culture, reshaping societal understandings and reactions, and hopefully eliminating sexual violence.

#MeToo: The Origins

As detailed in the introductory chapter, a media frenzy began on October 15, 2017, when Alyssa Milano sent out a tweet encouraging survivors of sexual harassment and abuse to reply with "me too" to demonstrate the widespread impact of sexual violence. In less than two days, Twitter reported that the #MeToo hashtag had been utilized 825,000 times (Santiago & Criss, 2017). Within a day, Facebook noted that 12 million posts, reactions, and comments concerning "me too" had been made, thus equating to the reality that nearly 50 percent of people in the United States were friends on Facebook with at least one person who had posted a "me too" message (Santiago & Criss, 2017).

Alyssa Milano's tweet would increase confidence and create a community for survivors of sexual violence to come forward and disclose their stories of abuse. What was believed to be a viral trend became a powerful movement seemingly overnight. Millions of people from around the world utilized the phrase and hashtag (Santiago & Criss, 2017). As A-list stars shared their own experiences with abuse in the industry, Hollywood, its celebrities, and the public could no longer deny the prevalence of sexual harassment and abuse that existed in Hollywood.

USA Today conducted a survey of women in the entertainment industry, and the results revealed 94 percent of the participants had experienced sexual assault or harassment on the job (Puente & Kelly, 2018). When examining the nature of the abuse, 21 percent said that at least once they had been forced to do something sexual in nature against their will. Only one-fourth of the women said they had reported their experience. The majority of women in the sample stated they had not come forward due to fear of retaliation and concern over job security or advancement. Of those women who did report their maltreatment, a mere 28 percent stated their work environment improved. When describing reporting tendencies, younger participants who had been in the industry for fewer than five years were more likely to report sexual misconduct than their older counterparts, even though many of the older participants had been exposed to more than one act of abuse.

Hollywood's Longtime Dirty Little Secret

Despite the recent public attention surrounding the topic of sexual misconduct in Hollywood, allegations, reports, and acknowledged abuse in the industry have long existed. Throughout its history, Hollywood executives seemed to assume that sex with females was simply a perk of their power (Clarke, 2000). One of the earliest incidents of known sexual abuse in the industry occurred in 1921. Roscoe "Fatty" Arbuckle, the highest paid actor of his time, is believed to have raped Virginia Rappe in a San Francisco hotel room. Rappe died days later from a ruptured bladder, and Arbuckle was charged with manslaughter. He was tried three times before being acquitted of the aspiring actress's death, yet the notoriety of his alleged behaviors was career-ending for Arbuckle (Associated Press, 2017).

Shirley Temple, America's darling known as "Curly Top," noted in her autobiography that sexual harassment and attempted abuse started for her at age 12 (Associated Press, 2017; Black, 1988). An MGM producer exposed himself to the child, saying, "I have something made just for you" (Chirico, 2018, para. 8). The young actress nervously laughed due to her lack of familiarity with the male body, and she was quickly thrown out of the producer's office. Temple recalled how at 17 she was once again trapped by a producer who attempted to assault her in his office. The dark reality that powerful men in the industry expected sexual favors from stars made Temple feel as if "casual sex could be a condition of employment" (para. 9). For her, the condition was not one she was willing to fulfill. So, when comedian George Jessel invited Temple to his office to discuss a role and attempted to assault her, she reacted by kneeing him in the groin.

Judy Garland, famously known for playing Dorothy in *The Wizard of Oz*, also was sexually harassed and abused as a child star (Adams, 2018). From age 16 to 20, Garland was plagued by attempts for sex, by unwanted harassment, and by advances from MGM studio executives (Associated Press, 2017; Clarke, 2000). In one incident, the head of the studio, Louis B. Mayer, placed his hand on Garland's left breast, noting that she sang with her "heart." After several attempts by Mayer, Garland defended herself by telling him she would no longer tolerate his abuse, leaving Mayer in tears. Not all of her abusers reacted in the same remorseful manner. An unnamed executive grew enraged when Garland turned down his advances, attempting to wield his power in the industry by warning that he would ruin her (Rosenwald, 2017).

In 1977, Samantha Geimer was a 13-year-old aspiring actress. On the set of a photo shoot in Los Angeles, she was given champagne and quaaludes by film-maker Roman Polanski before he raped and sodomized her. Polanksi pleaded guilty to statutory rape (Grady, 2017). However, days before he was sentenced, Polanksi fled to Europe and avoided extradition. He remains a fugitive from the U.S. criminal justice system. Despite the allegations and outstanding charges he faced, Polanski won the Academy Award for Best Director for *The Pianist* in 2003. Harrison Ford accepted the award on his behalf. Many interpreted the award and the many subsequent accolades for Polanski as the industry's blatant, public disregard for the protection of abuse victims. In 2017, California artist Marianne Barnard came forward with allegations that Polanski had raped her when she was just 10 years old, becoming the fifth woman to claim Polanski had sexually assaulted her as a child (Grady, 2017).

Not only has Hollywood protected those in power who have been accused of sexual harassment and abuse, but many victims note that when they refuse to stay silent about their abuse, they are threatened with being "blackballed" from projects or are retaliated against by being denied career-advancing opportunities. Joan Collins has been vocal about the repercussions of her refusal to trade sexual favors for roles (Collins, 2017). When Collins was just 21 years old, she was warned by Marilyn Monroe of the sexual harassment and abuse that existed in Hollywood. Monroe cautioned her about "wolves" in Hollywood who used their power to get what they wanted. Collins had already experienced the kind of sexual misconduct that Monroe warned of. She was 17 years old when she experienced her first episode of harassment. When she reached out to an older actress for help, Collins was told it was behavior she would have to tolerate, or else she should get out of the business. Monroe echoed this sentiment by telling Collins that if she refused advances from studio bosses, she would be dropped and replaced. For Collins, the harassment and abuse began when she was a teen and continued throughout her career. She recalled how entitled and threatening the men she encountered could be. After turning down one producer, she received a call from him with a warning, "You won't get much further in this business, kid, if you're going to be so high-hat!" (para. 41). Later, Collins was the front-runner for the leading role in *Cleopatra*. She read for several screen tests and was encouraged that the role was hers. Buddy Adler, the head of 20th Century Fox, promised her the part if she would simply be "nice" to him, a term commonly used in Hollywood to imply sexual favors. Refusing his advances, Collins was denied the role, which later went to Elizabeth Taylor (Associate Press, 2017; Collins, 2017). Collins recalled that sexual abuse was rampant throughout the ranks of Hollywood: "It wasn't just studio bosses and producers who were predatory. Many actors I worked with considered it their divine right to have sex with their leading lady" (Collins, 2017, para. 48).

Case Study: Harvey Weinstein

Harvey Weinstein has become known as one of the most predatory individuals in Hollywood, utilizing his power to sexually abuse women. On October 5, 2017, the *New York Times* shed light on Weinstein's actions and his practice of paying off his victims (Kantor & Twohey, 2017). The story detailed decades of abuse along with the multiple settlements the Hollywood mogul had reached with many of his accusers. Ashley Judd and Rose McGowan were two of the survivors featured in the piece (BBC News, 2019; Kantor & Twohey, 2017). Following the release of the story, Weinstein issued a public apology noting that he "has caused a lot of pain," but he denied allegations of harassment (BBC News, 2019).

Lauren O'Connor, an employee at the Weinstein Company, had written a scathing memo in 2014 accusing Weinstein of frequent sexual misconduct, harassment, and abuse and included specific details of known incidents (Kantor & Twohey, 2017), thus forcing his business partners and law enforcement to take notice. Subsequently, after a 2015 meeting with a model, Weinstein was caught making sexual comments and touching the woman's breasts. Law enforcement asked her to make a recording of their interaction, but later the district attorney refused to take the case. A settlement was reached with both women, and O'Connor, like many other victims of Weinstein, later retracted her claims and publicly praised Weinstein. Such retraction, denial, or failure to report alludes to Weinstein's control and untouchable nature. His victims were often up-and-coming actresses and individuals seeking to launch careers in Hollywood. Aligning with Weinstein opened doors for these individuals, but breaking into the industry with Weinstein's help came with the risk of sexual violence. As one of the most powerful men in Hollywood, his victims had little recourse, as speaking up would cause them to be denied future career opportunities (BBC News, 2019; Farrow, 2017; Kantor & Twohey, 2017).

Weinstein's public image made him out to be a humanitarian, a defender of women, and a supporter of the feminist movement (Kantor & Twohey, 2017). Yet behind the scenes he was a predator that used his employees and connections to lure vulnerable women to private rooms where he would demand sexual favors in return for career advancement, often forcing himself on those women who denied his requests. Many of those who surrounded Weinstein either knew about the abuse or participated in his recruitment, perpetration, or cover-up, but few came forward to disclose his behavior. Employees were required to sign a code of silence forbidding them from vocalizing criticism about the company or its leaders. He also silenced victims by meeting their claims with large payouts and nondisclosure agreements containing confidentiality clauses that forbade them from sharing their story (Farrow, 2017; Kantor & Twohey, 2017). Rumors of Weinstein's behavior had been a common discussion among women in Hollywood, but in time, a demand for the public to recognize his abuse was made.

The *New York Times* piece made it nearly impossible for those in Tinseltown to not take action. On October 8, 2017, Weinstein was released from his company (BBC News, 2019). An even more scathing piece was published in the *New Yorker* magazine on October 10, 2017, in which 13 women recounted their abuse at the hands of Weinstein, including 3 women who said they were raped by him (BBC News, 2019; Farrow, 2017). In the story, 16 previous and current associates of Weinstein noted they had personally witnessed or had intimate knowledge of unwanted sexual violence by Weinstein, noting that professional meetings were often a guise to gain access to young actresses and models whom Weinstein would pursue with his unwanted sexual advances and abuse. The associates referred to other women in the meetings as "honeypots," there to create a comfortable environment in order to relax the young actresses; a "honeypot" would then leave a meeting to allow Weinstein to isolate his victim (Farrow, 2017). All the individuals noted that Miramax and the Weinstein Company were aware of Weinstein's behavior and knew of the abusive patterns (Farrow, 2017). The same day, more A-list stars emerged with accounts of abuse by Weinstein, including Angelina Jolie and Gwyneth Paltrow. Even more celebrities and public figures, such as President Barack Obama and Leonardo DiCaprio, denounced the mogul (BBC News, 2019). Later, Georgina Chapman, his wife, announced that she was leaving Weinstein to protect and prioritize her children (BBC News, 2019).

It was more than seven months before Weinstein was charged for his actions (BBC News, 2019). On May 25, 2018, Weinstein walked into the New York Police Department to turn himself in on charges related to sexual misconduct, abuse, and rape of two women. He was released the next day on $1 million bail, agreeing to wear a monitor and to surrender his passport. He was indicted for rape and criminal sexual acts by a grand jury on May 31, 2018, formally pleading not guilty in the New York Supreme Court on June 5, 2018. A third case was brought forth on July 9, 2018, with Weinstein pleading not guilty. Several civil cases emerged from other women against Weinstein and his related companies (BBC News, 2019).

The reality in the Weinstein case is that money and position provided him the tools needed to sexually abuse women and get away with it. His actions were no secret, and many individuals directly or indirectly aided in his ability to perpetrate sexual violence (Farrow, 2017). Weinstein has continued to be protected as he fights litigation and criminal charges. Several cases have been dropped. For example, on October 11, 2018, one of the sexual assault cases was dropped, and Ashley Judd's sexual harassment case was dropped on January 9, 2019 (BBC News, 2019). Several motions to drop other charges have been filed by Weinstein and his attorneys, citing documentation that the accusers in these cases reported engaging in fond, affectionate, and appreciative communication with Weinstein following the incidents in which they claimed they were abused.

Weinstein reemerged in the news as he worked to build his "dream team" of attorneys, which included Jose Baez, most widely known for defending Casey Anthony as she faced charges for murdering her toddler (Johnson, 2019; Sykes, 2019). Reports claim that Weinstein was seeking to hire a "skirt" so that female attorneys would portray a softer image, but he refused to pay premium fees for their service, relying on a similar sentiment to the one he used with young actresses: it will be good for your career to work with me (Johnson, 2019; Sykes, 2019). In March 2020, Weinstein was sentenced to 23 years in prison after being convicted of sexual assault and rape (Levenson et al., 2020).

Hiding Behind a Famous Facade: The Case of Bill Cosby

Hollywood introduces its viewers to actors, actresses, and behind-the-scenes crews whom audiences come to identify with on a personal level. Through their works and their roles, celebrities take on identities that resonate with everyday citizens. Thus, when an accusation comes out about a well-known, wealthy celebrity, people are quick to question the authenticity of the allegation when it contrasts with the public figure they have come to "know" and love.

In 2018, comedian and "America's Dad" Bill Cosby was sentenced to 3 to 10 years in prison for sexual assault (BBC News, 2018; Kim et al., 2018; Leah, 2018). However, his methodical predatory behavior began many decades before. Kristina Ruehli was only 22 in 1965 when, she said, Cosby invited her to his home. After two drinks she passed out and later awoke to him taking off his clothes and forcing her to perform oral sex on him (Kim et al., 2018). His abuse would continue, with Cosby utilizing his power, his reputation, and drugs to gain access to women he would sexually assault. While some victims stayed silent until larger cases allowed them to share their story, many women spoke to the media and filed charges against Cosby. For years their accounts were denied due to lack of evidence or statutes of limitations.

Cosby evaded consequences for his predatory behavior until 2004 when Andrea Constand, a Temple University employee who was being mentored by Cosby, notified police that she had been assaulted one year earlier by Cosby in his home. In 2005, Cosby spoke to police and admitted to acquiring quaaludes to use to have sex with women but denied he provided Constand with the drug (Kim et al., 2018). In the years to come, other women came forward with similar claims of sexual assault by Cosby. Comedian Hannibal Buress drew significant attention to Cosby's actions in October 2014 when he joked that Cosby "gets on TV: 'Pull your pants up, black people, I was on TV in the 80s. I can talk down to you because I had a successful sitcom.' Yeah but you rape women, Bill Cosby, so turn it down a couple notches . . ." (Lockhart, 2018, para. 16). Stations and various programs began to pull Cosby's content from their lineups. One month later, nearly 45 women had come forward with accusations against Cosby. In December 2015, despite an initial rejection of the case, Pennsylvania authorities brought charges against Cosby in the 2004 sexual assault of Andrea Constand. The case resulted in a mistrial in 2017 due to a deadlocked jury but was retried in 2018. Cosby was found guilty of three charges of sexual assault against Constand, including lack of consent, penetration of an unconscious victim, and impairing Constand with drugs.

While Cosby was eventually held accountable in one of the cases, his abuse began some 53 years earlier. It is difficult to grasp why it took so long for the public to believe that Bill Cosby was a perpetrator, even after so many women came forward. It is possible that history is partially to blame. Particularly in the African American community, cautionary tales circulated of Black men being falsely accused of sexual assault against white women (Copeland, 2018). The accusations and charges surrounding Bill Cosby were initially interpreted as society's way of reminding African American men that they had forgotten their "place."

Unlike Weinstein, who was commonly known as a sexual predator, Cosby served as an iconic figure in American history, both as a healthy father figure and as a strong Black man (BBC News, 2018; Calkins, 2018; Copeland, 2018; Kim et al., 2018; Roig-Franzia, 2018). He served as role model for the African American community, breaking racial barrier lines in his career, exemplifying what it meant to be a good father, and encouraging people to dream big, do the right thing, and work hard to achieve their goals (Copeland, 2018). He developed a brand that was so strong he became an almost omnipresent, positive person in the minds of Americans (Calkins, 2018; Copeland, 2018). He was constantly in the public eye and always appeared joyful, thus reinforcing the values of virtue, approachability, and kindness (BBC News, 2018; Calkins, 2018; Copeland, 2018; Roig-Franzia, 2018). What people failed to see was the private Cosby, a man who was manipulative, demanding, selfish, and predatory. So when women made accusations against Cosby, the public chose to believe and defend the brand that Cosby had created instead of accepting the reality of the man he was off-screen (Calkins, 2018; Copeland, 2018). The women themselves were aware of the image and brand that surrounded Cosby. Many noted that they stayed silent and suffered in private after their abuse for this exact reason: who would believe that America's favorite dad raped them (Roig-Franzia, 2018)?

Tarana Burke, founder of the original Me Too movement, tweeted that we must begin to move away from stories about individuals and instead focus on the power differentials and privilege that give way to sexual violence (Arceneaux, 2018). Her tweet reminded followers that *who* the perpetrator is does not change the impact of the abuse and does not redefine the problem. Assailants can be any gender; can be our favorite actor/actress, humanitarian, or professor; and can hide behind false narratives. Burke argued that the issue at the end of the day is power and the harm done to victims when power is abused, regardless of the character or reputation of the perpetrator. While a possible three-year sentence for Cosby, a serial rapist with more than 60 women coming forward against him, is difficult to categorize as a victory, it highlights this needed shift to prioritize victims. Cosby's victims were called "gold diggers" and "liars," but they can now begin to heal and find peace as their truths were finally recognized (Leah, 2018).

Male Survivors

The #MeToo movement has largely focused on the protection and advancement of women, but men have also suffered sexual harassment and abuse in Hollywood. For young men entering the industry, many powerful executives would wield the casting couch as a tool to sexually exploit them while promising career success in return.

For male survivors, navigating the #MeToo movement can be incredibly difficult. Few have come forward publicly, and instead they often adopt a "keep your head down" and "get over it" attitude to survive their victimization (Arceneaux, 2018). The fear of feeling alone as a male survivor or of having their sexuality questioned keeps many male survivors silenced, thus forcing them to deal with their abuse without support (Bradley, 2018). The reality is, particularly in the United States, men are not allowed to be victims. Skepticism, mockery, and degradation surround male survivors who step forward and vocalize their victimization. Male survivors often have their sexuality or interpretation of the events questioned when coming forward about a male assailant or are praised when they are abused by older women (Arceneaux, 2018; Bradley, 2018).

Just as sexual abuse against females in Hollywood has been a long-standing issue, so has sexual violence against men. Henry Wilson was a talent agent from the 1940s through the 1960s known for using his power to abuse men seeking to launch careers in Hollywood (Adams, 2018). A closeted gay man, Wilson utilized the following tactic with his clients: "Come with me, do what I say and I'll make you a star" (para. 13). He is famously associated with the success of Rock Hudson, turning him from a truck driver into a Hollywood heartthrob. Abusing men provided Wilson with a significant power advantage. In fear of being outed as gay or of being blackmailed by Wilson, victims of his advances and abuse had a significant incentive to remain quiet about the agent's criminal practices.

On October 17, 2017, just two days after Alyssa Milano tweeted #MeToo, Terry Crews came forward noting his support for the survivors speaking out, because he knew the abuse they spoke of personally (Bradley, 2018). Crews—infuriated by people who were expressing a belief that the masses of women were coming forward with allegations of abuse only in order to gain fame—related how he had been groped by a powerful agency executive, Adam Venit, at a party. Venit had laughed when Crews protested the executive's advances. Many men questioned Crews's account of abuse, stating that his physical size prohibited him from being a victim. Other critics questioned why he did not defend himself by punching his abuser (Arceneaux, 2018; Bradley, 2018).

The public backlash that met male survivors, like it had female survivors, sheds light on why so many victims of sexual abuse are not able or willing to come forward with their stories. Crews noted that once you speak up, you are behind "enemy lines" and viewed as a problem that must be removed instead of as a victim who needs help and deserves to be heard (Bradley, 2018). Rapper 50 Cent and comedian D. L. Hughley mocked Crews for "allowing himself" to be abused, which further fueled the negative responses to male victims (Arceneaux, 2018; Bradley, 2018). To combat this issue, Crews sat before the Senate Judiciary Committee and described how manhood becomes a toxic, cultlike system that promotes men protecting one another but also attacks those who speak out against abuse (Arceneaux, 2018).

Despite the fact that the movement was centered on female victims of sexual violence, the #MeToo movement has been instrumental in shifting the dialog surrounding male sexual abuse as well. When Alex Winter saw the prevalence of sexual abuse and the strength of the women coming forward to share their stories, he said it broke the stigma of speaking up and removed the sense of isolation from his own abuse. For #MeToo to be a successful movement, gender must become a nonissue (Arceneaux, 2018). And the movement will be *most* successful when it is genderless, giving permission for survivors to come forward, demanding that people listen, and pushing to change a culture that will allow for freedom from sexual abuse for all (Arceneaux, 2018; Bradley, 2018).

Progress and Policy in Hollywood

Within two months of Alyssa Milano's use of the hashtag #MeToo, Hollywood executives began to seek ways to reduce sexual misconduct and abuse in the entertainment industry. Two dozen leaders, under the direction of Anita Hill, formed and funded the Commission on Sexual Harassment and Advancing Equality in the Workplace (Sun, 2017). Hill is known for her courage as a pioneering whistleblower who testified about sexual harassment at the hands of Clarence Thomas during his Supreme Court confirmation hearing in 1991.

As a result of the commission, a group of 300 women in the entertainment industry, many of whom were A-list celebrities, joined together to form Time's Up. The goal of the movement was to seek ways to improve working conditions, increase equity, and eliminate abuse of women in the workforce (Time's Up, 2018). What originally started as a mission to rid Hollywood of maltreatment of women diversified when nearly 750,000 female farmworkers wrote an open letter describing their support for the movement and their own experiences with gender inequality, sexual harassment, and assault. This letter and pledge of solidarity expanded the goals of Time's Up, recognizing that the women in Hollywood had a platform to promote change that would impact all women, regardless of privilege and power (Buckley, 2018; Calfas, 2018).

On January 1, 2018, the Time's Up initiative was unveiled in a letter that was published in a full-page ad in the *New York Times* and *La Opinion* that pledged to create change (Buckley, 2018). The ad, headed "Dear Sisters," recognized that the abuse of power and maltreatment of women is found in every corner of the globe and in all industries. It laid out a promise to push for equality, to hold perpetrators accountable, and to shift public opinions by demanding change. The ad served as a visible pledge that would rally women around the world by reminding them that those who experience sexual misconduct are not alone and no longer have to be silent. It ended with a powerful and symbolic note: "In Solidarity" (Time's Up, 2018).

Time's Up developed several initiatives to deliver on the promises it made in its open letter. One of its greatest contributions to the #MeToo movement was the establishment of the Time's Up Legal Defense Fund. Now run by the National Women's Law Center, the fund began with $13 million from donations to aid women around the globe. It provides legal and public resources to report and recover from sexual misconduct in the workplace, to protect women from retaliation, and to preserve their ability to advance their careers after coming forward with their experiences (Buckley, 2018; Calfas, 2018; Time's Up, 2018). Additionally, the movement called for women to wear black to the 2018 Golden Globes to show a united front and to serve as a beacon of support for all who had faced sexual maltreatment.

In the wake of the #MeToo and Time's Up movements, many changes are being made in Hollywood. In February 2018, codes of conduct across many guilds, including the Screen Actors Guild and the Producers Guild of America, were created to begin to improve conditions and ensure safety for women in the entertainment workplace (Melas, 2019). One of the major realizations in Hollywood was that women did not have fair representation and were predominantly excluded from many areas of the industry. For example, a study found that over 75 percent of Rotten Tomatoes critics were white men age 40 and older, thus failing to provide a diverse review of works and performances. In response, a call has been made to enhance the representation of minorities and underrepresented groups, including women, in the area of entertainment reporting and critical review. Along similar lines, in the last decade only 4 percent of the 1,200 highest earning studio films have had a female director (Fitzpatrick, 2019); thus, Time's Up and the Annenberg Inclusion Initiative have challenged Hollywood studios to break this cycle and, within the next 18 months, to develop a project that has a female director.

Conclusion

The big question is, What happens next for the #MeToo movement? Cases like Bill Cosby's remind us that our society has a way to go before being able to prevent, respond to, and help heal the survivors of sexual violence (Leah, 2018). As a society, we have also been conditioned to question accusers and to believe that women who make claims against powerful men are simply vindictive, seeking money, or seeking revenge (Copeland, 2018). The idea that a woman who comes forward and should be believed has, for much of history, been nonsensical. The next chapter of #MeToo should prioritize victims and the survivors of sexual violence and create healthy and healing responses to the trauma they have endured instead of quick, reactive responses that can often be jarring and retraumatizing (Leah, 2017). Treating sexual violence as a significant, serious problem and shifting attitudes and responses to be pro-survivor will be the most difficult and simultaneously the most powerful progress that the #MeToo movement can achieve. Much work is to be done, but thanks in part to the attention raised by the actors and actresses in Hollywood, sexual violence is being addressed on a national platform like never before.

References

Adams, T. (2018, October 5). Casting-couch tactics plagued Hollywood long before Harvey Weinstein. *Variety.* https://variety.com/2017/film/features/casting-couch-hollywood-sexual-harassment-harvey-weinstein-1202589895/

Arceneaux, M. (2018, August 28). If we want men to be a part of #MeToo, we have to stop gendering the movement. *Glamour.* https://www.glamour.com/story/me-too-movement-men-sexual-assault-survivors

Associated Press. (2017, October 10). *Hollywood's long ugly history with sexual harassment.* https://www.apnews.com/dea7a81f65e64db5ac9de6f30943a803

BBC News. (2018, September 25). *Bill Cosby: From "America's Dad" to disgraced comic.* https://www.bbc.com/news/entertainment-arts-30194819

BBC News. (2019, January 10). *Harvey Weinstein timeline: How the scandal unfolded.* https://www.bbc.com/news/entertainment-arts-41594672

Black, S. T. (1988). *Child Star: An Autobiography.* McGraw-Hill.

Bradley, L. (2018, October 4). "I was terrified, and I was humiliated": #MeToo's male accusers, one year later. *Vanity Fair.* https://www.vanityfair.com/hollywood/2018/10/metoo-male-accusers-terry-crews-alex-winter-michael-gaston-interview

Buckley, C. (2018, January 1). Powerful Hollywood women unveil anti-harassment action plan. *New York Times.* https://www.nytimes.com/2018/01/01/movies/times-up-hollywood-women-sexual-harassment.html?rref=collection%2Fbyline%2Fcara-buckley&action=click&contentCollection=undefined&region=stream&module=stream_unit&version=latest&contentPlacement=1&pgtype=collection&_r=0

Calfas, J. (2018, January 2). Hollywood women launch Time's Up to end sexual harassment. Here's their plan. *Time.* http://time.com/5083809/times-up-hollywood-sexual-harassment/

Calkins, T. (2018, April 30). Commentary: Everyone loved Bill Cosby. Did his brand cover his crimes? *Fortune*. http://fortune.com/2018/04/30/bill-cosby -rape-sexual-assault-trial-jail/

Chirico, R. (2018). *Though she suffered abuse, Shirley Temple's story is a model of child star resilience*. Ranker. https://www.ranker.com/list/tragic-shirley -temple-stories/rob-chirico

Clarke, G. (2000). *Get Happy: The Life of Judy Garland*. Dell Publishing.

Collins, J. (2017, October 13). Hollywood's casting couch and why I lost my part as Cleopatra to Liz Taylor: Joan Collins recalls hiding in wardrobes, dodging naked producers and heeding Marilyn's warning that all studio bosses were "wolves." *The Daily Mail*. https://www.dailymail.co.uk/femail/article-4979212 /Why-lost-Cleopatra-Liz-Taylor.html

Copeland, B. (2018, May 1). Why was it so hard to believe the women about Cosby? *San Francisco Chronicle*. https://www.sfchronicle.com/opinion/openforum /article/Why-was-it-so-hard-to-believe-the-women-about-12878970.php

Farrow, R. (2017, October 10). From aggressive overtones to sexual assault: Harvey Weinstein's accusers tell their stories. *New Yorker*. https://www.newyorker .com/news/news-desk/from-aggressive-overtures-to-sexual-assault-harvey -weinsteins-accusers-tell-their-stories

Fitzpatrick, H. (2019, January 29). *Stars are taking on a new Time's Up pledge to in-crease the number of female directors in Hollywood*. ABC News. https://abcnews .go.com/GMA/Culture/stars-taking-times-pledge-increase-number-female -directors/story?id=60675505

Grady, C. (2017, October 23). *Roman Polanski is now facing a 5th accusation of sexual assault against a child: The long history of Roman Polanski's child rape charges, from 1977 to the present*. Vox. https://www.vox.com/culture/2017/8/17 /16156902/roman-polanski-child-rape-charges-explained-samantha-geimer -robin-m

Johnson, T. (2019, February 25). *Harvey Weinstein "desperately trying to hire" a female lawyer*. Page Six. https://pagesix.com/2019/02/25/harvey-weinstein -desperately-trying-to-hire-a-female-lawyer/

Kantor, J. & Twohey, M. (2017, October 5). Weinstein paid off sexual harassment accusers for decades. *New York Times*. https://www.nytimes.com/2017/10/05/us /harvey-weinstein-harassment-allegations.html

Kim, K., Littlefield, C., & Etehad, M. (2018, September 25). Bill Cosby: A 50-year chronicle of accusations and accomplishments. *LA Times*. https://www.latimes .com/entertainment/la-et-bill-cosby-timeline-htmlstory.html

Leah, R. (2018, September 27). *Bill Cosby's prison sentence: Why the next phase of #MeToo should prioritize survivors*. Salon. https://www.salon.com/2018/09/27 /bill-cosbys-prison-sentence-why-the-next-phase-of-metoo-should-prioritize -survivors/

Levenson, E., del Valle, L., & Moghe, S. (2020, March 11). *Harvey Weinstein sentenced to 23 years in prison after addressing his accusers in court.* CNN. https://www.cnn.com/2020/03/11/us/harvey-weinstein-sentence/index.html

Lockhart, P. R. (2018, September 26). *The hypocritical moralizing of Bill Cosby: Years before being sentenced to prison for sexual assault, Cosby presented himself as a moral leader for Black America.* Vox. https://www.vox.com/identities/2018/5/1/17304196/bill-cosby-conviction-sentencing-hypocrisy-metoo

Melas, C. (2019, January 2). *Voices behind Time's Up.* CNN. https://www.cnn.com/interactive/2019/01/entertainment/times-up-movement-anniversary/index.html

Puente, M. & Kelly, C. (2018, February 20). How common is sexual misconduct in Hollywood? *USA Today.* https://www.usatoday.com/story/life/people/2018/02/20/how-common-sexual-misconduct-hollywood/1083964001/

Roig-Franzia, M. (2018, September 25). Bill Cosby sentenced to 3 to 10 years in state prison. *Washington Post.* https://www.washingtonpost.com/lifestyle/style/bill-cosby-sentenced-to-3-to-10-years-in-state-prison/2018/09/25/9aa620aa-c00d-11e8-90c9-23f963eea204_story.html?utm_term=.294f463883e5

Rosenwald, M. S. (2017, November 14). "I'll ruin you": Judy Garland on being groped and harassed by powerful Hollywood men. *Washington Post.* https://www.washingtonpost.com/news/retropolis/wp/2017/11/14/ill-ruin-you-judy-garland-on-being-groped-and-harassed-by-powerful-hollywood-men/?noredirect=on&utm_term=.d93a1fde0dbf

Santiago, C. & Criss, D. (2017, October 17). *An activist, a little girl and the heartbreaking origin of "Me too."* CNN. https://www.cnn.com/2017/10/17/us/me-too-tarana-burke-origin-trnd/index.html

Sun, R. (2017, December 15). Top Hollywood execs unveil anti-sexual harassment commission chaired by Anita Hill. *Hollywood Reporter.* https://www.hollywoodreporter.com/news/top-hollywood-execs-unveil-anti-sexual-harassment-commission-chaired-by-anita-hill-1068646

Sykes, T. (2019, February 26). *Harvey Weinstein tells female lawyers repping him at discount will be good for their careers: Report.* Daily Beast. https://www.thedailybeast.com/harvey-weinstein-tells-female-lawyers-repping-him-at-discount-will-be-good-for-their-careers-report

Time's Up. (2018). *Time's Up history.* https://www.timesupnow.com/history

8.   Sexual Abuse in Sport: Hegemonic Masculinity and Institutional Failures

Pamela J. Forman, Anne M. Nurse, and Lake D. Montie

The #MeToo movement has brought unprecedented attention to sexual victimization in a variety of institutions, including the institutions discussed throughout this book. Many of the most highly publicized cases have been in youth sports, an area that has long been considered a safe space for the healthy development of children. While many aspects of abuse are common across institutions, this chapter focuses on features of the sports environment that support abuse. Specifically, we look at the role of hegemonic masculinity and an accommodating organizational culture. The case studies of Penn State and Michigan State University provide vivid illustrations of how these factors protected and abetted both Jerry Sandusky and Larry Nassar in their abuse of children and adolescents.

Explanations for sexual assault in institutions often rely on the existence of a "bad apple." This is a convenient narrative for institutions to adopt; by blaming a corrupt "apple," the institution itself remains unblemished (Waterhouse-Watson, 2013). Cynthia Enloe (2004), however, has called on us to question this explanation. Her analysis of the U.S. military personnel's abusive treatment of prisoners in Abu Ghraib showed how the problem went much deeper than a few bad apples. In fact, Enloe found the whole barrel to be rotten, arguing that the military's organizational culture supported the abusive actions toward Iraqi prisoners. Her work revealed that institutional sex scandals are not as much about individuals with psychological problems as they are due to "institutional pathologies" and evidence of "institutional decay" (Gamson, 2001, p. 185). Our goal in this chapter is to take this sociological understanding and apply it to sexual abuse in sports.

Prevalence and Characteristics of Sexual Abuse in Sports

Sexual abuse "occurs when there is not mutual consent, or when consent cannot be given or is obtained in an aggressive, exploitative, manipulative or threatening manner" (Marks, 2013, p. 170). We know that it is a misuse of power that exists in relation to other types of exploitation, including sexual harassment, gender harassment, bullying, and hazing. While both authority figures and peers can engage in sexual abuse, here we concentrate on sexual abuse committed by people in authority like coaches, medical practitioners, athletic trainers, officials, and administrators.

International studies indicate that sexual abuse is a pervasive problem at all levels of sports—from recreational, to elite, to college athletics. The prevalence of abuse is impossible to calculate accurately, given that most experiences of abuse go unreported. Surveys of athletes also underestimate abuse levels, partially because they do not capture the experiences of former athletes who left their sports as a result of abuse (Kirby et al., 2008; Toftegaard Nielsen, 2001; Volkwein et al., 1997).

There is not a lot of research on the prevalence of sexual abuse in sports in the United States, but European studies have found that about 3 percent of athletes report victimization (Alexander et al., 2011; Timpka et al., 2018; Toftegaard Nielsen, 2001). At the same time, some studies have found much higher rates. For example, 31 percent of 210 female and 21 percent of 160 male elite athletes in Australia reported having been abused (Leahy et al., 2002, p. 31). A 1996 survey of 266 Canadian national athletes found that 8.6 percent of athletes had experienced rape or attempted rape in a sports context, and another 22 percent reported having had sex with an authority figure (many in this latter group did not perceive these encounters as sexual abuse) (Kirby et al., 2008, pp. 88–89).

Limited research from the United States suggests that abuse in athletics occurs at about the same rate as in other nations. For example, Volkwein et al. (1997) surveyed 210 U.S. female college athletes about their experiences with sexual harassment and found that 20 percent reported being "subjected to potentially threatening behaviors" by their coach (p. 291). Just under 2 percent reported that a coach had kissed them, stared at their breasts, or proposed a sexual encounter. In another study with 200 female college athletes and 200 nonathletes at three American universities, 1.92 percent of the athletes reported coaches making verbal or physical advances toward them (Volkwein-Caplan et al., 2002, p. 99).

Youth who are victimized in sports contexts are similar to people who are abused in other contexts. Offenders often choose victims because they have low self-esteem, weak family connections, or few friends (Brackenridge, 1997; Marks, 2013; Volkwein et al., 1997). In a study of athletes, Cense and Brackenridge (2001) found that offenders tend to choose athletes who have previous abuse histories (often in non-sports contexts). Disabled athletes and those who compete at high levels at young ages are at an increased risk (Alexander et al., 2011; Kirby et al., 2008).

As in the general population, female athletes are more likely to experience abuse than are males, and abuse is likely to be committed by a male offender. Research, however, tends to focus on the "male perpetrator–female victim" paradigm (Hartill, 2005, p. 287). Although females are underrepresented as offenders and overrepresented as victims, this does not justify the lack of attention to female perpetrators and male victims (Hartill, 2014; Parent & Bannon, 2012). Information is also extremely limited about sexual orientation and abuse victimization. The fact that levels of abuse against lesbian, gay, bisexual, and queer athletes are elevated in the general population, however, suggests that it is likely true in sports as well (Kirby et al., 2008).

Sports and Hegemonic Masculinity

The expression of masculinity varies across cultures and time periods, but there is usually one form held up as the ideal in any given society. Called hegemonic masculinity, this ideal includes strength, dominance over women, winning, violence, and heterosexuality (Connell, 1987). The institution of sport has become central to the construction and contestation of hegemonic masculinity (Bryson, 1987; Messner & Sabo, 1994; Messner & Stevens, 2002). With their emphasis on winning, strength, and violence, sports provide men with a compelling way to "do gender." Additionally, since sports are commonly sex-segregated, they free male athletes to subscribe to standards of hegemonic masculinity more strongly than is possible in mixed-gender groups (Crosset, 2016).

Undoubtedly, football remains the team sport most associated with hegemonic masculinity in the United States (Anderson & Kian, 2012). Football asks its athletes to gut out physical pain and inflict physical violence upon others. This hypermasculine environment teaches young men to distance themselves from homosexuality, and it becomes very hard for young men or coaches who are gay to come out. At Pennsylvania State University, it is quite possible that a homophobic culture helped harbor Sandusky, a same-sex perpetrator.

Similarly, emphasized femininity works with hegemonic masculinity to reify ideologies that denigrate women and accentuate their identities as heterosexuals committed to pleasing men (Connell, 1987). Within women's athletics, gymnastics epitomizes emphasized femininity. Nubile adolescent females compete in skintight sparkly leotards; their hair is perfectly coiffed, their faces are made up, and glitter appears on their faces, in their hair, and even on their fingernails. Perennially, women's artistic gymnastics is one of the most watched Olympic sports; men's gymnastics, however, struggles to find its audience. Even though men's gymnastics takes strength and skill, hegemonic masculinity feeds into its unfair perception as a "gay" sport, while viewers see women gymnasts as eye candy. Gymnastics is a rare sport where female athletes sign up in far greater numbers than males and outshine them in popularity.

As more female athletes have entered the masculine domain of athletics, hegemonic masculinity impedes them from gaining much more than a foothold. Ironically, women's participation supports masculine supremacy in sports and other institutions by existing as a second-class venture. In contradiction to the National Collegiate Athletic Association's (NCAA) rhetoric in support of gender equity, men's collegiate sports receive more funding and much more attention. In 2018, women remained the minority of NCAA student-athletes (44 percent) (Schwarb, 2018) despite making up over half of the undergraduate students. The media compounds this relative invisibility; men's sports receive 96 percent of sports media coverage (Springer, 2019). The NCAA and youth sport organizations need to expand opportunities for girls and women in sports and to spend more energy promoting their accomplishments. Otherwise, negative publicity about sexual predators like Nassar will predominate supposed women's sports coverage.

Organizational Context of Sexual Abuse in Sports

Youth sports organizations face many unique challenges when trying to prevent abuse. For example, coaches spend significant periods of time with their players, who may lean on them for intellectual and emotional support. Travel time and stay during competitions allows emotional intimacy to develop and creates open opportunities for abuse (Brackenridge, 2001; Cense & Brackenridge, 2001; Kirby et al., 2008). Locker rooms become sites for sexualized conversations and activities that go beyond changing and showering (Hartill, 2009). Whereas a coach making sexualized comments about players would stand out as sexual harassment in other educational settings, in team practices it might become "normalized" behavior. When such situations combine with opportunities for one-on-one interactions in offices, athletic complexes, or even hotels, it is not surprising that boundaries blur and abuses of power ensue.

Abusive coaches are often admired community figures who take on a parental role with their athletes (Marks, 2013; Stirling & Kerr, 2009). Parents tend to trust their children's coaches (Marks, 2013; McMahon & Thompson, 2011; Pinheiro et al., 2014). When an athlete comes forth with sexual abuse allegations, administrators, parents, and team members may side with the coach. Thus, children fear that if they report abusive behaviors, they will not be believed or will be ostracized by their peers for reporting their beloved coach (Brackenridge, 2001).

Athletes are at most risk for sexual abuse within a few years of reaching their peak performance (Cense & Brackenridge, 2001; Kirby & Wintrup, 2002), which is referred to as the "stage of imminent achievement" (Brackenridge & Kirby, 1997, p. 407). For female athletes whose sexual maturity usually coincides with career peak, the potential risks are heightened. Marks (2013) has claimed that the prevalence of sexual harassment and violence is highest in elite athletics. The intensity of the sport at this level means that athletes spend enormous amounts of time training for, traveling to, and participating in competitions (Parent & Fortier, 2018). Unfortunately, elite athletes oftentimes weigh the risk of jeopardizing their careers by divulging inappropriate behavior against the burden of pleasing their parents and various stakeholders (like coaches, trainers, agents, sponsors, and sport associations).

Athletes are not likely to report sexual abuse due to the configuration of power within the organizational structure of sport and the cultural environment of competitive athletics. The coach-athlete relationship offers coaches control over athletes' lives both on and off the field (Hargreaves, 1994). Coaches have the authority to decide who makes the team, who receives special training or special opportunities, and how much playing time each athlete receives (Sand et al., 2011). Because coaches have more training, knowledge, and previous athletic experience than the athletes they instruct, they can legitimately touch athletes to help them learn new skills, to apply ice or strapping to an injury, or to congratulate them for their performances. Consequently, athletes are often reluctant to object to how coaches touch them because boundaries between acceptable and unacceptable touch are blurred (Parent & Demers, 2011). Finally, coaches have physical power over athletes, especially when an adult male coaches young females (Sand et al., 2011).

Young athletes quickly learn that to be successful in sports, they must relinquish power over their bodies to the coach. They do not get to make decisions about training—in fact, they are taught to believe that the door to the elite levels of sports involves pushing their bodies to the limits demarcated by adults (Hartill, 2010). Regulation of athletes' bodies is not confined to training, however. Coaches, peers, and parents constantly monitor athletes' physiques to ensure that their bodies take on the form considered ideal in their sports (McMahon & Thompson, 2011).

While there are many reasons why athletes do not report sexual victimization, a number of factors are relevant to the sports context. Athletes are taught to embrace their identity as part of a team and to prioritize athletic performance over well-being (Parent & Bannon, 2012). Boys and girls are socialized to respect masculinity and heteronormativity (Hartill, 2010). For boys who suffer abuse by other males, the "threat of being labeled as a faggot, homosexual, or queer may ensure silence against reporting sexual abuse" (Holland, 2015, p. 30) or delay its disclosure for years. Finally, athletic administrators silence allegations by situating violations as personal or private (Burton Nelson, 1994). The resultant code or dome of silence (Kirby et al., 2008) perpetuates cycles of victimization and supports institutional violence.

The following sections focus on the institutional failures that allowed Jerry Sandusky's transgressions at Pennsylvania State University and Larry Nassar's egregious behavior at Michigan State University to continue for decades. While Nassar's abuse falls into the common pattern of sexual abuse—men taking advantage of young women—Sandusky's atrocities fall into a lesser studied category, same-sex victimization (Hartill, 2009). Due to the voluminous media coverage of these sexual abuse scandals, we offer relatively few details about the crimes for which Sandusky and Nassar are serving time in prison. Instead, we examine the institutional culture and shortcomings at these universities and suggest ways that sport organizations and institutions of higher education can work to protect the welfare of children and adolescents.

Pennsylvania State University's Sexual Abuse Scandal

There are a lot of little boys around the country today who are watching this game. And they're trying to figure out what the definition of manhood is all about. Father, this is it right here. I pray that this game will be a training ground of what manhood looks like. . . . May the truth be known, may justice be known. May you protect the victims. . . . (Fernandez, 2011, para. 2)

Assistant coach Ron Brown of Nebraska brought his team and Penn State's together for this prayer prior to PSU's first game after it fired its legendary football coach, Joe Paterno. The irony of a prayer and moment of silence was not lost upon the media. Jeff Greenfield, a political journalist, tweeted, "Moment of silence for the children at Penn State? Why not? Just about everyone who might have saved them was silent for more than a decade" (as cited in Fernandez, 2011, para. 3).

Jerry Sandusky assisted head football coach Joe Paterno during his thirty-four years at PSU and also founded the Second Mile Foundation, a nonprofit organization for under-resourced youth in 1977. Second Mile was where, until 2010, he groomed many of his victims. In 1998, a boy returned home from the Penn State campus with wet hair, admitting to his mother that he had showered with Sandusky. She filed a report; however, the university police did not press charges (Klein & Tolson, 2015). The senior officials at PSU were complicit with the police department in not treating suspected child sexual abuse as a potential crime. Senior Vice President for Finance and Business Gary Schultz, the executive in charge of the university's police department, did not enter the reported sex offense in the crime log because Chief Thomas Harmon "believed there was no clear evidence of a crime" (Moore, 2016, p. 17). Further, Schultz, university president Graham

Spanier, and Athletic Director Tim Curley did not inform the school's board of trustees, interrogate Sandusky, or restrict his campus access.

Sandusky retired in 1999 with emeritus status, a status it was later determined he did not deserve (Moore, 2016). His retirement package provided him continued access to the school's football facilities. In 2001 a former PSU quarterback and graduate assistant in the football program, Mike McQueary, told his father and Paterno that he witnessed a naked Sandusky standing behind a 10- to 12-year-old boy and heard "rhythmic slapping" in the Lasch Football Building's showers (Moore, 2016, p. 21). He later offered Schultz and Curley additional details. Although Paterno also contacted Schultz and Curley, neither felt the situation warranted more than a warning to Sandusky and to Second Mile.

Their denial allowed Sandusky to continue violating children in PSU facilities. Spanier concurred with Curley and Schultz's decision not to alert the board of trustees and took no further action. Curley's office allowed Sandusky to continue running youth camps on Penn State campuses (Moore, 2016), and Sandusky went on to molest at least two more children on the campus. In violation of the Jeanne Clery Disclosure of Campus Security Policy and Campus Crime Statistics Act (Clery Act), these allegations were not logged in the campus crime statistics (Moore, 2016).

Penn State finally took action after Curley was placed on administrative leave and Schultz officially retired. The trustees fired Spanier, and Interim President Rodney Erickson placed assistant football coach McQueary on paid leave and then fired him a few days later (Nesbitt, 2016). McQueary settled his whistleblower claim against PSU for $7.3 million. The board of trustees fired Joe Paterno in a telephone conversation. Originally, Paterno tried to chart his own course, promising to resign at the season's end. His resignation statement was contrite, stating, "It is one of the great sorrows of my life. . . . I wish I had done more" in connection to the victims (Gustini, 2011, para. 5). This sympathy for the victims departed from his past protection of Sandusky, such as when Paterno had told PSU leaders to feel sorry for Sandusky and not to report him to the police (Alderfer, 2013).

Paterno's legions of supporters protested his dismissal after an illustrious 46-year tenure as head football coach, lamenting that PSU and the media had treated him unfairly (Cooky, 2012). Over 5,000 angry students, alumni, and community members poured into the streets, necessitating police in riot gear to disperse them (Logan, 2011). They carried signs and chanted, "We are JoePa," their affectionate truncation of his name. Paterno had put PSU football on the map for guiding the Nittany Lions to two national championships, 409 wins, and five undefeated seasons. His legacy went beyond football on the State College campus. He endowed a $5 million library wing that bears his name, the health center, a spiritual center, and professorships in English and the library (Pennington, 2011).

Paterno held tremendous informal power at PSU. As Alderfer (2013) pointed out, "Key individuals represent collective entities (e.g., the university, the football program, and the university police)" (p. 118). After a losing season, Spanier, Curley, and the head of the board of trustees finally arrived on Paterno's doorstep to secure his resignation, but they relented after Paterno refused to bow down.

Institutional Failures at Penn State

PSU's response to the abuse centered on the individuals or "bad apples" who had allowed Sandusky to remain on campus despite allegations against him (Alderfer, 2013; Altheide & Johnson, 2012; Holland, 2015; Ott, 2012). The university even attempted to pass off Sandusky's abuses as "normal crimes" in an effort to minimize harm to the institution (Altheide & Johnson, 2012). And senior officials kept information about an alleged sexual offender from the institution's board of trustees.

In the wake of this scandal, the board of trustees hired a law firm led by former FBI director Louis Freeh to complete an independent investigation. The Freeh Group concluded that senior leaders had accommodated instead of prevented Sandusky's molestation of male child victims (Freeh Sporkin & Sullivan, 2012). The Freeh report supported an explanation of individual misdeeds; seldom did it fault institutional complicity in the inattention to Sandusky's alleged misconduct.

Institutional deviance in the case of Sandusky can be traced to the 1970s when suspicions originated (Klein & Tolson, 2015). Later, Vice President Schultz and Athletic Director Curley engaged in a "conspiracy of silence" by colluding with President Spanier to cover up Sandusky's delinquency (Eder, 2012, para. 3). The board lacked necessary reporting procedures and committee structures to guide its actions (Freeh Sporkin & Sullivan, 2012). Board members trusted Spanier to lead the institution; instead he sanitized and withheld information.

The insular culture of the leadership at Penn State contributed to the cover-up of Sandusky's abuse. Loyalty was expected from long-standing employees. Curley and McQueary grew up in State College. Sandusky, McQueary, and Curley had all played football under Paterno. Spanier was a PSU professor from 1973 to 1982, returning in 1995 as the president (Dowler et al., 2014). Curley was in his 19th year as athletic director (Alderfer, 2013). Schultz had two degrees from PSU, where he served for four decades (Dowler et al., 2014). McQueary, the assistant coach, was in his 12th year on the staff. Paterno was in his seventh decade as a coach and seemingly had power over the top-ranking officials at PSU. The Athletic Department became an island where the staff "lived by their own rules" (Freeh Sporkin & Sullivan, 2012, p. 139) with low employee turnover and a tendency to promote within the department. Nepotism and its "incestuous nature" abetted a culture of violence within the department (Dowler et al., 2014, p. 389).

Legitimate organizations can act in illegitimate ways, forcing us to question their integrity (Altheide & Johnson, 2012). In the case of PSU, fraternal leadership "prioritized the reputation of the University over the welfare of his [Sandusky's] victims" (Dowler et al., 2014, pp. 388–389). Further, the athletic culture predominated over the educational values. "There is an over-emphasis on the 'Penn State Way' as an approach to decision-making, a resistance to outside perspectives, and an excessive focus on athletics" (Freeh Sporkin & Sullivan, 2012, p. 129), and football was the epicenter of the athletic culture in the region known as Happy Valley.

Penalties Assessed against Penn State

The NCAA penalized Penn State in 2012. Initially, the NCAA wiped out the 112 football victories that Penn State had won over a 14-year period, imposed a 4-year postseason ban, assessed a 5-year probation, and reduced its program by 80 football scholarships over the next 4 years (Britt & Timmerman, 2013). In an interesting twist, a lawsuit from the State of Pennsylvania argued that the NCAA had overstepped its jurisdiction; under pressure the NCAA dissolved many of the penalties (New, 2016). A $60 million fine did go toward child sexual abuse prevention programs with another $12 million used to endow a PSU research center for detection and prevention of child abuse.

In addition to the legal fines, the U.S. Department of Education fined Penn State a record $2.4 million for 11 violations of the Clery Act (New, 2016). One recommendation was that the university train all of its employees, especially the police, on the Clery Act's provisions (Alderfer, 2013). Prior to this, the board of trustees had addressed just one Clery Act issue over the 14-year review period (Kiss & Feeney White, 2016).

The Penn State football team recovered quickly with a Rose Bowl appearance in 2017. Repairing the university's reputation, however, is a continuing project. PSU has had to contract with a global public relations firm, Ketchum, to appease the school's current corporate sponsors (Proffitt & Corrigan, 2012). In the words of a barbershop owner in State College, Pennsylvania, "Happy Valley is not going to be Happy Valley anymore" (Altheide & Johnson, 2012, p. 306).

Michigan State University's Sexual Abuse Scandal

Situated within a comparable university culture of indifference, Lawrence (Larry) Nassar's mistreatment of Michigan State University athletes draws attention to institutional patterns of neglect toward sexual abuse. Nassar, a former USA Gymnastics medical coordinator, MSU osteopathic physician and associate professor in the College of Osteopathic Medicine, the women's gymnastics and women's crew physician, and volunteer at East Lansing's Twistar Gymnastics Club, had access to multiple sites for grooming his victims. He faces life in prison after receiving three concurrent sentences for federal pornography charges and criminal sexual conduct. Although Nassar was convicted on charges from elite gymnasts he treated as a part of his work with USA Gymnastics, we focus on his malfeasance while employed by Michigan State University.

The first Title IX complaint against Nassar's conduct came in 2014. MSU graduate Amanda Thomashow told an MSU doctor that Nassar "massaged her breast and rubbed her vagina despite her protestations" (Forsyth, 2018, p. 9). Nassar admitted to touching Thomashow, passing off his actions as part of his regular treatment (Casarez et al., 2018). He was given a three-month suspension, although MSU's investigation into Nassar's clinical practices concluded,

> We cannot find that the conduct was of a sexual nature. Thus, it did not violate the sexual harassment policy. However, we find the claim helpful in that it allows us to examine certain practices at the MSU Sports Medicine Clinic. (para. 31)

This report was based on consultation with Nassar's colleagues at the clinic, not with independent medical practitioners (Forsyth, 2018, p. 14). Thomashow later testified, "Michigan State University, the school I loved and trusted, had the audacity to tell me that I did not understand the difference between sexual assault and a medical procedure" (Correa & Louttit, 2018, para. 12). MSU warned Nassar to properly discuss his procedures with patients, because they were "opening the practice up to liability and . . . exposing patients to unnecessary trauma based on the possibility of perceived sexual misconduct" (Casarez et al., 2018, para. 36). MSU cleared Nassar after his suspension.

Nassar's legal convictions are for crimes he committed over two decades. In August 2016, the *Indianapolis Star* investigated USA Gymnastics for its handling of sexual abuse complaints against coaches. After reading its report, former Olympic gymnast Rachael Denhollander expressed her willingness to cooperate in the newspaper's investigation. She filed the first criminal complaint with the MSU police as well as a Title IX complaint. She claimed that in 2000, when she was 15 years old, Nassar had abused her during treatment for lower back pain. The *Star* published a story about the accusations by Denhollander and another former Olympian (who later was identified as Jamie Dantzscher) (Alesia et al., 2016). MSU fired Nassar in September, a month after removing him from clinical and teaching responsibilities.

In July 2017, Nassar pleaded guilty to three federal charges of child pornography as well as seven counts of sexual assault. FBI investigators discovered at least 37,000 child pornographic images on computers in his home, including video of his sexual assault of girls in a swimming pool. In 2017, preliminary hearings determined there was enough evidence to try Nassar on three sexual assault charges. Additionally, warrants for 22 new sexual assault charges were filed against him, with over half associated with his MSU medical practice.

Before rendering her sentence, Judge Rosemarie Aquilina presided over a #MeToo watershed hearing including seven days of devastating testimony. In January 2018 a total of 156 women delivered victim-impact statements, speaking of the sexual assault and abuse they had been subjected to under the guise of medical treatment for sports injuries. For example, 16-year-old gymnast Amy Labadie had been molested by Nassar at the MSU Sports Medicine clinic and later at an invitational meet in Lansing. She testified, "My vagina was sore during my competition because of this man. How disgusting is that to even say out loud?" (Correa & Louttit, 2018, para. 4). Nassar was sentenced to 40 to 175 years in prison on charges of sexual assault.

Since his sentencing, the #MeToo movement continues to push to eradicate what Valorie Kondos Field, a UCLA women's gymnastics coach, dubbed a "culture of abuse" in the sport (Correa, 2018, para. 2). All five members of the winning 2012 Olympic women's gymnastics team made public statements about Nassar's abuse through various social media platforms (Arnold, 2018). Nassar, like other prominent people accused of sexual abuse by women using the #MeToo hashtag, represented institutions that engaged in a culture of silence to protect themselves instead of safeguarding youth and young adults.

Institutional Failure at Michigan State

Like Penn State, Michigan State University lacked proper institutional control mechanisms. Its negligence in disciplinary responses to student allegations of sexual abuse allowed Nassar to continue his exploitative medical practices. Despite abuse allegations reported against Nassar beginning in 1997, MSU employees failed to use the reporting practices mandated by Title IX and the Clery Act (Jenkins, 2018).

President Lou Anna Simon was one of 14 MSU representatives who knew about allegations of Nassar's sexual abuse prior to his conviction (Kozlowski, 2018). She received her doctorate at MSU in 1974 and spent her professional career at the university, becoming president in January 2018. In her resignation statement she said, "As tragedies are politicized, blame is inevitable. As president, it is only natural that I am the focus of this anger" (Simon, 2018, para. 5). Her resignation came after public pressure from victims and a threat of a no-confidence vote from faculty and eventually from the MSU Board of Trustees. Simon has stated that, while she received a Title IX complaint about a university physician, she was not told it was Nassar. "I told people to play it straight up, and I did not receive a copy of the report. That's the truth" (Thomason, 2018, para. 9).

The cover-up of Nassar's misconduct, however, extends beyond upper-level administrators. Notably, MSU women's gymnastics coach Kathie Klages was suspended in February 2017 and later retired. Klages contends she did not dissuade two members of the Spartan Youth Gymnastics team from reporting abuse by Nassar in 1997 (Mencarini, 2018a). She was convicted of lying to police about her knowledge of sexual assault allegations against Nassar and sentenced to 90 days in jail (Murphy & Barr, 2020). MSU graduate Mark Hollis, the athletic director, retired in January 2018, though he denied having previous knowledge of accusations against Nassar (Connor & Stelloh, 2018). Brooke Lemmen, an MSU doctor, resigned in March 2017 after accusations that she had known since 2015 that USA Gymnastics was investigating Nassar. While the Department of Licensing and Regulatory Affairs cleared her of violations, it is investigating six more doctors from the MSU clinic (Mencarini, 2018b). Finally, Robert Noto, MSU's head lawyer— accused of downplaying Nassar's actions in order to strengthen the university's legal defense strategy— resigned in February 2018 after 23 years at MSU (Jesse, 2018; Brown, 2018).

Nassar was not the only person accused of sexual violations at MSU. Dr. William Strampel, former dean of the College of Osteopathic Medicine, was found guilty of misconduct in office and two counts of willful neglect of duty in July 2019 (Joseph & del Valle, 2019). He was charged with evading his supervisory responsibilities over Nassar and with sexual harassment and solicitation of nude photos from four female students. Strampel's actions highlight the severity of the culture of sexual harassment and violence that persisted unchecked by university or outside officials.

After President Simon's resignation, John Engler, former Michigan governor and MSU graduate, spent a tempestuous year as the interim president. While his first decision was not controversial—he revoked Strampel's tenure and removed him from his position as dean of the College of Osteopathic Medicine—he spent the rest of his appointment fending off criticism. A member of MSU's board of trustees referred to his leadership as a "reign of terror" after he claimed that Nassar's victims were "enjoying the spotlight" and harming the university's ability "to go back to work" (Jesse, 2019, para. 11). He was also accused of attempting to pay off Nassar's victims (Hobson, 2018).

The final settlement with the 332 Nassar accusers was believed to be the largest involving sexual abuse and higher education. Its $500 million dwarfed the Penn State settlement of $109 million. One of the lawyers for the accusers, John Manly, emphasized, "When you pay half a billion dollars, it's an admission of responsibility" (Smith & Hartocollis, 2018, para. 3).

The university staff and faculty who failed to protect MSU's students and community members acted in the interest of institutional protection. Michigan attorney general special prosecutor William Forsyth claimed that MSU harbored a "culture of indifference toward sexual assault, motivated by its desire to protect its reputation" (Forsyth, 2018, p. 2), and a "culture of anti-transparency" that facilitated the abuse of countless girls and women (p. 4). Additionally, the university "stonewall[ed] the very investigation it pledged to support" (p. 2) by admitting to withholding or redacting documents and releasing inaccurate public statements. And despite the board of trustees' promise of cooperation, Forsyth contended the "university has largely circled the wagons" (p. 5). Members of the independent special counsel's team found that 13 of the 280 survivors they interviewed had reported Nassar's sexual abuse to an MSU employee between 1997 and 2015. The report explained,

> That so many survivors independently disclosed to so many different MSU employees over so many years, each time with no success, reveals a problem that cannot be explained as mere isolated, individual failures; it is evidence of a larger cultural problem at the MSU Sports Medicine Clinic and MSU more broadly. (p. 10)

Similar to Penn State, Michigan State conducted an internal review. At first, MSU hired a former federal prosecutor, Patrick Fitzgerald, to investigate MSU's handling of the Nassar accusations. Fitzgerald claimed that university officials were unaware of the abuse until the media reported on it in 2016 (Brown, 2018). The special counsel report, however, revealed that Fitzgerald was hired to "protect the institution in forthcoming litigation" (Forsyth, 2018, p. 3) and found that MSU employees consistently dismissed each accuser's allegations against Nassar, likely unwilling to confront someone with Nassar's good reputation.

The full repercussions of the MSU sexual abuse scandal are not yet known. The federal Department of Education is still conducting its investigation (Smith & Hartocollis, 2018), and the FBI is completing its own review of its agents' knowledge of allegations against Nassar. Finally, in June 2018, almost two years after the scandal broke, MSU succumbed to public pressure and hired McDermott Will & Emery to conduct an independent investigation of MSU's handling of Nassar's abuse and of other sexual assault claims (Brown, 2018).

MSU is clearly a case of institutional failure with negligence at all levels of administration. The special counsel report concluded that "policies are no better than the people implementing them. . . . Until there is a top-down cultural change at MSU, survivors and the public would be rightly skeptical of the effectiveness of any set of written policies" (Forsyth, 2018, p. 16). In the words of Amanda Thomashow, the former gymnast who filed the first Title IX complaint against Nassar in 2014,

I hope that our experiences at MSU have opened up the world's eyes to the suffering that survivors of sexual assault deal with every day. . . . And I hope that we can change our attitude toward victims. And I hope that our culture shifts from enabling predators to empowering survivors. (Smith & Hartocollis, 2018, para. 12)

To ensure that institutional cultures do shift, we offer policy suggestions.

Policy Suggestions

Until recently, sports organizations have resisted implementing measures to prevent and stop abuse. Sports hold a particularly esteemed and trusted space in American culture; the institution is framed as always being in the best interest of children (Brackenridge, 2003). Sports administrators and coaches are invested in maintaining this image and consequently may have difficulty admitting or even recognizing sexual abuse (Bowker, 1998; Brackenridge, 1997). When asked about abuse prevention, sports administrators say that they want to protect children but fear that bringing up the topic might result in false accusations. They also say they lack training and competence to tackle the problem (Malkin et al., 2000; Parent & Demers, 2011). These situations are compounded by the fact that sports have complicated organizational structures; leagues operate with relative autonomy, and there is often a communication gap between the local and national levels of sport (Brackenridge, 2002).

Despite these barriers, there has been considerable progress in addressing sexual abuse in sports. To lessen the chances of inappropriate relationships, many players and coaches are mandated to attend training workshops on sexual abuse prevention. These training and prevention efforts have been shown to increase knowledge and confidence in participants' abilities to detect and stop abuse, and they may also slowly shift the culture that "normalizes" sexual assault (Hazzard et al., 1991; Nurse, 2018; Parent & Demers, 2011; Rheingold et al., 2015). This will not happen, however, unless they are properly funded, contain current information, and are imparted by trained professionals. Crosset (2016) cited the case of a university that received a three-year start-up grant for athlete-specific sexual assault education. The year after the funding expired, the university ceased the program. After three years of no reported assaults, an assault occurred.

Another way that sports organizations can improve prevention efforts is by requiring criminal background checks for volunteers and coaches. While these checks do not flag offenders who avoid prosecution, they identify people with previous child abuse convictions. Sports organizations can also create and publicize new codes of conduct to address travel to competitions and accepted types of touch. This step is important because coaches have been found to be unaware of the rules and to hold "lax attitudes toward intimacy" with athletes (Toftegaard Nielsen, 2001). These kinds of interventions, however, address "'getting the right people in sport' (an individual approach) rather than 'getting sport right' (a systems approach)" (Brackenridge & Rhind, 2014, p. 333). Systems approaches of creating more accountability are more likely to have a durable impact in safeguarding athletes.

Federal policies have the potential to encourage or force educational institutions to take prevention seriously. The U.S. Department of Education's Office of Civil Rights (OCR) oversees Title IX, a federal law that views the sexual assault of a student as a civil rights violation. The OCR's 2011 policy stipulated that educational institutions are responsible for sexual harassment or assault that they either know about or "reasonably should know about" (Blanchard, 2018, p. 259). Unfortunately, Title IX is basically a law without teeth. Although institutions have paid fines to the OCR for noncompliance, no college or university has ever had its federal funding withheld. This situation may worsen as the OCR is currently considering changes to Title IX that would give more rights to perpetrators and further disempower victims (Melnick, 2018).

Another important piece of federal legislation is the Clery Act, which mandates that educational institutions report cases of sexual abuse. The Clery Act is not student-specific, meaning that Title IX extends beyond college students to community members and elite athletes. Faculty and staff are responsible for reporting cases of sexual assault committed on a campus to authorities. After Penn State's mishandling of the Jerry Sandusky sexual abuse allegations, critics underscored the importance of "technical *and* moral compliance" (Kiss & Feeney White, 2016, p. 103). Both assistant football coach Mike McQueary and head coach Joe Paterno fulfilled the technical requirements by notifying their superiors but failed to take extra steps to inform the campus lawyers, the university administration, or city police of Sandusky's misconduct. Similarly, Michigan State administrators did little to penalize Nassar's behavior. When employees do not report sexual assaults, the university assumes vicarious liability; however, the OCR failed to charge either PSU or MSU for evading this responsibility (Breeland, 2018).

The current governmental infrastructure in the United States is insufficient to address sexual assault in athletics. Gaps in jurisdiction exist between Title IX, the Clery Act, and the U.S Center for SafeSport, the disciplinary body created for arbitration of sexual misconduct in Olympic sports in 2017. SafeSport is poorly funded and inundated with abuse complaints that it cannot promptly handle (Jenkins, 2018). Further, it is a conflict of interest to expect employees connected to institutions of higher education and national governing bodies in sport to conduct objective investigations of sex abuse.

The creation of a federal agency, perhaps a Safe Athletics Commission, would help ensure athletes at all levels are protected against sexual assault (Breeland, 2018). Such an agency would draft regulations for mandatory reporting, conduct investigations, and develop education and training programs for athletes and employees. By placing collegiate athletics under the Amateur Sports Act, which already oversees the United States Olympic Committee and national governing bodies, the Safe Athletics Commission would have the authority to sue universities and national governing bodies for mishandling sexual assault cases. While we are not optimistic this solution will be implemented, it speaks to the need to entirely overhaul our existing structures in the interest of child and youth welfare.

A dilemma with preventing abuse is determining the degree to which regulations safeguard sport. Intrusive regulations risk creating collateral damage; an emphasis on eradicating "'all things bad' makes 'anything good' less accessible" (Piper, 2015, p. 177). When an athletic program rids itself of "bad apples," it may deter "good apples" from seeking positions. Our attempts to sanitize sport from risks could stop warm and inspired coaches from entering the profession. Another possibility is that these "good apples" may deflect us from confronting sex abuse scandals (Dowler et al., 2014). As noted earlier, Penn State funded a research institute on sexual abuse. Hiring more faculty to address child welfare is important; however, it must be accompanied by confronting the resistant cultures within existing university departments and programs. The goal is to change sports cultures to be inclusive and aware rather than simply regulatory and reactive.

Conclusion

The #MeToo movement is encouraging more victims to reports incidents of sexual abuse (Milligan, 2018). Although the Sandusky scandal erupted before #MeToo went viral in October 2017, the movement reignited interest in the Penn State case. The fact that Sandusky abused boys contributed to denial of his abuse and to downplaying his crimes as "horseplay." #MeToo is giving male victims a voice and punctuating the need for more research and awareness of same-sex sexual victimization. The contrast in the gender of the victims in the crimes at Penn State and MSU underscores that gender oppression works with heterosexism to create a sports culture that favors heteronormative masculinities and debases femininities.

The timing of the #MeToo movement propelled Nassar's extensive history of abuse to the forefront of media coverage. Regardless of repeated abuse allegations against him, these reports did not gain traction until #MeToo shifted the discourse from denial to belief (Correa, 2018). #MeToo is empowering victims to speak up and defenders to support them in their efforts for justice.

While #MeToo may not succeed in softening hegemonic masculinity, this movement is fostering opportunities for college campuses to have difficult conversations about gender and power. It is no coincidence that Tarana Burke spoke at both PSU and MSU in 2018. In March, the PSU Student Programming Association hosted Burke as a distinguished speaker; the following month she spoke at Michigan State as part of its Transformative Justice Speaker Series. When asked for suggestions for how institutions of higher education can improve and reform policies for addressing sexual violence, Burke insisted that students and survivors participate in the decision-making process (Wolcott, 2018).

In response to these scandals, both universities are working to establish a culture of commitment to public safety. At Penn State, all employees undergo background checks and receive abuse training. Programs for students and children require additional supervision to ensure that participants are not left alone with one person. Michigan State pledged $10 million to a Counseling and Mental Health Services Fund for victims (Guerrant, 2019). The university is reviewing its Title IX program and medical services for student athletes. These changes in policies and practices may redirect its institutional culture from one that enabled sexual predators to one that prioritizes the safety of its faculty, staff, students, and community members (Staller, 2012).

Administrators at both institutions collaborated in cover-ups to protect their university's reputation. This tells us that we cannot focus solely on perpetrators. Management scholars argue that when departments operate independently and a high degree of group loyalty is present, administrators are allowed to act with relative impunity (Hearn & Parkin, 2001). At Penn State and Michigan State, the athletic departments operated in relative isolation from the remainder of the university.

Athletic departments and sport organizations must be integrated into larger systems that engage in active oversight. We need "'sportspeople' to construct new narratives, and to become whistleblowers and advocates for children's rights rather than bystanders to their abuse" (Hartill, 2013, p. 252). But it will take more than these sportspeople to do their due diligence. Authorities in amateur and elite sports need to work with higher education, health, family, and recreation institutions to create policies that detect and prevent sexual abuse.

Ultimately, the federal government oversees compliance with sexual abuse prevention efforts. At the time of this writing, Congress has failed to reauthorize the Violence against Women Act, which includes significant modifications of the Clery Act. If the Violence against Women Act is not extended, it is likely that Clery Act enforcement will suffer. "There can be no safe sport in an unsafe society: expecting sport to be held to a higher standard than the political, social and cultural environment in which it operates is a forlorn hope" (Brackenridge & Rhind, 2014, p. 334). In other words, change in sports will require a change in the larger society as well.

References

Alderfer, C. P. (2013). Not just football: An intergroup perspective on the Sandusky scandal at Penn State. *Industrial and Organizational Psychology, 6*(2), 117–133. https://doi.org/10.1111/iops.12022

Alesia, M., Kwiatkowski, M., & Evans, T. (2016, September 20). Michigan State University fires former USA Gymnastics doctor Larry Nassar. *IndyStar.* https://www.indystar.com/story/news/2016/09/20/michigan-state-fires-former-usa-gymnastics-doctor/90735722/

Alexander, K., Stafford, A., & Lewis, R. (2011). *The experiences of children participating in organised sport in the UK.* NSPCC.

Altheide, D. L., & Johnson, J. M. (2012). Normal crimes at Penn State. *Cultural Studies ↔ Critical Methodologies, 12*(4), 306–308. https://doi.org/10.1177/1532708612446428

Anderson, E., & Kian, E. M. (2012). Examining media contestation of masculinity and head trauma in the National Football League. *Men and Masculinities, 15*(2), 152–173. https://doi.org/10.1177/1097184X11430127

Arnold, A. (2018, August 16). *Every "Fierce Five" gymnast has now claimed that Larry Nassar abused them.* The Cut. https://www.thecut.com/2018/08/larry-nassar-fierce-five-sexual-abuse.html

Blanchard, J. (2018). Sexual violence on college campuses. In J. Blanchard (Ed.), *Controversies on Campus: Debating the Issues Confronting American Universities in the 21st Century* (pp. 257–268). Praeger.

Bowker, L. H. (Ed.). (1998). *Masculinities and violence.* Sage Publications.

Brackenridge, C. H. (1997). "He owned me basically . . .": Women's experience of sexual abuse in sport. *International Review for the Sociology of Sport, 32*(2), 115–130.

Brackenridge, C. H. (2001). *Spoilsports: Understanding and preventing sexual exploitation in sport.* Routledge.

Brackenridge, C. H. (2002). ". . . So what?" Attitudes of the voluntary sector towards child protection in sports clubs. *Managing Leisure, 7*(2), 103–123. https://doi.org/10.1080/13606710210139857

Brackenridge, C. H. (2003). Dangerous sports? Risk, responsibility and sex offending in sport. *Journal of Sexual Aggression, 9*(1), 3–12.

Brackenridge, C. H., & Kirby, S. (1997). Playing safe: Assessing the risk of sexual abuse to elite child athletes. *International Journal for the Sociology of Sport, 32*(4), 407–418.

Brackenridge, C. H., & Rhind, D. (2014). Child protection in sport: Reflections on thirty years of science and activism. *Social Sciences, 3*(3), 326–340. https://doi.org/10.3390/socsci3030326

Breeland, N. R. (2018). *"The army you created": Combating the issue of sexual assault in college and quasi-professional sports.* SSRN. https://papers.ssrn.com/sol3/papers.cfm?abstract_id=3174478

Britt, M., & Timmerman, M. (2013). Penn State University, Title IX, Clery Act and sexual harassment: Was the old boy network at work? *Journal of Applied Management and Entrepreneurship, 18*(4), 64–112.

Brown, S. (2018, April 17). Here's a list of who has left Michigan State since the Nassar scandal erupted. *Chronicle of Higher Education.* https://www.chronicle.com/article/Here-s-a-List-of-Who-Has/243145

Bryson, L. (1987). Sport and the maintenance of masculine hegemony. *Women's Studies International Forum, 10*(4), 349–360. https://doi.org/10.1016/0277-5395(87)90052-5

Burton Nelson, M. (1994). *The stronger women get, the more men love football.* Harcourt Brace.

Casarez, J., Grinberg, E., Moghe, S., & Tran, L. (2018, February 1). *She reported Larry Nassar in 2014. Nothing happened.* CNN. https://www.cnn.com/2018/02/01/us/msu-amanda-thomashow-complaint-larry-nassar/index.html

Cense, M., & Brackenridge, C. H. (2001). Temporal and developmental risk factors for sexual harassment and abuse in sport. *European Physical Education Review, 7*(1), 61–79. https://doi.org/10.1177/1356336X010071006

Connell, R. W. (1987). *Gender and power: Society, the person and sexual politics.* Cambridge University Press.

Connor, T., & Stelloh, T. (2018, January 26). *Larry Nassar scandal: MSU athletic director Mark Hollis resigns.* NBC News. https://www.nbcnews.com/news/us-news/larry-nassar-scandal-msu-athletic-director-mark-hollis-resigns-n841391

Cooky, C. (2012). Success without honor: Cultures of silence and the Penn State scandal. *Cultural Studies ↔ Critical Methodologies, 12*(4), 326–329. https://doi.org/10.1177/1532708612446432

Correa, C. (2018, January 25). The #MeToo moment: For U.S. gymnasts, why did justice take so long? *New York Times.* https://www.nytimes.com/2018/01/25/us/the-metoo-moment-for-us-gymnasts-olympics-nassar-justice.html

Correa, C., & Louttit, M. (2018, January 24). More than 160 women say Larry Nassar sexually abused them. Here are his accusers in their own words. *New York Times.* https://www.nytimes.com/interactive/2018/01/24/sports/larry-nassar-victims.html

Crosset, T. W. (2016). Athletes, sexual assault, and universities' failure to address rape-prone subcultures on campus. In S. C. Wooten & R. W. Mitchell (Eds.),

The crisis of campus sexual violence: Critical perspectives on prevention and response (pp. 74–92). Routledge.

Dowler, L., Cuomo, D., & Laliberte, N. (2014). Challenging "The Penn State Way": A feminist response to institutional violence in higher education. *Gender, Place & Culture, 21*(3), 387–394.

Eder, S. (2012, November 1). Former Penn State president is charged in Sandusky case. *New York Times.* https://www.nytimes.com/2012/11/02/sports /ncaafootball/graham-b-spanier-former-penn-state-president-charged-in -sandusky-case.html

Enloe, C. (2004). Wielding masculinity inside Abu Ghraib: Making feminist sense of an American military scandal. *Asian Journal of Women's Studies, 10*(3), 89–102.

Fernandez, M. E. (2011, November 18). *Penn State saga: Most noteworthy moments in Jerry Sandusky coverage.* Daily Beast. https://www.thedailybeast.com /penn-state-saga-most-noteworthy-moments-in-jerry-sandusky-coverage

Forsyth, W. (2018). *Status of the independent special counsel's investigation into Michigan State University's handling of the Larry Nassar matter.* Mlive.com . https://www.mlive.com/news/2018/12/read-investigation-report-on-michigan -state-universitys-handling-of-nassar-scandal.html

Freeh Sporkin & Sullivan. (2012). *Report of the Special Investigative Counsel regarding the actions of the Pennsylvania State University related to the child sexual abuse committed by Gerald A. Sandusky.* Freeh Sporkin & Sullivan, LLP.

Gamson, J. (2001). Normal sins: Sex scandal narratives as institutional morality tales. *Social Problems, 48*(2), 185–205. https://doi.org/10.1525/sp.2001.48.2.185

Guerrant, E. (2019, June 21). *Trustees make Nassar-related announcements.* MSU Today. http://msutoday.msu.edu/news/2019/trustees-make-nassar-related -announcements/

Gustini, R. (2011, November 9). Joe Pa exits the Valley. *The Atlantic.* https://www. theatlantic.com/entertainment/archive/2011/11/joe-paterno-exits-valley /335693/

Hargreaves, J. (1994). *Sporting females: Critical issues in the history and sociology of women's sports.* Routledge.

Hartill, M. (2005). Sport and the sexually abused male child. *Sport, Education and Society, 10*(3), 287–304.

Hartill, M. (2009). The sexual abuse of boys in organized male sports. *Men and Masculinities, 12*(2), 225–249. https://doi.org/10.1177/1097184X07313361

Hartill, M. (2010). The sexual subjection of boys in sports: A theoretical account. In C. H. Brackenridge & D. Rhind (Eds.), *Elite child athlete welfare: International perspectives* (pp. 85–92). Brunel University Press.

Hartill, M. (2013). Concealment of child sexual abuse in sports. *Quest, 65*(2), 241–254. https://doi.org/10.1080/00336297.2013.773532

Hartill, M. (2014). Suffering in gratitude: Sport and the sexually abused male child. In J. Hargreaves & E. Anderson (Eds.), *Routledge handbook of sport, gender and sexuality* (pp. 426–434). Routledge.

Hazzard, A., Webb, C., Kleemeier, C., Angert, L., & Pohl, J. (1991). Child sexual abuse prevention: Evaluation and one-year follow-up. *Child Abuse & Neglect, 15*(1), 123–138.

Hearn, J., & Parkin, W. (2001). *Gender, sexuality and violence in organizations: The unspoken forces of organization violations.* Sage.

Hobson, W. (2018, July 24). Congress questions Michigan State interim president over sex abuse scandal. *Washington Post.* https://www.washingtonpost.com /sports/congress-questions-interim-michigan-state-president-over-sex-abuse -scandal/2018/07/24/cdc22e8a-8f6a-11e8-b769-e3fff17f0689_story.html?utm _term=.bdcade6479be

Holland, A. R. (2015). *The Pennsylvania State University child sexual abuse scandal: An analysis of institutional factors affecting response.* Widener University.

Jenkins, S. (2018, December 20). Larry Nassar was just a symptom. Congress must cure a sick Olympic culture. *Denver Post.* https://www.denverpost .com/2018/12/20/larry-nassar-symptom-olympic-culture/

Jesse, D. (2018, April 10). Former MSU head lawyer walks away with $430K retire-ment payout. *Detroit Free Press.* https://www.freep.com/story/news/local /michigan/2018/04/10/robert-noto-michigan-state-nassar/504301002/

Jesse, D. (2019, May 15). Michigan State sends out surveys: Do we sound sincere about Nassar fallout? *Detroit Free Press.* https://www.freep.com/story/news /education/2019/05/15/michigan-state-larry-nassar-survivors/3665774002/

Joseph, E., & del Valle, L. (2019, June 13). *William Strampel: Former Michigan State dean guilty of misconduct in office.* CNN. https://www.cnn.com/2019/06/12/us /msu-strampel-conviction-nassar/index.html

Kirby, S. L., Greaves, L., & Hankivsky, O. (2008). *The dome of silence: Sexual ha-rassment and abuse in sport.* Zed Books.

Kirby, S. L., & Wintrup, G. (2002). Running the gauntlet: An examination of initiation/hazing and sexual abuse in sport. *Journal of Sexual Aggression, 8*(2), 49–68. https://doi.org/10.1080/13552600208413339

Kiss, A., & Feeney White, K. N. (2016). Looking beyond the numbers: Understand-ing the Jeanne Clery Act and sexual violence. In S. C. Wooten & R. W. Mitchell (Eds.), *The crisis of campus sexual violence: Critical perspectives on prevention and response* (pp. 95–112). Routledge.

Klein, J. L., & Tolson, D. (2015). Wrangling rumors of corruption: Institutional neutralization of the Jerry Sandusky scandal at Penn State University. *Journal of Human Behavior in the Social Environment, 25*(5), 477–486. https://doi.org/10 .1080/10911359.2014.983258

Kozlowski, K. (2018). What MSU knew: 14 were warned of Nassar abuse. *Detroit News*. https://www.detroitnews.com/story/tech/2018/01/18/msu-president -told-nassar-complaint-2014/1042071001/

Leahy, T., Pretty, G., & Tenenbaum, G. (2002). Prevalence of sexual abuse in organized competitive sport in Australia. In C. H. Brackenridge & K. Fasting (Eds.), *Sexual harassment and abuse in sport: International research and policy perspectives* (pp. 19–46). Whiting & Birch.

Logan, G. (2011, November 10). Joe Paterno firing sparks student protest. *Newsday*. https://www.newsday.com/sports/college/joe-paterno-firing-sparks-student -protest-1.3310476

Malkin, K., Johnston, L., & Brackenridge, C. H. (2000). A critical evaluation of training needs for child protection in UK sports. *Managing Leisure, 5*(3), 151–160.

Marks, S. I. (2013). Sexual harassment and abuse in sport. In D. A. Baron, C. L. Reardon, & S. H. Baron (Eds.), *Clinical sports psychiatry: An international perspective* (pp. 169–179). John Wiley & Sons.

McMahon, J., & Thompson, M. D. (2011). "Body work—regulation of a swimmer body": An autoethnography from an Australian elite swimmer. *Sport, Education and Society, 16*(1), 35–50. https://doi.org/10.1080/13573322.2011.531960

Melnick, R. S. (2018). *The transformation of Title IX: Regulating gender equality in education*. Brookings Institution Press.

Mencarini, M. (2018a, August 30). Klages charges tied to 2 teens' reports of Nassar sexual abuse in '97. *Lansing State Journal*. https://www.lansingstatejournal .com/story/news/local/2018/08/30/kathie-klages-charges-arraignment-larry -nassar/1124034002/

Mencarini, M. (2018b, November 27). Ex-MSU doctor with ties to Nassar scandal cleared in licensing inquiry. *Lansing State Journal*. https://www. lansingstatejournal.com/story/news/local/2018/11/27/ex-msu-doctor-ties -nassar-scandal-cleared-licensing-inquiry/2129659002/

Messner, M. A., & Sabo, D. F. (1994). *Sex, violence & power in sports: Rethinking masculinity*. Crossing Press.

Messner, M. A., & Stevens, M. A. (2002). Scoring without consent: Confronting male athletes' violence against women. In M. Gatz & S. J. Ball-Rokeach (Eds.), *Paradoxes of youth and sport* (pp. 225–239). State University of New York Press.

Milligan, S. (2018, December 27). Sexual assault reports spike in #MeToo era. *US News & World Report*. https://www.usnews.com/news/national-news/articles /2018-12-27/sexual-assault-reports-spike-in-metoo-era

Moore, J. L. (2016). *Campus crime final program review determination report*. U.S. Department of Education.

Murphy, D., & Barr, J. (2020, August 4). *Judge sentences ex–Michigan State gymnastics coach Kathie Klages to jail*. ESPN. https://www.espn.com/college-sports

/story/_/id/29594880/judge-sentences-ex-michigan-state-gymnastics-coach
-kathie-klages-jail

Nesbitt, S. J. (2016, November 5). Fallout from Penn State scandal continues to upend Mike McQueary's life. *Pittsburgh Post-Gazette.* https://www.post-gazette.
com/sports/psu/2016/11/06/Fallout-from-Penn-State-scandal-upended-assistant
-coach-s-life-sandusky/stories/201611040207

New, J. (2016, November 4). Education Department's historic sanction against Penn
State for Clery violations, Sandusky's abuse. *Inside Higher Education.* https://
www.insidehighered.com/news/2016/11/04/education-departments-historic
-sanction-against-penn-state-clery-violations

Nichols, A. L. (2018, November 26). Ex-MSU president Simon arraigned on two
felonies, two misdemeanors. *State News* (Michigan State). https://statenews
.com/article/2018/11/lou-anna-k-simon-is-arraigned

Nurse, A. M. (2018). Coaches and child sexual abuse prevention training: Impact
on knowledge, confidence, and behavior. *Children and Youth Services Review,
88,* 395–400.

Ott, B. L. (2012). Unnecessary roughness: ESPN's construction of hypermasculine
citizenship in the Penn State sex abuse scandal. *Cultural Studies ↔ Critical
Methodologies, 12*(4), 330–332. https://doi.org/10.1177/1532708612446433

Parent, S., & Bannon, J. (2012). Sexual abuse in sport: What about boys? *Children
and Youth Services Review, 34*(2), 354–359. https://doi.org/10.1016/j.childyouth
.2011.11.004

Parent, S., & Demers, G. (2011). Sexual abuse in sport: A model to prevent and protect athletes. *Child Abuse Review, 20*(2), 120–133. https://doi.org/10.1002/car.1135

Parent, S., & Fortier, K. (2018). Comprehensive overview of the problem of violence
against athletes in sport. *Journal of Sport and Social Issues, 42*(4), 227–246.
https://doi.org/10.1177/0193723518759448

Pennington, B. (2011, November 8). Paterno, the king of Pennsylvania, until now.
New York Times. https://www.nytimes.com/2011/11/09/sports/ncaafootball
/paterno-the-king-of-pennsylvania-until-now.html

Pinheiro, M. C., Pimenta, N., Resende, R., & Malcolm, D. (2014). Gymnastics and
child abuse: An analysis of former international Portuguese female artistic
gymnasts. *Sport, Education and Society, 19*(4), 435–450. https://doi.org/10.1080
/13573322.2012.679730

Piper, H. (2015). Fear, risk, and child protection in sport: Critique and resistance.
In H. Piper (Ed.), *Touch in sports, coaching and physical education: Fear, risk,
and moral panic* (pp. 167–187). Routledge.

Proffitt, J. M., & Corrigan, T. F. (2012). Penn State's "success with honor": How
institutional structure and brand logic disincentivized disclosure. *Cultural
Studies ↔ Critical Methodologies, 12*(4), 322–325. https://doi.org/10.1177
/1532708612446431

Rheingold, A. A., Zajac, K., Chapman, J. E., Patton, M., de Arellano, M., Saunders, B., & Kilpatrick, D. (2015). Child sexual abuse prevention training for childcare professionals: An independent multi-site randomized controlled trial of stewards of children. *Prevention Science, 16*(3), 374–385. https://doi.org/10.1007/s11121-014-0499-6

Sand, T. S., Fasting, K., Chroni, S., & Knorre, N. (2011). Coaching behavior: Any consequences for the prevalence of sexual harassment? *International Journal of Sports Science & Coaching, 6*(2), 229–241. https://doi.org/10.1260/1747-9541.6.2.229

Schwarb, A. W. (2018, October 10). *Number of NCAA college athletes reaches all-time high.* NCAA. http://www.ncaa.org/about/resources/media-center/news/number-ncaa-college-athletes-reaches-all-time-high

Simon, L. A. K. (2018, January 24). *President Simon announces resignation from MSU.* MSU.edu. https://msu.edu/issues-statements/2018-01-24-simon-resignation

Smith, M., & Hartocollis, A. (2018, May 16). Michigan State's $500 million for Nassar victims dwarfs other settlements. *New York Times.* https://www.nytimes.com/2018/05/16/us/larry-nassar-michigan-state-settlement.html

Springer, S. (2019, January 7). 7 ways to improve coverage of women's sports. *Nieman Reports.* https://niemanreports.org/articles/covering-womens-sports/

Staller, K. M. (2012). Missing pieces, repetitive practices: Child sexual exploitation and institutional settings. *Cultural Studies ↔ Critical Methodologies, 12*(4), 274–278. https://doi.org/10.1177/1532708612446420

Stirling, A. E., & Kerr, G. A. (2009). Abused athletes' perceptions of the coach-athlete relationship. *Sport in Society, 12*(2), 227–239. https://doi.org/10.1080/17430430802591019

Thomason, A. (2018, January 25). 5 Moments that led to Lou Anna Simon's resignation at Michigan State. *Chronicle of Higher Education.* https://www.chronicle.com/article/5-Moments-That-Led-to-Lou-Anna/242338

Timpka, T., Janson, S., Jacobsson, J., Dahlström, Ö., Spreco, A., Kowalski, J., Bargoria, V., Mountjoy, M., & Svedin, C. G. (2018). Lifetime history of sexual and physical abuse among competitive athletics (track and field) athletes: Cross sectional study of associations with sports and non-sports injury. *British Journal of Sports Medicine, 53*(22), 1412–1417. https://doi.org/10.1136/bjsports-2018-099335

Toftegaard Nielsen, J. (2001). The forbidden zone: Intimacy, sexual relations and misconduct in the relationship between coaches and athletes. *International Review for the Sociology of Sport, 36*(2), 165–182. https://doi.org/10.1177/101269001036002003

Volkwein, K. A. E., Schnell, F. I., Sherwood, D., & Livezey, A. (1997). Sexual harassment in sport: Perceptions and experiences of American female student-athletes. *International Review for the Sociology of Sport, 32*(3), 283–295.

Volkwein-Caplan, K., Schnell, F., Devlin, S., Mitchell, M., & Sutera, J. (2002). Sexual harassment of women in athletics vs. academia. In C. H. Brackenridge & K. Fasting (Eds.), *Sexual harassment and abuse in sport: International research and policy perspectives* (pp. 91–110). Whiting & Birch.

Waterhouse-Watson, D. (2013). *Athletes, sexual assault, and trials by media: Narrative immunity*. Routledge.

Wolcott, R. J. (2018, April 19). #MeToo founder Tarana Burke speaks at MSU: "This is a survivor's movement." *Lansing State Journal*. https://www.lansingstatejournal.com/story/news/local/2018/04/19/metoo-msu-burke/534083002/

9. How Mass Media Industries Have Enabled Sexual Misconduct and Harassment—and How They Also Exposed Them

Jacqueline Lambiase, Tracy Everbach, and Carolyn Bronstein

Mass communication industries—including journalism, advertising, and public relations in traditional and digital channels—in recent years have provided a front-row seat for sexual harassment investigations, coverage of the #MeToo movement, and advocacy for awareness and change. Yet historically, the American mass media field is not a newcomer to these problems, nor is it merely an observer of their consequences. The earliest suffragist critique of women's working conditions overlapped and combined with the work of abolitionists in the 1800s. These critiques were often created and distributed by journalists and by publicity-seeking pamphleteers, advertisers, and public speakers. Indeed, the act of garnering publicity, for both agitation and advocacy, served as a precursor to the 20th-century profession of public relations and included the work of suffragists, abolitionists, and other activists, many of whom were women (Lamme & Russell, 2009). Women have also been present in printshops and newsrooms since the American Revolution, and they and male allies both participated in investigative reporting and created literature exposing working conditions for women, immigrants, children, and others outside the circle of power in the late 1800s and early 1900s (Whitt, 2008). These writers described rape, harassment, and discrimination in the workplace based on gender and race.

In 1970, during feminism's second wave, the work of women in the communication industry turned inward when women employees of *Newsweek* sued the publication for sexual discrimination during the same week the magazine's cover featured other protests from the feminist movement (*Newsweek* staff, 2016; Povich,

2012). At that time, *Newsweek* had only one female reporter on a 52-member staff (Povich, 2012). In 1972, women at the *New York Times* followed with their own lawsuit demanding equal rights (Robertson, 1992). Through these legal actions and others, women gained more entry into newsrooms such as those of the Associated Press, NBC, and other news outlets. But access to newsrooms did not guarantee that women would receive equal or humane treatment there.

During this same period, in 1974, journalist-activist Lin Farley provided leadership for a collective of women at Cornell University that coined the term "sexual harassment" (Brown, 2018; Farley, 2017). When the #MeToo movement went viral in 2017, after having been founded in 2006 by civil rights activist Tarana Burke, Farley again weighed in on the term "sexual harassment." She condemned its widespread and banal use by corporations, calling instead for more talk about the "excruciating, unforgettable" details of sexual harassment (2017, para. 11). In other words, sexual harassment must be more than a term used by companies to avoid lawsuits. In the spirit of Farley's advice, journalists and activists again have engaged in investigative work to uncover and recover the voices of those affected by sexual harassment. Yet, in this latest iteration of journalism and activism, the media industries themselves once again have received needed scrutiny for sexual abuse and misconduct.

In 2017 and 2018, insiders of the advertising and journalism industries began their work. *Ad Age* publicized a call to action originally posted on Facebook by Cindy Gallop, an advertising industry insider, who made comparisons between behavior in advertising firms and Hollywood. Gallop asked others to expose "the Harvey Weinsteins of [the advertising] industry once and for all" (Stein, 2017b). In March 2018, after Time's Up Hollywood had formed, Time's Up/Advertising was founded, announcing an initial public meeting in May 2018 (Bronstein & Lambiase, 2018). In April 2018, the Pulitzer Prize board awarded a joint prize in public service to the *New York Times*, for investigations into Fox News host Bill O'Reilly's history of sexual harassment and his network's multimillion-dollar settlements over many years, and to the *New York Times* and the *New Yorker*, for investigations into years of sexual harassment by Harvey Weinstein within the Hollywood motion picture industry (Grynbaum, 2018). One of the harassment survivors, former Fox News anchor Gretchen Carlson, published a book in 2017 about her experiences. These high-profile investigations and industry actions have offered insight into media industries and the "excruciating, unforgettable" details of sexual harassment, as Lin Farley has noted are necessary for change to occur (Farley, 2017).

In this chapter, we seek to shed light on sexual harassment in the mass media industry, especially on the experiences of journalists inside news organizations and of creative workers and managers inside advertising technology companies. First, we will provide background and context for the #MeToo movement by analyzing content produced by these industries and focusing on industry data and norms leading up to the 2017 #MeToo movement. Next, using Farley's suggested framework that emphasizes the details of sexual harassment, we will employ the case study method to examine two high-profile cases within journalism and advertising and will apply a theme analysis of other cases reported in industry publications between 2016 and 2018. Inquiry more broadly will focus on two cases and the patterns discerned among a collection of cases in mass media industries as these unfolded in the courts, behind the scenes, and in the details and stories shared by women affected by sexual harassment.

Background

Using both legal casework and histories of activism, Siegel (2003) outlined the harsh conditions, the violence endured, and the double bind of American women workers, during and after slavery and influenced by patriarchy, showing its continuation through the rise of industrialization and mass media. A century ago, socialist-feminist Emma Goldman reflected on the practice of so-called legal prostitution, which was an inevitable part of women's experience in the workforce in the 1800s (Siegel, 2003). Goldman asserted in an essay that "nowhere is woman treated according to the merits of her work, but rather as a sex. It is therefore almost inevitable that she would pay for her right to exist, to keep a position in whatever line, with sex favors" (Siegel, 2003, p. 7). Her perspective is fresh today.

A backdrop to modern sexual violence against women at work is the generalized violence present in American workplaces. Overall, among all workers in the United States, male and female, "violence occurred at over 60% of companies with more than 2,500 employees—and 91% of companies with 25,000 or more employees" (Society for Human Resource Management, 2012). Another national study shows that, on average, 40 percent of workers experience psychological aggression— screaming, insults, threats— during a year of employment, with about 13 percent of workers experiencing those conditions on a weekly basis (Schat et al., 2006). Bearing witness to workplace violence impacts performance as much as being abused oneself, according to Harris et al. (2013). Additionally, sex-based harassment is the most reported type of harassment complaint made to the U.S. Equal Employment Opportunity Commission (Feldblum & Lipnic, 2016), with sexual harassment described as widespread by policy researchers (Shaw et al., 2018). Yet, speaking out against sexual violence in any workplace—as an activist-journalist, as a digital influencer, or simply as a woman who has experienced harassment— carries a high price. Accusers and journalists who have shared sexual harassment stories have been sued by the accused men and/or harassed on social media; and some of the accused have retained their jobs or have secured exit packages (Corbet,

2019; Vox, 2019). In general, 71 percent of sexual harassment charges in the United States includes information about retaliation (Shaw et al., 2018).

In today's digital media environment, online retaliation and misogyny have reached epidemic levels, with women journalists becoming targeted by "gendertrolls," a term coined by scholar Karla Mantilla (2015). Rape and death threats by gendertrolls are sent to women journalists, often via social media, with the intent to intimidate and silence them. "Journalists no longer can avoid being part of the story, as they are trained to do," noted Sheila Gibbons (2018, p. 402), editor of *Media Report to Women*. Women are specifically targeted for this abuse: women journalists receive three times the abuse of their male counterparts. In addition, many news organizations do little to nothing to protect women journalists from online harassment (Vickery & Everbach, 2018). The effects of such harassment can cause emotional and physical trauma, but women journalists often cannot leave social media because it is a vital tool for their jobs. For instance, feminist writer Jessica Valenti temporarily left Twitter in 2016 after someone threatened her five-year-old daughter with rape and death. "I am sick of this shit," she tweeted. "Sick of saying over and over how scary this is, sick of being told to suck it up" (Valenti, 2016). Valenti later returned to Twitter, but one look at her account, @JessicaValenti, shows that men continue to regularly troll and threaten her. Social media companies such as Google, Twitter, Instagram, and Facebook, under the guise of free speech, have taken only cursory actions to stop harassment of women online (Gibbons, 2018; Vickery & Everbach, 2018).

Conditions and Representations in Journalism

While women journalists may be harassed online, sexual harassment of women undoubtedly occurs more commonly inside newsrooms or while on the job. In surveys from the 1990s, between 60 percent and 70 percent of women reported being sexually harassed on the job (Brown & Flatow, 1997; Flatow, 1994; McAdams & Beasley, 1994; Walsh-Childers et al., 1996). A 2005 study by Hardin and Shain found that more than half of women sports journalists experienced on-the-job discrimination, and a subsequent study by the same authors found that women sports journalists encountered "a gender-related lack of respect from male colleagues and fans as a routine part of their work experiences" (2006, p. 28). Three years later, a study found that half of women sports journalists surveyed experienced sexual harassment on the job (Pederson et al., 2009). Seven years after that, nothing had improved; a 2016 study found that more than half of women journalists had been sexually harassed at work (North, 2016). In 2018, an international study found that two-thirds of women journalists had been harassed, and one-third reported that they considered leaving the profession because of harassment (International Women's Media Foundation, 2018). The same study found that harassment and attacks on women journalists occurred both online and physically and that women were targeted much more often than men. A majority of women do not report harassment to their superiors for fear they may be told simply to tolerate it, they may be labeled as troublemakers, they may be doubted, or they may lose their jobs (Vickery & Everbach, 2018).

Coverage of sexual violence and harassment by news media reflects the conditions of women journalists. In their survey of research about news media portrayals of violence against women—which includes sexual harassment—Easteal et al. (2015) concluded that "mutuality of responsibility" is often a theme of news media coverage, reflecting "male dominance, sexism, and misogyny" (para. 1), which prohibits change and continues a cycle of violence. Other themes include violence as an "isolated incident" and complaints that are always described as "on the rise" (para. 19). In much news coverage,

> victim-blaming resonates in the narratives of domestic violence, rape, and sexual harassment. Media reporting of violence against women may be simplistic, misleading, and overly reliant on clichéd characters. This can be seen as a shorthand method of reinforcing dominant social values about gender (and the law). (para. 60)

Conditions and Representations in Advertising

The 3% Movement (formerly the 3% Conference), so named for the low percentage of women executive creative directors in advertising in the early 21st century (Windels, 2008), has brought needed attention to the contemporary working conditions of women in advertising. The founder of the 3% Movement, Kat Gordon, uses the conference and other events to focus on sexism and racism in the ad business, as well as to support women so that they may more easily claim leadership positions within the industry (Maheshwari, 2017). Her work and the efforts of others have paid off; over the past decade, the number of female creative directors in 31 agencies has risen to nearly 30 percent. Yet problems remain. A 2016 survey by the American Association of Advertising Agencies revealed that 70 percent of women creatives in advertising agencies had never worked for a female creative director (Hill, 2016), and the same survey showed that more than half of women in the industry have dealt with sexual misconduct (Jaramillo, 2016), many involving "rainmakers," meaning, in this case, men in powerful agency positions. Sexual harassment policy makers Elyse Shaw, Ariane Hegewisch, and Cynthia Hess (2018) have explained that the presence of "rainmakers" is a common condition of workplaces in which sexual harassment and misconduct may likely occur.

For women working for advertising technology companies such as Google, the realities of sexual harassment may be worse (Dishman, 2016). In their *Elephant in the Valley* study, Vassallo et al. (2016) discovered that among more than 200 women surveyed who had worked at least 10 years, many for large tech-media companies in Silicon Valley, 90 percent had witnessed sexist behavior, and 65 percent reported "unwanted sexual advances . . . received from a superior, with half receiving advances more than once" (para. 8); one in three women "felt afraid for their personal safety because of work-related circumstances" (para. 10). The same study showed that 60 percent of women who reported sexual harassment "were dissatisfied with the course of action" taken after their complaints, with 39 percent not reporting because of feared repercussions and 30 percent not reporting because they did not want to think about the harassment any longer (para. 11).

Representations of women created by the advertising and media industries have long been the subject of feminist, gender, race, and intersectional studies scholars. Pioneering feminist media critic Jean Kilbourne observed that "the ideal image of beauty is more tyrannical and unattainable than ever . . . [and] the obsession with thinness continues to devastate many women and girls" (2019, p. xii). In a historical study of 50 years of feminist activism and scholarship against sexist advertising, researchers outlined the types of sexism found in advertising, including hierarchy, sexualization and racist sexualization, violence, objectification, limited and stereotyped role schema, heterosexism, infantilization, and passivity (Lambiase et al., 2017). A 2017 study by the Geena Davis Institute on Gender and Media and J. Walter Thompson showed that men featured in advertising still receive four times as much screen time and are spoken about seven times more often than women; the same study showed that 25 percent of ads feature men only, with only 5 percent of ads featuring women only (Gee, 2017).

Case Studies

Women are at a distinct, systematic disadvantage compared with men, as shown by a preponderance of research, in two types of sexist spaces: the working environments of newsrooms and advertising companies, and the media content produced by these industries. The details of sexual harassment contained in the following case studies, sadly, come as no surprise to the women who have worked in these mass media industries, which often include "significant power differentials" and elevate men as rainmakers (Shaw et al., 2018, para. 10). From the media organizational standpoint, the highest profile cases until recently involved settlements with complainants and exit packages for top executives, usually with silence from the organizations for which they worked. From the viewpoint of women at these organizations, the "excruciating, unforgettable" details—as requested by Lin Farley—fit patterns, too, now that some women have been believed by these organizations: behind-the-scenes sex assaults, unwanted touching, verbal harassment, objectification, constant pressure for sexual relationships, lower pay than men, payments for silence, and a sexist and hostile work environment, where subordination of others by top executives was part of a company's culture (for a review, see Vox, 2019). Two case studies, plus broader analyses of other cases, illustrate contemporary working conditions for women in media industries.

Fox News and CEO Roger Ailes

In 2016, Gretchen Carlson, a former Fox News anchor, filed a sexual harassment complaint against Fox chairman and CEO Roger Ailes. Shortly thereafter, a number of other women who worked at Fox News, including anchors Megyn Kelly and Andrea Tantaros, also came forward publicly with sexual harassment allegations against Ailes. He was removed as head of Fox News, which eventually settled with Carlson for $20 million. Ailes had engaged in predatory behavior for decades, propositioning and harassing women since the 1960s. After he launched Fox News in 1998, he offered over the years to "mentor" women who worked there, many of whom he targeted with unwanted sexual advances (Sherman, 2016). Carlson's lawsuit alleged that Ailes fired her from the network after she wouldn't comply with his sexual demands. In her complaint, she noted that Ailes had "sabotaged her career because she refused his sexual advances" (Carlson v. Ailes, 2016, p. 2).

Carlson previously had reported to her supervisor at Fox News that Steve Doocy, her cohost on the show *Fox & Friends*, had caused a hostile work environment by "treating her in a sexist and condescending way" (Carlson v. Ailes, 2016, p. 3). She said that Doocy put his hand on and pulled her arm to "shush her" on the air, mocked her during commercial breaks, refused to engage with her on-air, and belittled her. When Carlson reported Doocy, Ailes responded by calling Carlson a "man hater" and "killer" and said she "needed to get along with the boys" (p. 3). Ailes removed her from *Fox & Friends* and reduced her on-air appearances. Carlson also reported that Ailes made sexist comments to her, including ogling her in his office and "asking her to turn around so he could view her posterior," noting that specific outfits enhanced her figure, remarking on her legs, and "stating that if he could choose one person to be stranded with on a desert island, she would be that person" (p. 5). When Carlson met with Ailes in his office to ask him to stop the harassment, he replied, "I think you and I should have had a sexual relationship a long time ago and then you'd be good and better and I'd be good and better" (p. 6). Her legal complaint contended she was punished for refusing him. While she did receive a settlement, she never faced Ailes in court; he died in May 2017.

After Carlson left Fox News, she wrote *Be Fierce: Stop Harassment and Take Your Power Back*, which offered advice to women and men on ways to combat sexual harassment. "In spite of the lingering doubt and guilt that most women feel, it's not about something *you* did," she wrote. "It's about what somebody else did to you" (2017, p. 5). She also noted that remaining silent about abuse allows the harassment to continue. Carlson alluded to hegemonic masculinity in her book by discussing the "boys' club" mentality in the workplace. She noted that men use their advantage in a male-dominated culture to reinforce their status over women and added that some women accept and allow sexual harassment so they may gain higher status within the culture.

Google, Andy Rubin, and Other Top Executives

Whereas one woman, Gretchen Carlson, offered personal testimony in a lawsuit and a book about her treatment by Ailes and other men at Fox News, the voices of many women at advertising technology giant Google were amplified by investigative journalists at the *New York Times*. The first story about the real reason for Andy Rubin's exit from Google, published on technology-insider website The Information, did not "elaborate on the specific nature of the woman's complaint" (Albergotti, 2017, para. 3). Unlike stories in 2014, when Rubin left Google apparently to start a new company, The Information's story cited an inappropriate relationship as the cause of his departure, because the relationship involved a woman working in his division. After The Information's story, Rubin took a leave of absence from Essential, the company he founded after leaving Google.

In several investigative stories in 2017 and 2018, the *New York Times* detailed the treatment of women employees at Google over two decades (Wakabayashi, 2017; Wakabayashi & Benner, 2018), providing those "excruciating, unforgettable" details demanded by journalist-activist Farley. Much of the *New York Times'* reporting focused on Rubin. While married to someone else he had met at Google, according to sources at the company, he coerced another Google employee into oral sex in 2013, which led to his departure in 2014 with a $90 million exit package (Wakabayashi & Benner, 2018). After the story was published, Rubin denied the incident took place, despite an investigation by Google that concluded the claim "was credible" (Wakabayashi & Benner, 2018, para. 3). Other evidence accumulated by the *Times'* investigation revealed the discovery of "bondage sex videos on Mr. Rubin's work computer" (para. 44); his dating other Google employees while married; his dating a woman on Google's Android team, which was in his division and explicitly prohibited by the company; and "ownership relationships" with women, with evidence from 2015 after he left Google when he told a woman through a text that "being owned is kinda like you are my property, and I can loan you to other people" (para. 47). Yet when he left Google in 2014, not only did he receive the $90 million exit package, but also Google "went out of its way to make Mr. Rubin's departure seem amicable," including a "public statement of gratitude" (para. 65).

The *New York Times* investigation targeted other top executives at Google and its culture, revealing stories of sexual harassment found credible by the company, including these:

- The chief legal officer of Google's parent company, David Drummond, while married, also engaged in a relationship with a woman who worked in the legal division; they had a son in 2007, and only then did he disclose the relationship to the company. The woman was moved to another part of the company, and she eventually left before the two severed their relationship; he still works for the company. She told the *Times* that "Google felt like I was the liability" (Wakabayashi & Benner, 2018, para. 26).
- Another top executive, Richard DeVaul, invited a prospective woman employee to attend the Burning Man event and "asked her to remove her shirt and offered a back rub," which she refused (Wakabayashi & Benner, 2018, para. 31); DeVaul resigned from the company after the article was published (D'Onfro, 2018).
- A senior vice president, Amit Singhal, groped an employee in 2015 at a party; Singhal received an exit package in 2016.
- Google was a "permissive workplace culture from the start" of the company in 1998 (Wakabayashi & Benner, 2018, para. 18).

The newspaper's investigative report, published October 25, 2018, prompted Google to issue a statement on the same day, saying that "the company had fired 48 people for sexual harassment over the last two years and that none of them received an exit package" (Wakabayashi & Benner, 2018, para. 14). The report also sparked global protests by 20,000 of the company's own employees—about 20 percent of the company's workforce—in 50 cities on November 1 (Segarra, 2018). Those protests spurred a comment from the company's CEO, Sundar Pichai, who sent an internal email to Google's employees on November 8. It stated in part that "going forward, we will provide more transparency on how we handle concerns. . . . And we will double down on our commitment to be a representative, equitable, and respectful workplace" (Pichai, 2018, para. 3).

Patterns from Other Cases

The #MeToo and Time's Up movements particularly affected the journalism and media industry by bringing forward sexual abuse allegations against a number of high-profile newsmen and rainmakers who ended up losing their jobs between

2016 and 2018. These included not only Roger Ailes but also Bill O'Reilly, who hosted one of the most popular shows on Fox News; Les Moonves, chairman and CEO of the CBS network; Charlie Rose, cohost of *CBS This Morning* and of his eponymous PBS network show; and Matt Lauer, longtime cohost of NBC's *Today* show, among others (for a review, see Vox, 2019). O'Reilly was fired after he was sued multiple times by women who had worked with him and who later received multimillion-dollar settlements. Moonves resigned from CBS after 12 women accused him of sexual harassment and dozens of others filed complaints of sexual misconduct in the company. Rose was fired after more than 30 women accused him of sexual harassment over several decades. Lauer was fired from NBC after allegations of sexual misconduct, also over decades (Disis, 2017; Farrow, 2018; Lee, 2018).

Described in the spring of 2017 as still "a boys' club" by the influential trade publication *Ad Age,* the advertising industry also struggles with an intransigent sexism and discrimination problem (Stein, 2017a). As Kat Gordon, the founder of the 3% Movement, has noted, targeted work is needed to "eradicate harassment in an industry that's been mythologized for its misogyny" (Gordon, 2018, para. 3). The industry has been rocked in recent years by revelations about predatory behaviors in leading agencies, some of which have led to the dismissal of prominent male agency heads. In March 2016, Erin Johnson, chief communications officer at the venerable Madison Avenue advertising agency J. Walter Thompson, filed a federal lawsuit that revealed a culture of sexual harassment within the agency. She alleged that CEO Gustavo Martinez had unleashed "an unending stream of racist and sexist comments" and subjected employees to "unwanted touching and other unlawful conduct" (Ember, 2016, para. 15). She reported that Martinez characterized Jews and African Americans in offensive ways and made "numerous comments about rape" (O'Reilly, 2016). These included Martinez telling Johnson in front of other employees that he wanted to rape her in the bathroom. The accusations provided outsiders a window into the toxic masculinity that has long characterized Madison Avenue culture. It revealed the lack of gender and racial diversity within agency leadership ranks and an environment where discriminatory and predatory behaviors flourished. Martinez resigned one week after the lawsuit was filed. *Ad Age* described the J. Walter Thompson lawsuit as "the flash point [that] vaulted sexism in the ad world to the forefront of nearly every conversation" (Stein, 2017a). These highly publicized cases and their "excruciating, unforgettable" details have helped to shine a light on the hazardous working conditions in the media industries.

In addition to sexually violent and racist behavior from agency colleagues, a 2018 lawsuit showed that employees could fall victim to client misconduct as well. In early 2018, Nancy Mucciarone, a former associate director at the media-buying agency Initiative, owned by Interpublic Group, filed a lawsuit claiming that a media manager at Dr Pepper, an agency client, had sexually assaulted her (O'Reilly, 2018). Mucciarone reported the incident to her supervisors, who decided to solve the problem by removing her from the Dr Pepper account to protect the business. After she voiced her intent to file legal charges, Mucciarone claimed that her agency colleagues turned against her, creating a hostile environment. The *Wall Street Journal* reporter covering the case opined that what happened to Mucciarone was a basic business practice in the advertising industry: keep the client happy at all costs. Yet, the lawsuit shows the downside of this philosophy and the damage it can wreak on individuals. Employees may be vulnerable in their work with clients, forced together in a situation where the power dynamic is terribly lopsided and some actors consider themselves untouchable.

Discussion and Conclusions

These case studies, which include "excruciating, unforgettable" details from women in mass media industries, demonstrate the willingness and ease of a privileged and patriarchal system to ignore what was right under its nose. The case studies for Fox News and Google contain examples of the ways systemic problems are rooted in a toxic cultural setting. At Fox News, the system provided settlements to keep men in place and to keep women silent for years, and while outsiders may have caught hints of problems prior to the #MeToo movement, men were still protected by their privilege and by other men until Gretchen Carlson's lawsuit. The Fox News case illustrates that harassment and abuse usually are addressed only when women complainants themselves are rainmakers, with the means and resources not only to file a lawsuit but also to garner publicity about the misconduct. Other women—particularly women of color, young professionals, and non-celebrity workers—continue to have little to no recourse when it comes to sexual abuse on the job in media industries.

At Google, the system provided settlements to men who were asked to leave and to women who were shunted aside and silenced. Unlike the Fox News case, women at Google were shown to be less able to request that their concerns be addressed because of power differentials and a culture built by other powerful men who protected their own. Compounding the protection offered to Google's rainmakers is the reality of women working in a male-dominated industry such as advertising or technology (or a combination of the two businesses). Only the power of investigative journalism, led first by The Information and followed by the *New York Times*, caused Google to stop business as usual and proceed with remedies. The women's stories within the larger investigative story, which contrasted the exit package offered to Andy Rubin with the "excruciating, unforgettable" details of women's experiences, sparked the outrage and walkouts by Google's workers worldwide. Carlson's lawsuit and Google workers' walkouts mark a turning away, at least in the short term, from the patterns discerned in these media industry cases.

Leigh Gilmore (2017) argued in her book *Tainted Witness: Why We Doubt What Women Say about Their Lives* that modern and ancient cultures have discredited, shamed, and dismissed women's words and testimony. "Doubting women is enshrined in the law, represented in literature, repeated in culture, embedded in institutions, and associated with benefits like rationality and objectivity" (pp. 19–20). But, Gilmore noted, the #MeToo movement has challenged and disrupted this pattern of silencing women. The social media movement has given women the ability to draw attention publicly to sexual violence without mass media filters. "MeToo breaks down the isolation that sexual violence and its aftermath imposes," Gilmore wrote, and "it opens a pathway of identification and begins to replace shame and stigma with the possibility of new affiliations" (p. 20).

While the #MeToo movement in social media and off-line activism has raised awareness of the difficulties and abuse of women in the workplace, more support will be necessary to continue the momentum and gains of the past few years so that all women will reap the benefits of changed workplaces. Universities and other school settings must provide information and training to young professionals so that they will understand their rights and be more able to navigate a difficult workplace, should issues arise. One example of pre-professional training is contained in a brochure distributed to students at the University of North Texas before students begin internships. Awareness for new and younger employees, however, is only a start to addressing sexual misconduct and harassment. In corporate settings and newsrooms, training must begin and be sustained for all employees and supervisors so that they may become more responsive and communicate more frequently about reporting procedures, penalties, and support for harassment survivors (Shaw et al., 2018). Executive training must be mandatory, especially for corporate leadership or workers with celebrity status, for as the case studies in the chapter demonstrate, they are among the most high-profile harassers and most reported in mass media industries. Agreements with contractors, vendors, and clients should include expectations for conduct, as well.

Fortunately, the movement has been intersectional, giving voice to people of different races, ethnicities, sexualities, socioeconomic status, and gender identities. New communities of support for women and others allow them to bypass those who silence them and to have their voices heard. Such momentum represents feminist and intersectionalist solidarity and activism against the status quo. In addition, the industries themselves must take more steps to protect their workers from sexual abuse in the workplace and from online attackers and trolls. Social media companies also should continue efforts to quash "gendertrolling" and other abuse. While the larger problem of sexual harassment is societal, based on a misogynistic and patriarchal structure that has yet to be dismantled, mass media industries need only to look within their own workplaces to find the unforgettable details of abuse and then to turn from awareness to action against harassment.

References

Albergotti, R. (2017, November 28). *Android's Andy Rubin left Google after inquiry found inappropriate relationship.* The Information. https://www.theinformation.com/articles/androids-andy-rubin-left-google-after-inquiry-found-inappropriate-relationship

Bronstein, C., & Lambiase, J. (2018). "Mythologized for its misogyny": Fighting gender discrimination in the advertising industry. *Feminist Media Histories, 4*(4), 184–197.

Brown, C. M., & Flatow, G. M. (1997, Spring). Targets, effects, and perpetrators of sexual harassment in newsrooms. *Journalism and Mass Communication Quarterly 74*(1), 160–183.

Brown, L. (2018, November). Long live the queen: Legendary feminist and human-rights advocate Gloria Steinem takes a rare step into the spotlight with an upcoming play and movie about her exceptional life. *InStyle,* pp. 172–175, 185.

Carlson, G. (2017). *Be fierce: Stop harassment and take your power back.* Hachette Book Group.

Carlson v. Ailes. (2016, July 6). Civil action in the Superior Court of New Jersey, Law Division: Bergen County. https://assets.documentcloud.org/documents/2941009/Carlson-Complaint-Filed-003.pdf

Corbet, S. (2019, February 4). *6 French women on trial for alleging lawmaker harassed them.* AP News. https://apnews.com/article/16b3a60916bc4d8eb2bcdd512e91b46b

Dishman, L. (2016, January 13). *60% of women in Silicon Valley have been sexually harassed.* Fast Company. https://www.fastcompany.com/3055395/60-of-women-in-silicon-valley-have-been-sexually-harassed

Disis, J. (2017, November 30). *The media men who have been accused of sexual misconduct.* CNN. https://money.cnn.com/2017/11/29/media/media-men-accused-of-sexual-misconduct/index.html

D'Onfro, J. (2018, October 30). *Alphabet exec accused of sexual misconduct resigns.* CNBC. https://www.cnbc.com/2018/10/30/google-x-exec-richard-devaul-resigns-sexual-misconduct-accusations.html

Easteal, P., Holland, K., & Judd, K. (2015). Enduring themes and silences in media portrayals of violence against women. *Women's Studies International Forum, 48,* 103–113.

Ember, S. (2016, March 18). Accusations of sexism and racism shake ad agency and industry. *New York Times.* https://www.nytimes.com/2016/03/19/business/j -walter-thompson-gets-new-chief-after-departure-over-suit.html

Farley, L. (2017, October 18). I coined the term "sexual harassment." Corporations stole it. *New York Times.* https://www.nytimes.com/2017/10/18/opinion/sexual -harassment-corporations-steal.html

Farrow, R. (2018, August 6 & 13). Les Moonves and CBS face allegations of sexual misconduct. *New Yorker.* https://www.newyorker.com/magazine/2018/08/06 /les-moonves-and-cbs-face-allegations-of-sexual-misconduct

Feldblum, C., & Lipnic, V. (2016). *EEOC select task force on the study of harassment in the workplace: Report of co-chairs Chai R. Feldblum and Victoria A. Lipnic.* U.S. Equal Employment Opportunity Commission. https://www.eeoc.gov/eeoc /task_force/harassment/

Flatow, G. M. (1994, Summer). Sexual harassment in Indiana daily newspapers. *Newspaper Research Journal 15,* 32–45. https://doi.org/10.1177 /073953299401500304

Gee, R. (2017, June 21). The representation of women in advertising hasn't improved in a decade. *Marketing Week.* https://www.marketingweek.com/2017/06/21 /representation-women-ads/

Gibbons, S. (2018). Conclusion: What can we do about mediated misogyny? In J. R. Vickery & T. Everbach (Eds.), *Mediating misogyny: Gender, technology, and harassment* (pp. 401–403). Palgrave Macmillan.

Gilmore, L. (2017). *Tainted witness: Why we doubt what women say about their lives.* Columbia University Press.

Gordon, K. (2018, March 22). Five stages in addressing #TimesUp advertising. *Ad-Week.* https://www.adweek.com/agencies/5-stages-in-addressing-timesup -advertising/

Grynbaum, M. M. (2018, April 16). *New York Times* and *New Yorker* share Pulitzer for public service. *New York Times.* https://www.nytimes.com/2018/04/16 /business/media/pulitzer-prizes.html

Hardin, M., & Shain, S. (2005). Female sports journalists: Are we there yet? "No." *Newspaper Research Journal 26*(4), 22–35.

Hardin, M., & Shain, S. (2006). "Feeling much smaller than you know you are": The fragmented professional identity of female sports journalists. *Critical Studies in Media Communication 23*(4), 322–338.

Harris, K. J., Harvey, P., Harris, R. B., & Cast, M. (2013). An investigation of abusive supervision, vicarious abusive supervision, and their joint impacts. *Journal of Social Psychology 153*(1), 38–50.

Hill, N. (2016, August 11). *More than 50% of women in advertising have faced sexual harassment, says 4A's study.* American Association of Advertising Agencies. https:// www.aaaa.org/50-women-advertising-faced-sexual-harassmment-says-4as-study/

International Women's Media Foundation. (2018). *Attacks against female journalists are career-altering, survey says*. https://www.iwmf.org/2018/09/attacks-against-female-journalists-are-career-altering-survey-says/

Jaramillo, C. (2016, August 11). More than 50% of women in advertising have faced sexual harassment, study finds. *Wall Street Journal*. https://www.wsj.com/articles/more-than-50-of-women-in-advertising-experience-sexual-harassment-study-finds-1470938770

Kilbourne, J. (2019). Forward. In K. Golombisky (Ed.), *Feminist perspectives on advertising: What's the big idea?* (pp. xi–xiv). Lexington.

Lambiase, J., Bronstein, C., & Coleman, C. (2017). Women vs. brands: Sexist advertising and gender stereotypes motivate transgenerational feminist critique. In K. Golombisky & P. J. Kreshel (Eds.), *Feminists, feminisms, and advertising: Some restrictions apply* (pp. 29–59). Lexington.

Lamme, M. O., & Russell, K. M. (2009). Removing the spin: Toward a new theory of public relations history. *Journalism and Communication Monographs 11*(4), 280–362.

Lee, E. (2018, September 9). CBS chief executive Les Moonves steps down after sexual harassment claims. *New York Times*. https://www.nytimes.com/2018/09/09/business/les-moonves-longtime-cbs-chief-may-be-gone-by-monday.html

Maheshwari, S. (2017, November 5). 3% Conference spotlights hurdles for women at ad agencies. *New York Times*. https://www.nytimes.com/2017/11/05/business/media/women-advertising-3-percent.html

Mantilla, K. (2015). *Gendertrolling: How misogyny went viral*. Praeger.

McAdams, K., & Beasley, M. (1994, Winter). Sexual harassment of Washington women journalists. *Newspaper Research Journal 15*, 127–132.

Newsweek staff. (2016, October 28). "Women in revolt": A *Newsweek* cover and lawsuit collide. *Newsweek*. https://www.newsweek.com/women-revolt-newsweek-cover-and-lawsuit-collide-514891

North, L. (2016). Damaging and daunting: Female journalists' experiences of sexual harassment in the newsroom. *Feminist Media Studies 16*(3), 495–510. https://doi.org/10.1080/14680777.2015.1105275

O'Reilly, L. (2016, March 11). Lawsuit alleges top agency boss joked about raping colleagues and called black people "monkeys." *Business Insider*. http://uk.businessinsider.com/jwt-ceo-gustavo-martinez-lawsuit-2016-3?r=US&IR=T

O'Reilly, L. (2018, January 23). Sexual harassment suit naming ad agency shines light on client dealings. *Wall Street Journal*. https://www.wsj.com/articles/sexual-harassment-suit-naming-ad-agency-shines-light-on-client-dealings-1516746191

Pedersen, P. M., Lim, C. H., Osborne, B., & Whisenant, W. A. (2009). An examination of the perceptions of sexual harassment by sport print media professionals. *Journal of Sport Management 23*, 335–360.

Pichai, S. (2018, November 8). A note to our employees. *The Keyword.* https://www.
blog.google/inside-google/company-announcements/note-our-employees/

Povich, L. (2012). *The good girls revolt: How the women of* Newsweek *sued their bosses and changed the workplace.* Public Affairs.

Robertson, N. (1992). *The girls in the balcony: Women, men, and* The New York Times. Random House.

Schat, A. C. H., Frone, M. R., & Kelloway, E. K. (2006). Prevalence of workplace aggression in the U.S. workforce: Findings from a national study. In E. K. Kelloway, J. Barling, & J. J. Hurrell (Eds.), *Handbook of workplace violence* (pp. 47–89). Sage.

Segarra, L. M. (2018, November 3). More than 20,000 Google employees participated in walkout over sexual harassment policy. *Fortune.* http://fortune.com/2018/11/03/google-employees-walkout-demands/

Shaw, E., Hegewisch, A., & Hess, C. (2018, October 15). *Sexual harassment and assault at work: Understanding the costs.* Institute for Women's Policy Research. https://iwpr.org/iwpr-publications/briefing-paper/sexual-harassment-and-assault-at-work-understanding-the-costs/

Sherman, G. (2016, September 5). The revenge of Roger's angels. *New York Magazine.* http://nymag.com/intelligencer/2016/09/how-fox-news-women-took-down-roger-ailes.html

Siegel, R. B. (2003). A short history of sexual harassment. In C. A. MacKinnon and R. B. Siegel (Eds.), *Directions in sexual harassment law* (pp. 1–39). Yale University Press.

Society for Human Resource Management. (2012, February 29). *Workplace violence.* SHRM. https://www.shrm.org/hr-today/trends-and-forecasting/research-and-surveys/Pages/workplaceviolence.aspx

Stein, L. (2017a, May 30). Advertising is still a boys' club: 15 months after Martinez, little has changed. *Ad Age.* http://adage.com/article/news/advertising-a-boy-s-club/309166/

Stein, L. (2017b, October 20). Cindy Gallop asks for "Harvey Weinsteins of our industry" to be exposed—and people are answering. *Ad Age.* https://adage.com/article/agency-news/cindy-gallop-asks-advertising-expose-harvey-weinsteins/310976/

Valenti, J. [@JessicaValenti]. (2016, July 27). *I am sick of this shit. Sick of saying over and over how scary this is, sick of being told to suck it up.* [Tweet]. Twitter. https://twitter.com/JessicaValenti/status/758347558003544065

Vassallo, T., Levy, E., Madansky, M., Mickell, H., Porter, B., Leas, M., & Oberweis, J. (2016). *Elephant in the valley.* Stanford University and Women in Tech 2017. www.elephantinthevalley.com

Vickery, J. R., & Everbach, T. (Eds.) (2018). *Mediating misogyny: Gender, technology, and harassment.* Palgrave Macmillan.

Vox. (2019, January 9). *263 celebrities, politicians, CEOs, and others who have been accused of sexual misconduct since April 2017.* https://www.vox.com/a/sexual -harassment-assault-allegations-list/other

Wakabayashi, D. (2017, November 29). Andy Rubin, Android creator, steps away from firm amid misconduct report. *New York Times.* https://www.nytimes .com/2017/11/29/technology/andy-rubin-android-google-misconduct.html

Wakabayashi, D., & Benner, K. (2018, October 25). How Google protected Andy Rubin, the "father of Android." *New York Times.* https://www.nytimes.com /2018/10/25/technology/google-sexual-harassment-andy-rubin.html

Walsh-Childers, K., Chance, S., & Herzog, K. (1996). Sexual harassment of women journalists. *Journalism and Mass Communication Quarterly 73*(3), 559–581.

Whitt, J. (2008). *Women in American journalism: A new history.* University of Illinois Press.

Windels, K. F. (2008). *Proportional representation and regulatory focus: The case for cohorts among female creatives* [Unpublished doctoral dissertation]. University of Texas at Austin. https://repositories.lib.utexas.edu/bitstream/handle/2152 /17824/windelsk.pdf

10. #MeToo and Social Media

Tania G. Levey

In response to multiple allegations of sexual assault by film producer Harvey Weinstein, on October 15, 2017, actor Alyssa Milano posted to Twitter, "If you've been sexually harassed or assaulted write 'me too' as a reply to this tweet." Along with the tweet, Milano posted an image that read "Me too. Suggested by a friend: If all the women who have been sexually harassed or assaulted wrote 'Me too.' as a status, we might give people a sense of the magnitude of the problem." As discussed in the introduction, the phrase "me too" was first used by civil rights activist Tarana Burke on MySpace in 2006 in response to a 13-year-old African American girl who had shared her experience of sexual assault (Garcia, 2017). However, it was not until 2017 that #MeToo became a global phenomenon due to the growth of social media, the hashtag feature, the involvement of celebrities, and a cultural context rife with anger at the election of a president who was accused of sexual harassment and assault.

The reaction to Milano's tweet was extraordinary. Within 24 hours, 500,000 Twitter users had responded to it. By the end of November 2017, Twitter confirmed that over 1.7 million tweets using the hashtag or a translation had been posted globally (Thorpe, 2017). And the response was not limited to Twitter; Facebook reported that 4.7 million people around the world had engaged with #MeToo, posting, commenting, and reacting more than 12 million times (Khomami, 2017). Additionally, 50 percent of Facebook users are friends with someone who posted about experiences of harassment and assault (Tambe, 2018). By December 2018, #MeToo had been used 1.5 million times on Instagram, making it the most-used advocacy hashtag of the year.

Although the #MeToo movement is new and empirical evidence for its effects are limited, social media has become central for social movements and thus requires a nuanced understanding. The openness and reach of social media create tremendous opportunities for political organizing. This chapter explores the ability of social media to challenge and upend hetero-feminine norms and patriarchal power structures. At the same time, social media has become associated with rampant online sexual harassment, including name-calling, unsolicited sexual material, and rape and death threats. This chapter also examines the social media policies that Facebook and Twitter[1] are putting into place to protect users from online sexual harassment. I conclude with recommendations for making social media more conducive to the exchange of ideas and to progressive social change.

Social Media

Social media refers to "sites and services that emerged during the early 2000s, including social network sites, video sharing sites, blogging and microblogging platforms, and related tools that allow participants to create and share their own content" (boyd, 2014, p. 6). As a hashtag campaign, #MeToo calls for the public to report their experiences of sexual harassment and assault via social media using a hashtag that collects responses for searches. Large numbers of people using a hashtag can turn it into a trending topic.

Currently, 77 percent of people in the United States have a social media account, and this number increases to 90 percent for 18- to 29-year-olds (Statista, 2019a). The Pew Research Center has reported that 72 percent of online adults use Facebook and 23 percent use Twitter (Duggan, 2015). By the end of 2018, Facebook had over 2 billion monthly active users. Twitter monthly active users have leveled off at 67 million, partly due to purging and people leaving the site. Use varies by country, with the average person in the United States spending 1.7 hours a day on social media, compared with 3.7 hours in the Philippines, the country with the highest usage (Statista, 2019b).

Much of the scholarly work on social media draws from the work of Jürgen Habermas's analysis of bourgeois society (1962/1989). Debates emerge about whether social media revitalizes Habermas's public sphere, which is central to deliberative democracies (Kruse et al., 2018). Essential to progressive social change is civil debate in a public forum. However, features of social media platforms may thwart meaningful and civil discourse. Certain features of the platforms, such as anonymity, a broad audience, the low threat of punishment, and ideas about free speech, may encourage bullying and uncivil behavior.

According to philosopher Regina Rini, people change their behavior by acting bolder or more boisterous because they are performing for the public (Talisse,

2019). Thus, they use tactics that are not conducive to real debate, such as claiming moral superiority or immediately dismissing a differing opinion. Furthermore, for social media to be a public forum, people must have chance encounters with opinions incongruous with their own. But instead, people insulate themselves from differing opinions in what is called speech niches or echo chambers (Sunstein, 2017).

Moreover, online interactions may simply mirror power dynamics that exist off-line, with educated, white males dominating discourse. Additionally, Habermas (2006) argued that communicative action is not happening, because equal access to technology is unavailable to all. Much of the conversation is also occurring in English, though #MeToo has been translated into other languages. Finally, in order to have an effective public forum, people would have to be free of institutional influences, because ultimately, social media platforms are run by private entities with corporate interests. In his book *Zucked* (2019), early Facebook investor Roger McNamee worried about Facebook's influence on our behaviors and emotions through the company's deliberate design choices and its decision to operate on a consumer model. Fuchs (2014) drew on Marxian theory to highlight the exploitation that occurs when we provide content, including personal information, on sites like Facebook for free.

Swisher (2018) argued that social media platforms such as Facebook and Twitter are as guilty as other platforms such as Gab[2] for spreading hate speech and inciting violence, due to their fear of losing users and alienating funding coming from countries with human rights abuses. Similarly, the editorial board of the *New York Times* (2018) contended that social media plays a role in violent right-wing extremism by rewarding certain kinds of engagement and creating feedback loops for toxic ideas. Apple's chief executive, Tim Cook, was quoted as saying, "Platforms and algorithms that promised to improve our lives can actually magnify our worst human tendencies" (Bruni, 2018, para. 14). Despite the notion that, for social movements, posting online may offer a safer conduit in which to protest for progressive social change, users may put themselves at risk when posting publicly.

Online Sexual Harassment

Since the beginning of the Internet, women have experienced relentless sexual harassment on blogs, video games, and social media sites such as 4Chan, Facebook, Reddit, and Twitter. Like street and workplace harassment, online sexual harassment serves to limit women's participation and maintain patriarchal power structures. Women have been harassed so often online that 2014 was referred to as "the year of Internet misogyny." A poll from Ipsos MORI for Amnesty International found that 23 percent of women ages 18–55 in eight countries, including the United States, have experienced online abuse or harassment, and this number increases to 33 percent for women in the narrower age range of 18–24 (Magill, 2017). Threats can extend into real life through stalking and the posting of personal information, known as doxing. A Centre for the Analysis of Social Media study argued that misogyny is prevalent across all forms of social media (Demos, 2016). Tracking data over a three-week period, the researchers at Demos found that 200,000 aggressive tweets that contained the keywords "slut" and "whore" targeted 80,000 people around the world. I found that words such as "slut" and "whore" were used on average 418,655 and 21,018 times a day on Twitter, respectively, though careful analysis of the meaning of tweets revealed that not all were sent with the intent to harass (Levey, 2018). Words like "slut" and "bitch" have also been reclaimed, used endearingly among friends and to educate about misogyny.

Early well-known cases of online sexual harassment include blogger Ariel Waldman, who received a flood of tweets calling her a "cunt" and a "whore," as well as a string of threatening tweets that revealed private information in 2007. Writer Cheryl Lindsey Seelhoff was another early recipient of doxing in 2007, which led to coordinated rape and death threats through forums such as 4Chan. Throughout 2013, journalist and feminist activist Caroline Criado-Perez was inundated with rape threats on Twitter for campaigning for a female figure to appear on a Bank of England note. "Gamergate" began in 2014, with women video game developers, players, and commentators such as Zöe Quinn, Anita Sarkeesian, and Brianna Wu experiencing rape and death threats (Mantilla, 2015).

Recounting online threats against women writers, blogger Amanda Hess (2014) recalled message after message hoping for women to be violently raped and killed. Activist Feminista Jones has been continually threatened for her street harassment #YouOkSis Twitter campaign. *The Guardian* revealed that since 1999, 8 out of 10 blocked comments were directed toward women writers, with the most going to Jessica Valenti, feminist blogger and founder of Feministing.com (Valenti, 2016). Threats of stalking and violence caused 41 percent of women to feel physically unsafe on at least one occasion (Magill, 2017). Several women had to change their behaviors or move due to threats. In an example of a direct attack, a brick was thrown through Wu's home window. For detailed accounts of online sexual harassment, see Citron (2014) and Mantilla (2015).

Posting about feminist issues attracts the most abuse. However, women have been sexually harassed for discussing a broad range of topics. Women who speak about topics traditionally perceived as men's domain, such as sports, technology, and video games, experience a great deal of online harassment, but so do women who discuss economic policy, immigration, and even subjects traditionally seen as women's domain, such as cooking and parenting. An Amnesty International study of members of British Parliament found all women in Parliament received harassing messages, but an overwhelming majority went to the first Black woman member of Parliament, Diane Abbott (Dhrodia, 2017). In addition to the most commonly targeted public figure, Hillary Clinton, the majority of celebrity women targeted for online harassment were identified or perceived as women of color or as immigrants to the United States, such as Ariana Grande, Leslie Jones, Kim Kardashian, and Amber Rose (Levey, 2018).

Online sexual harassment has become so widespread that a United Nations report called for a "world-wide wake-up call," recommending sensitization programs and policies to safeguard users and sanction abusers (Broadband Commission for Sustainable Development, 2015). The extensive use of the Internet makes it more difficult to escape harassment, particularly if a person's job requires using social media. Concerns exist regarding the chilling effect of women in politics and other positions that involve visibility and power.

Social Media Policies

Due to declining users and complaints of harassment, Facebook and Twitter were encouraged to abandon their claim that they are just platforms and therefore not responsible for the actual content posted to their sites. This issue became even more critical after two Senate Intelligence Committee reports released on December 17, 2018, confirmed that Russian operatives had used social media, including Instagram, to influence the 2016 presidential election by spreading disinformation attacking Hillary Clinton and sowing dissent over issues like immigration and gun control (Roose, 2018).

Consequently, Facebook and Twitter began to crack down on fake accounts and bots, software designed to behave like real people. Removing fake accounts had some effect on harassment. However, Facebook and Twitter had to improve monitoring and reporting functions to specifically address harassment. New policies and algorithms for detecting prohibited content emerge often, so the information presented here represents only a snapshot of the world of social media. This section explores the main ways that Facebook and Twitter are addressing harassment through terms of use agreements and community standards as posted on their websites as of January 2019—with the recognition that these documents will change many times in the future.

Facebook's Community Standards policy (Facebook 2019) outlines what is and is not allowed on the platform. Facebook establishes the importance of providing a platform where people "feel empowered to communicate" (para. 2) and states that moderators take their role in keeping abuse off Facebook seriously. Both Facebook and Twitter address free speech arguments by banning speech that limits the speech of others. Facebook's policies were developed in consultation with the community and experts in the field and are rooted in safety, voice, and equity, recognizing that adhering to one of these elements could violate another and also that different cultures have varying ideas of what counts as objectionable. Because of this recognition, Facebook allows itself to apply these principles on a case-by-case basis due to the need to understand context, unless the content is a severe violation, such as making a violent threat against a protected group, explained below. Facebook also acknowledges that its policies can change over time.

Under the section on Safety,[3] Community Standards #9, #10, and #12 relate most closely to sexual harassment. Community Standard #9 refers to "Bullying," which Facebook defines as ranging from making statements and degrading someone's character to posting inappropriate images and threatening someone. There are heightened protections for minors. The document reiterates the company's commitment to making everyone feel safe and respected on the platform. In order to allow discussions of public issues, Facebook does not apply these protections to public figures. A link to a "Bullying Prevention Hub" offers resources to teens, parents, and educators on how to address bullying and other conflicts. "Read More" lists specific content that constitutes bullying, which includes claims about sexual activity, ranking people's physical appearance, threats of nonconsensual sexual touching, using derogatory terms such as "slut" and "whore" as attacks, and calling for violence. "Harassment" is #10. In the "Read More" section, harassment includes targeted cursing, calling for harm, bullying, and claiming that someone is lying about being a victim of violence. Users are allowed to post content that may be considered malicious if the purpose is to condemn or draw attention to a problem. Much overlap exists with the bullying section, though here public figures are included as potential victims.

Number 12 prohibits "Hate speech," which is defined as a direct attack on a person on the basis of protected characteristics. The concern is that online attacks could incite real-world violence. Protected characteristics include race, ethnicity, national origin, religious affiliation, sexual orientation, caste, sex, gender, gender identity, and serious disease or disability. "Attack" is defined as violent or dehumanizing speech, statements of inferiority, or calls for exclusion or segregation. Facebook recognizes that people may be raising awareness about an issue or using the words self-referentially, and therefore users must be clear about their intent. Attacks are divided into three tiers based on severity. Tier 1 attacks include violent threats, dehumanizing individuals by comparing them to an animal in written or visual form, and joking about hate crimes. Tier 2 attacks include statements of inferiority or cursing at a person in a protected group. Tier 3 attacks include calls to exclude or segregate a person in a protected group or to describe that person with slurs, defined as insulting labels for the above-listed characteristics. Facebook also has a "Safety Center" that offers resources in the form of videos and downloadable files, both in multiple languages, on how to prevent bullying and precautions for protecting personal information.

Depending on severity of the violation, Facebook may issue a warning, restrict the ability to post content, or disable a profile. A violent threat may also warrant notifying law enforcement. When prohibited content permeates the site, Facebook relies on users to report content, a task that is now easier to accomplish. Users can also customize their experience by blocking or hiding people or certain kinds of posts. Consequences for violations depend on the severity of the violation and the offender's history.

The Twitter user agreement (Twitter 2019b) includes the terms of service, privacy policy, Twitter Rules, and all incorporated policies for users living in the United States. Individuals living outside the country may have slightly different forms of these policies. Twitter takes less responsibility for the content on its platform than Facebook by warning users early in the document that they may encounter offensive, harmful, and deceptive content. However, the user agreement states Twitter's right to remove content that violates the agreement. A link to the Help Center outlines specific policies and the process for reporting or appealing violations.

The Twitter Rules (2019a) apply to users in all countries and include regulations against graphic violence and adult content, abusive behavior, violence and physical harm, abuse and hateful conduct, and private information and intimate media. In the section on abusive behavior, Twitter reaffirms its belief

> in freedom of expression and open dialogue, but that means little as an underlying philosophy if voices are silenced because people are afraid to speak up. In order to ensure that people feel safe expressing diverse opinions and beliefs, we prohibit behavior that crosses the line into abuse, including behavior that harasses, intimidates, or uses fear to silence another user's voice. (p. 31)

This section of the Twitter Rules goes on, like Facebook, to recognize that context matters when determining if content is abusive. Users may not make "specific threats of violence or wish for the serious physical harm, death, or disease of an individual or group of people" or "target anyone with abuse or encourage others to do so," defining abusive behavior as "an attempt to harass, intimidate, or silence someone else's voice" (Twitter, 2019a, pp. 31–32). Users also cannot send unwanted sexual content, objectify someone in a sexually explicit manner, or otherwise engage in sexual misconduct. Hateful conduct means promoting violence or harassing people on the basis of race, ethnicity, national origin, sexual orientation, gender, gender identity, religious affiliation, age, disability, or serious disease. Users also cannot create additional accounts for the goal of harassment, as opposed to creating fan pages to publicize businesses, for example. Twitter provides a link to read more about its "Hateful Conduct Policy," which confirms the platform's commitment to combating hatred, prejudice, and intolerance, particularly when used to silence historically marginalized people.

Twitter offers links to report tweets or direct messages that violate its Hateful Conduct Policy, and in response, moderators will review and take action depending on the type of content. The zero-tolerance policy for violent threats results in immediate and permanent suspension of an account. Twitter will also review desires for harm to come to a person, references to violence in order to harass, the act of inciting fear about a protected category, repeated and/or nonconsensual degrading language such as slurs, and hateful imagery. Reactions to these occurrences depend on the severity of the violation and the user's history of rule violations and can range from asking the user to take the content down to enforcing read-only periods to permanent suspension. Users can submit an appeal. The final level of defense is made up by other Twitter users. Self-reporting tools include blocking, filtering, geofencing, and educational materials (Milosevic, 2016). When offensive content penetrates filters, social media companies hope users will flag it, because the users know more about the particular interaction under question.

Discussion of Policies

This section is based on research and personal conversations and focuses on Facebook because of its more rigorous regulation of content and the ability of users to post more content relative to Twitter. Flagging allows people to report harassment; however, a lack of transparency clouds how flagged material is handled (Crawford & Gillespie, 2016). Facebook's "Community Standards on Hate Speech" links to a page, *Hard Questions: Who Should Decide What Is Hate Speech in an Online Global Community?* by Richard Allan (2017), a vice president of public policy. The page reiterates much of what was written previously but also reveals that in the two months prior to this post, Facebook had deleted 66,000 posts reported as hate speech per week. Complaints emerged that some legitimate pages were deleted in this purge.

The document written by Allan (2017) claims that Facebook attempts to create a balance between condemning hate speech and censorship and will fix mistakes, citing the example of removing civil rights activist Shaun King's repost of hate mail. The language in Facebook's and Twitter's rules deliberately leaves room for interpretation, and the platforms recognize the potential mistakes when applying rules without knowing intent or context. The importance of intent and context is confirmed by my research on misogynist terms that may be reclaimed or have different connotations in different cultures (Levey, 2018). However, personal conversations have revealed many complaints from people reported and punished for using derogatory language to condemn attitudes such as white supremacy. Facebook's response is that the platform does not want to stifle political debate, but users should make their intentions to condemn clear and in a way that does not violate standards. However, the users noted that the original posts they intended to condemn were allowed to remain on Facebook.

For our purposes, when thinking about whether social media can act as an instrument of social change for gender, the male bias criticism is the most relevant and concerning. First, violent threats still occur, although it is much harder to set up fake accounts since the Senate reports on election interference. However, I have heard stories where complaints about harassment go unanswered on Facebook and Twitter. To combat harassment, Facebook plans to increase the number of reviewers by two-thirds (Allan, 2017, para 31). The platform also is trying to train artificial intelligence but still relies on the community and a team of reviewers, who, as Facebook indicates, are experts in many languages and work 24 hours a day.

One of the problematic areas is male bias when applied to nudity. Pictures of women breastfeeding have been removed, even if the nipple is more covered than when a woman appears in a bathing suit. Images of childbirth are not allowed due to nudity, but pictures of menstrual blood have been removed even though women were fully clothed. Photographer Michael Stokes (2018) landed in "Facebook jail" for six months after someone reported his photos of male amputees. Their genitals were not showing, while pictures of women such as Kim Kardashian showing much more skin were allowed to remain. Stokes concluded that the community standards reflect the heterosexual male gaze. All child nudity is forbidden, but Facebook took back its decision to censor the "Napalm Girl" photo because of its historical significance. Who decides what is historically or culturally significant? It is not enough to simply hire more reviewers; those reviewers have to come from diverse cultural and demographic backgrounds. This should help users feel safer; and the safer people feel on these sites, the more likely they are to use social media to contribute to progressive social change.

Social Media and Social Change

Despite the rampant sexual harassment and controversies over social media's responses, the case can also be made that social media can advance progressive social movements, particularly when considering the long-term effects of the #MeToo movement. Online activity allows for action outside of existing power structures and the dissemination of information outside of mainstream media, as shown in empirical studies of the effect of social media on protests that were part of the Arab Spring (Howard & Hussain, 2013), Black Lives Matter (Eligon, 2015), and Occupy Wall Street, Indignados, and Vinegar movements (Bastos et al., 2015). Contributors to Berenger's edited collection (2013) found that Twitter allowed citizens to share information and circumvent government control in Egypt. Italian activists used social media to support connective actions and create a sense of identity, even when the platform conflicted with their core values (Comunello et al., 2016). The platform mattered, with a preference for Facebook due to the greater room for content.

Critiques of inequality notwithstanding, Shirky (2008, 2011) has argued that social media is free of cost and anyone can contribute, allowing for wide dissemination of a message, a multiplicity of voices, an intersectional analysis, and the attraction of people previously unaware of or uninterested in an issue. Khomami (2017) found translations of #MeToo, including the French #balancetonporc, the Spanish #YoTambien, and in Arab countries the hashtags انا_كمان # and #اناو_ىاضى#, showing that knowing English is unnecessary for participation. Concerns about the reach and influence of tweets have been challenged by Cappella (2017), who argued that even those at the periphery of networks are crucial to spreading messages beyond more active participants in social movements. Thus, the term "slacktivist" is a mischaracterization (see also Barberá et al., 2015).

Social media allows people to respond in real time. In 2017, immediately after then Senator Kamala Harris, Senator Elizabeth Warren, and Representative Maxine Waters were silenced in Congress and an Uber board member commented that women talk too much, people posted personal experiences and research on the silencing of women to social media. While I have been writing this chapter, people are tweeting #WontBeErased in response to the Trump administration's plans to define gender as the sex assigned at birth, effectively erasing nonbinary and trans people. Hollaback![4] allows women to share stories of harassment and assault, which has led to the development of an app that even includes geolocation. Finally, Facebook's and Twitter's policies to allow banned language in order to condemn leaves room for political criticism, though the intent to condemn must be completely clear.

#MeToo and Society

#MeToo is not the first hashtag critiquing gender inequality to go viral. The 2014 Commentary and Criticism section of *Feminist Media Studies* was dedicated to hashtags invoked by feminist causes, such as #YesAllWomen, #BringBackOur Girls, and #Direnkahkaha, arguing they have made an "indelible mark on the popular vernacular and mainstream discourse" (Portwood-Stacer & Berridge, 2014, p. 1090). After a 2014 shooting spree in Isla Vista, California, where the killer claimed to be seeking revenge against women for being rejected, the millions of responses to #YesAllWomen spread the message that misogyny and structural sexism leads to violence by men against women (Solnit, 2014; Thrift, 2014). The Yes AllWomen hashtag led to a Facebook page, numerous articles and think pieces, a Wikipedia entry, an edited collection of tweets, and the Tumblr blog *WhenWomen Refuse* (Ceron, 2014). When Donald Trump's comments about touching women without their consent went public, writer Kelly Oxford tweeted on October 7, 2016, "Women: tweet me your first assaults. they aren't just stats. I'll go first: Old man on city bus grabs my 'pussy' and smiled at me, I'm 12." Millions responded to Oxford's tweet in one day, many using #NotOkay.

Hashtags such as #freethenipple and #shoutyourabortion raise awareness of female agency, body shaming, and reproductive rights. Hashtags such as #Say HerName highlight the intersections between gender and race to protest police brutality against Black women, and #BlackGirlMagic, #BlackManJoy, #CareFree BlackKids2k16, and #HeyBlackGirl help counteract negative media images and remind the Black community of self-care (Finley, 2016). Hashtag campaigns address women's issues around the world, including #MyStealthyFreedom, which accompanied Iranian journalist Masih Alinejad appearing in public without a hijab and was shared on average 1 million times per week (Novak, 2014).

The hashtag feature on social media allows for the collection of stories in one place, enabling people to view others with similar experiences. Tarana Burke's motivation for saying "me too" was to show the girls she worked with the pervasiveness of sexual assault so that they would know they were not alone. Power is present in numbers (Penny, 2017). The sheer numbers of stories encourage others to come forward (Boland, 2018), particularly women outside of "whisper networks," where information is passed privately among women. #MeToo seems to be changing the way the general public looks at those accused of harassment or assault. With so many testimonials, it is hard to believe women are making up stories. Ann Snitow (2018) wrote,

> For a feminist activist like me, after 45 years, #MeToo is simply marvelous: "We believe the women!" Although this is an absurd, generic statement, once again sealing one inside a restrictive existential category that can't hold still, what a change. To be believed, to have what one says make things move. Yes, marvelous. (p. 88)

Hashtag campaigns also allow for providing support and giving advice, which can be considered political action. Social movements start with people sharing their lives and realizing that they have experiences in common that they want to change (Jaffe, 2018). Rentschler (2014) considered women's use of social media to respond to street harassment and sexualized violence a form of "networked activist subjectivity" (p. 68). Sharing stories as a method of raising consciousness has been a practice of the Second Wave in U.S. feminism. By posting online, women are responding to harassers and rapists in a way law enforcement, workplaces, and the media have not.

The purpose of consciousness-raising is not only to enlighten the individual but to create an awareness of patterns—the sociological imagination. The grouping function of #MeToo has shown the world the pervasiveness of sexual harassment and assault (Boland, 2018). Seeing a pattern of harassment and assault makes it impossible to blame only a few individual perpetrators or to see harassment or assault as rare, isolated incidents rather than as structural power made possible by a culture that normalizes gender-based violence and sexual entitlement.

To address sexual harassment, Abigail Saguy argued that "the law is a necessary but not sufficient condition for justice. . . . The #MeToo movement is making the law more powerful not by revising the laws but by changing people's attitudes" (interviewed in Sweet, 2018, p. 6). Social media can be more effective than the political system as it allows previously excluded people to engage in social movements outside of formal systems. Seidman (2013), whose "I Need Feminism Because" exercise went viral, considered hashtag campaigns a new model of political activity that combines earlier forms of political organizing with new media. According to Conley (2014),

> Hashtags compel us to act. They are political actors, and most importantly, hashtags represent evidence of women and people of color resisting authority, opting out of conforming to the status quo, and seeking liberation, all by way of documentation in digital spaces. (p. 1111)

While the contributors to the 2014 issue of *Feminist Media Studies* recognized that the media's use of hashtags was central to activism around violence against women, they were also cautionary due to the unequal access to social media and different amounts of coverage. The phrase "me too" became an international phenomenon because of the involvement of white, attractive celebrities. Other than coverage of women working at Ford's Chicago Assembly Plant (Chira & Einhorn, 2017) and the publication of a letter by 700,000 women farmworkers (*Time* staff, 2017), white middle-class women's claims of harassment and assault have generated more coverage because they receive more attention, as does the downfall of powerful men.

The lack of inclusion of Black women and an intersectional feminist framework prompted hashtags such as #YesAllWhiteWomen, #WhatAboutUs, and #EachEveryWoman (Rodino-Colocino, 2014). Gender cannot be the only category examined, as women of color, religious minority women, LGBT women, nonbinary individuals, and women with disabilities experience additional abuse targeting those identities (Dhrodia, 2018). The lack of news coverage may be precisely why social media activism appeals to groups lacking institutional power and misrepresented by the media, as with the protests in Ferguson, Missouri, in 2014 (Bonilla & Rosa, 2015). Kasana (2014) argued that social media solidarity is essential for women of color, particularly for Muslim women's representation and agency. Naming and shaming circumvent the legal system, which has often failed women and hurt people of color. On the other hand, Tambe (2018) has pointed out that shaming and criminalization, the primary methods of the #MeToo movement, have proved problematic for Black men.

Conclusion

Social media companies cannot afford to tolerate hostile climates for women, especially in the #MeToo era. I agree with Dhrodia (2018) that "ensuring that everyone can participate freely online and without fear is vital to ensuring that the internet promotes freedom of expression equally" (p. 385). Companies like Facebook and Twitter are private companies that can develop their own rules and community standards without violating a constitutional right to free speech. However, social media companies lack the ability to eliminate all abusive speech or images on their sites. The key is to encourage these sites to remain responsive to users and transparent about their decisions. Above all, social media companies need diverse people making these decisions. Threats must also be taken seriously by law enforcement, which has historically overstated the distinction between online and offline threats.

Despite rampant sexual harassment, social media has also ushered in the most powerful challenge to sexual harassment seen in decades. As a hashtag campaign, #MeToo shows the potential for social media to directly influence society through cultural attitudes and institutional change. The available empirical evidence points to the fact that the #MeToo movement has transformed workplace responses to sexual harassment, suggesting we are at the beginning of a cultural shift. The #MeToo movement is directly responsible for the firing and resignation of prominent men, predominantly cisgender, heterosexual, and white, in powerful positions in entertainment. #MeToo has also reached companies in a range of industries around the world, including academia, the arts, business, the sciences, and technology. One year after exposés by Kantor and Twohey (2017) and Farrow (2017) documented scores of allegations of sexual harassment and assault by Harvey Weinstein, Traister (2017) documented the "year of reckoning" with details on investigations, firings, resignations, and arrests. Careful analysis by the *New York Times* found that within a year of the exposés, #MeToo took down 201 powerful men (Carlsen et al., 2018). It is significant that 43 percent, or 54 out of 124 replacements, have been women. To get a sense of the change that came after the exposés, Carlsen et al. (2018) reminded us that in the year preceding the Weinstein reports, fewer than 30 high-profile people made the news for resigning or being fired after accusations of sexual misconduct. The sheer magnitude of the response and the willingness to go public led to the December 18, 2017, issue of *Time* magazine featuring #MeToo Silence Breakers at its Person of the Year (Zacharek et al., 2017).

Consensus suggests that #MeToo will have long-lasting effects only if the root causes of power imbalances are addressed and workplace policies, such as nondisclosure agreements, change. However, change is also uneven, and most companies have not gone far enough. Furthermore, long-term change will not occur if racism and classism are not at the heart of this movement. It is notable that Tarana Burke, the originator of the phrase "me too," was excluded from *Time* magazine's "Silence Breakers" photo. Furthermore, social change has been uneven. Brett Kavanaugh was confirmed to the Supreme Court despite allegations of sexual assault. Google searches for "toxic masculinity" increased 50 percent at the same time that deadly attacks were perpetrated by men identifying as involuntarily celibate, or "incel" (Kohn, 2018).

The question remains whether the #MeToo movement can create genuine and long-lasting shifts in thinking about women, sexuality, and work, or will we go back to business as usual, as with the last "year of the woman" in 1992?[5] One thing we know is that the world has changed because of social media. While it is difficult to predict the outcome of a movement like #MeToo while it is happening, it is clear that it has permeated our culture so much that many are describing the late 2010s as the "#MeToo era." Social media exerts contradictory effects on power, both facilitating harassment and creating opportunities for empowerment. Whether social media is used for progress or regress in the social world will depend on how people use such new tools, as well as on decisions made by developers and on external forces like governments, news outlets, and openness to cultural change. Not everyone has accounts on Facebook or Twitter, but the amount of feminist commentary and news coverage has extended the reach of #MeToo even further. One thing we know: things will never be the same.

Notes

1. This chapter focuses on Facebook and Twitter because they are popular platforms and have been most associated with both online sexual harassment and feminist campaigns. Established in 2004, Facebook allows people to interact and share content with friends, and groups and pages allow people to expand their networks around similar interests or causes. Groups and pages can be public, creating a larger audience. Twitter was founded in 2006 and allows users to tweet publicly or privately; to share images, videos, and website URLS; and to collect information through the use of a hashtag (#).

2. Gab is a social media site established in 2016 that promotes free speech and attracts primarily far-right users. Gab came under scrutiny after it was discovered that the man responsible for the mass shooting of the Pittsburgh synagogue posted about it on Gab beforehand.

3. See https://www.facebook.com/communitystandards/safety.

4. Hollaback! is a "global, people-powered movement to end harassment" (https://www.ihollaback.org/).

5. The year 1992 was labeled "the year of the woman" because there was a significant increase in women elected to Congress.

References

Allan, R. (2017). *Hard questions: Who should decide what is hate speech in an online global community?* Facebook. https://newsroom.fb.com/news/2017/06/hard-questions-hate-speech/

Barberá, P., Wang, N., Bonneau, R., Jost, J. T., Nagler, J., Tucker, J., & González-Bailón, S. (2015). The critical periphery in the growth of social protests. *PloS ONE, 10*(11), e0143611 https://doi.org/10371/ journal.pone.0143611

Bastos, M. T., Mercea, D., & Charpentier, A. (2015). Tents, tweets, and events: The interplay between ongoing protests and social media. *Journal of Communication, 65,* pp. 320–350.

Berenger, R. D. (Ed). (2013). *Social media go to war: Rebellion and revolution in the age of Twitter.* Marquette Books.

Boland, S. (2018). The power problem. *IPPR Progressive Review, 24*(4), pp. 274–279.

Bonilla, Y., & Rosa, J. (2015). #Ferguson: Digital protest, hashtag ethnography, and the racial politics of social media in the United States. *American Ethnologist, 42*(1), pp. 4–17.

boyd, d. (2014). *It's complicated: The social lives of networked teens.* Yale University Press.

Broadband Commission for Sustainable Development. (2015). *Combatting online violence against women and girls: A worldwide wake-up call.* ITU/UNESCO Report. http://www.broadbandcommission.org/publications/Pages/bb-and-gender-2015.aspx

Bruni, F. (2018, October 30). The Internet will be the death of us. *New York Times.* https://www.nytimes.com/2018/10/30/opinion/internet-violence-hate-prejudice.html

Cappella, J. N. (2017). Vectors into the future of mass and interpersonal communication research: Big data, social media, and computational social science. *Human Communication Research, 43*(4), pp. 545–558.

Carlsen, A., Salam, M., Miller, C., Lu, C., Ngu, D., Patel, A., Jugal, K., & Wichter, Z. (2018, October 23). #MeToo brought down 201 powerful men. Nearly half of their replacements are women. *New York Times.* https://www.nytimes.com/interactive/2018/10/23/us/metoo-replacements.html?emc=edit_th_181024&nl=todaysheadlines&nlid=505602651024

Ceron, E. (2014). *#YesAllWomen: A collection.* Thought Catalogue.

Chira, S., & Einhorn, C. (2017, December 19). How tough is it to change a culture of harassment? Ask women at Ford. *New York Times.* https://www.nytimes.com/interactive/2017/12/19/us/ford-chicago-sexual-harassment.html

Citron, D. K. (2014). *Hate crimes in cyberspace.* Harvard University Press.

Facebook. (2019). *Community Standards.* https://www.facebook.com/communitystandards/

Comunello, F., Mulargia, S., & Parisi, L. (2016). The "proper" way to spread ideas through social media: Exploring the affordances and constraints of different social media platforms as perceived by Italian activists. *Sociological Review, 64,* pp. 515–532.

Conley, T. L. (2014). From #Renishamcbride to #Rememberrenisha: Locating our stories and finding justice. *Feminist Media Studies, 14*(6), pp. 1111–1113.

Crawford, K., & Gillespie, T. (2016). What is a flag for? Social media reporting tools and the vocabulary of complaint. *New Media and Society, 18*(3), pp. 410–428.

Demos. (2016). *The use of misogynist terms on Twitter.* Demos.co.uk. https://www.demos.co.uk/wp-content/uploads/2016/05/Misogyny-online.pdf

Dhrodia, A. (2018). Unsocial media: A toxic place for women. *IPPR Progressive Review, 24*(4), pp. 380–387.

Duggan, M. (2015, August 19). *The demographics of social media users.* Pew Research Center. http://www.pewinternet.org/2015/08/19/the-demographics-of-social-media-users

Editorial Board. (2018, November 24). The new radicalization of the Internet. *New York Times.* https://www.nytimes.com/2018/11/24/opinion/sunday/facebook-twitter-terrorism-extremism.html?emc=edit_th_181125&nl=todaysheadlines&nlid=505602651125

Eligon, J. (2015, November 18). One slogan, many methods: Black lives matter enters politics. *New York Times.* http://www.nytimes.com/2015/11/19/us/one-slogan-many-methods-black-lives-matter-enters-politics.html

Farrow, R. (2017, October 10). From aggressive overtures to sexual assault: Harvey Weinstein's accusers tell their stories. *New Yorker.* https://www.newyorker.com/news/news-desk/from-aggressive-overtures-to-sexual-assault-harvey-weinsteins-accusers-tell-their-stories

Finley, T. (2016, July 13). *Black Twitter countered tragedy with these 6 uplifting hashtags.* HuffPost. https://www.huffpost.com/entry/black-twitter-countered-tragedy-with-these-6-uplifting-hashtags_n_5783a034e4b0c590f7ea090a

Fuchs, C. (2014). *Social media: A critical introduction.* Sage.

Garcia, S. E. (2017, October 20). The woman who created #MeToo long before hashtags. *New York Times*. https://www.nytimes.com/2017/10/ 20/us/me-too -movement-tarana-burke.html

Habermas, J. (1989). *The structural transformation of the public sphere: An inquiry into a category of bourgeois society* (T. Burger & F. Lawrence, Trans.). Polity. (Original work published 1962)

Habermas, J. (2006). Political communication in media society: Does democracy still enjoy an epistemic dimension? The impact of normative theory on empirical research. *Communication Theory, 16*, pp. 411–26.

Hess, A. (2014, January 6). Why women aren't welcome on the Internet. *Pacific Standard*. https://psmag.com/why-women-aren-t-welcome-on-the-internet -aa21fdbc8d6#.8587ngx71

Howard, P. N., & Hussain, M. M. (2013). *Democracy's fourth wave? Digital media and the Arab Spring*. Oxford University Press.

Jaffe, S. (2018, Spring). The collective power of #MeToo. *Dissent Magazine*. https:// www.dissentmagazine.org/article/collective-power-of-me-too-organizing -justice-patriarchy-class

Kantor, J., & Twohey, M. (2017, October 5). Harvey Weinstein paid off sexual harassment accusers for decades. *New York Times*. https://www.nytimes.com /2017/10/05/us/harvey-weinstein-harassment-allegations.html

Kasana, M. (2014). Feminisms and the social media sphere. *Women's Studies Quarterly, 42*(3/4), pp. 236–249.

Khomami, N. (2017, October 20). #MeToo: How a hashtag became a rallying cry against sexual harassment. *The Guardian*. https://www.theguardian.com /world/2017/oct/20/women-worldwide-use-hashtag-metoo-against-sexual -harassment

Kohn, I. (2018, November 15). *Inside the movement to reprogram masculinity*. Vice. https://broadly.vice.com/en_us/article/vbad3y/toxic-masculinity-classes -rethinking-men?utm_source=vicefbus&fbclid=iwarlenaownsbe9b8qqh91 tr4hxa11_00yrac-26vecu9h55crhos4bolpoky

Kruse, L. M., Norris, D. R., & Flinchum, J. R. (2018). Social media as a public sphere? Politics on social media. *Sociological Quarterly, 59*(1), pp. 62–84.

Levey, T. G. (2018). *Sexual harassment online: Shaming and silencing women in the digital age*. Lynne Rienner Publishers.

Magill, T. (2017). *Online Abuse and Harassment*. Ipsos MORI. https://www.ipsos .com/ipsos-mori/en-uk/online-abuse-and-harassment

Mantilla, K. (2015). *Gendertrolling: How misogyny went viral*. Praeger.

McNamee, R. (2019). *Zucked: Waking up to the Facebook catastrophe*. Penguin House.

Milosevic, T. (2016). Social media companies' cyberbullying policies. *International Journal of Communication, 10*, pp. 5164–5185.

Novak, A. N. (2014). The stealthy protestor: Risk and the female body in online social movements. *Feminist Media Studies, 14*(6), pp. 1094–1095.

Penny, L. (2017, October 18). #MeToo forces us to see pervasiveness of abuse. *Time Magazine.* http://time.com/4987390/me-too-shows-pervasive-sexual-abuse/

Portwood-Stacer, L., & Berridge, S. (2014). Introduction: The year in feminist hashtags. *Feminist Media Studies, 14*(6), pp. 1090–1115.

Rentschler, C. A. (2014). Rape culture and the feminist politics of social media. *Girlhood Studies, 7*(1), pp. 65–82.

Rodino-Colocino, M. (2014). #YesAllWomen: Intersectional mobilization against sexual assault is radical (again). *Feminist Media Studies, 14*(6), pp. 1113–1115.

Roose, K. (2018, December 17). Social media's forever war. *New York Times.* https://www.nytimes.com/2018/12/17/technology/social-media-russia-interference.html?emc=edit_th_181218&nl=todaysheadlines&nlid=505602651218

Seidman, R. F. (2013). Who needs feminism? Lesson from a digital world. *Feminist Studies, 39*(2), pp. 549–562.

Shirky, C. (2008). *Here comes everybody: The power of organizing without organizations.* Penguin Press.

Shirky, C. (2011). The political power of social media technology, the public sphere, and political change. *Foreign Affairs, 90*(1), pp. 28–41.

Snitow, A. (2018, Spring). Talking back to the patriarchy. *Dissent, 65*(2), pp. 88–93.

Solnit, R. (2014, June 3). Why #YesAllWomen matters. *Mother Jones.* http://www.motherjones.com/politics/2014/06/yesallwomen-shape-conversation-isla-vista-massacre-violence-against-women

Statista. (2019a). *Average number of hours per day spent by social media users on all social media channels as of 4th quarter 2015, by country.* https://www.statista.com/statistics/270229/usage-duration-of-social-networks-by-country/

Statista. (2019b). *Percentage of U.S. population with a social media profile from 2008 to 2018.* https://www.statista.com/statistics/273476/percentage-of-us-population-with-a-social-network-profile/

Stokes, M. (2018, December 11). The (straight) male gaze rules on sanitized social media. *The Advocate.* https://www.advocate.com/commentary/ 2018/12/11/straight-male-gaze-rules-sanitized-social-media?utm_source =facebook&utm_medium=social&utm_campaign=commentary&utm_term=media

Sunstein, C. R. (2017). *#Republic: Divided democracy in the age of social media.* Princeton University Press.

Sweet, P. (2018, July). Interview with Abigail Saguy. *Sex and Gender News,* pp. 5–6. https://asasexandgender.files.wordpress.com/2018/07/july20183.pdf

Swisher, K. (2018, October 30). I thought the web would stop hate, not spread it. *New York Times.* https://www.nytimes.com/2018/10/30/opinion/cesar-sayoc-robert-bowers-social-media.html?emc=edit_th_181031&nl=todaysheadlines&nlid =505602651031

Talisse, R. (Producer). (2019, January 22). *Why we argue: Is social media killing democracy?* [Audio podcast]. https://whyweargue.libsyn.com/is-social-media-killing-democracy-with-regina-rini

Tambe, A. (2018). Reckoning with the silences of #MeToo. *Feminist Studies, 44*(1), pp. 197–202.

Thorpe, J. R. (2017, December 1). *This is how many people have posted "me too" since October, according to new data.* Bustle. https://www.bustle.com/p/this-is-how-many-people-have-posted-me-too-since-october-according-to-new-data-6753697

Thrift, S. C. (2014). #YesAllWomen as feminist meme event. *Feminist Media Studies, 14*(6), pp. 1090–1092.

Time staff. (2017, November 10). 700,000 female farmworkers say they stand with Hollywood actors against sexual assault. *Time.* http://time.com/5018813/farmworkers-solidarity-hollywood-sexual-assault/

Traister, R. (2017, December 10). This moment isn't (just) about sex. It's really about work. *New York Magazine.* https://www.thecut.com/2017/12/rebecca-traister-this-moment-isnt-just-about-sex.html

Twitter. (2019a). *The Twitter Rules.* https://help.twitter.com/en/rules-and-policies/twitter-rules

Twitter. (2019b). *Twitter Terms of Service.* https://twitter.com/en/tos

Valenti, J. (2016, April 14). Insults and rape threats. Writers shouldn't have to deal with this. *The Guardian.* https://www.theguardian.com/commentisfree/2016/apr/14/insults-rape-threats-writers-online-harassment

Zacharek, S., Dockterman, E., & Sweetland Edwards, H. (2017). The silence breakers. *Time.* http://time.com/time-person-of-the-year-2017-silence-breakers/

Conclusion: Where Do We Go from Here?

Kendra N. Bowen and Jason D. Spraitz

Just as no two organizations are the same, the reasons for and explanations of institutional sexual abuse differ. The authors who contributed chapters to this volume expertly noted those differences. Yet, despite the various administrative hierarchies seen in institutes of higher learning and religious organizations or the distinct power structures seen in Hollywood, government and politics, and the world of media and advertising, there is a constant: the pain caused by sexual misconduct, abuse, violence, and harassment. While the institutions discussed are different, the traumatic effects of institutional sexual abuse are consistent, and nobody should have to endure them. While society has not seen the eradication of sexual violence, researchers and policy makers, as well as victims and advocates, aspire toward that goal. The 16 contributing authors highlighted stories of advocacy, findings of evidence-based research, and policy changes related to institutional sexual misconduct in relation to the #MeToo movement. Below, we offer our ideas for what the continued response should entail, both in terms of activism and of organizational policy.

Activism and Institutional Sexual Abuse

Tarana Burke started the "Me Too" movement in 2006. From that time to 2015, approximately 11 percent of adults in the United States had at least one social media account (Perrin, 2015). In 2019, that percentage rose to 77 percent, and many of these users were on social media daily (Pew Research Center, 2019).

Recent research suggests that more people get news from social media than from newspapers (Haselton, 2018). The substantial growth in social media users in the United States allows strangers to connect with one another and keeps the average person abreast of what is going on in society. For example, 65 percent of users say they have seen content that pertains to sexual harassment or assault while on social media (Anderson & Toor, 2018).

Alyssa Milano's request for Twitter users to tweet "me too" popularized the movement on October 15, 2017 (Pflum, 2018). The hashtag was used more than 19 million times by September 30, 2018, an average of approximately 55,000 uses per day (Anderson & Toor, 2018). Suk et al. (2019) have suggested that digital spaces give individuals an alternative avenue to share their experiences of trauma. This allows for a connection among people with similar stories as well as with those who want to understand what is happening but are not otherwise connected (Clark, 2016). This is a *network of acknowledgment* (Suk et al., 2019). This network has helped sustain and reinforce the #MeToo movement. Other social media movements have emerged, both before and after, that are related to #MeToo. Christine Fox created #WhatWereYouWearing in 2014 to combat victim blaming after a Twitter follower suggested that women who wear revealing clothes are at fault for sexual violence. Adrienne Simpson turned it into a visual campaign with the hashtag #RapeHasNoUniform (Dockterman, 2014). In 2018, after Brett Kavanaugh was nominated to the Supreme Court, the hashtag #WhyIDidntReport went viral on social media, highlighting reasons why many survivors do not report after they are victimized (Fortin, 2018).

These are just a few examples of viral movements similar to the #MeToo movement. Yet, #MeToo has remained at the forefront of social media. Not only that, but it has also expanded into other institutional domains, thus becoming a prominent social movement in this century (see Suk et al., 2019). As detailed in this book, the #MeToo movement has increased the level of awareness and knowledge surrounding institutional sexual violence and encouraged people to take a stand or get involved in reducing sexual violence.

Reducing Sexual Violence, Abuse, and Harassment

The activism affiliated with the #MeToo movement has demonstrated the need for better policies to combat sexual violence. As the chapters in this book have detailed, numerous investigations have been launched, media stories published, and legislation and policies proposed or amended as a result of this social movement. However, there is much more that should be done to reduce institutional sexual violence.

Legal Policy

Though the #MeToo movement has gained attention throughout society, legal ramifications are minimal (Tuerkheimer, 2019). Aside from criminal statutes, federal laws prohibiting sexual violence focus on places or settings. For example, Title IX prohibits sexual violence on college campuses, while Title VII focuses on sexual misconduct in the workplace. These laws call for regulatory systems in these institutions, though most victims do not report misconduct (see RAINN, 2020a; Tuerkheimer, 2019). As contributors to this book have discussed, when victims report their abuse to these institutional regulatory systems, perpetrators are rarely held accountable.

Regarding violations of criminal law, few victims of sexual violence report to law enforcement (RAINN, 2020b). In fact, rape and sexual assault are among the most underreported violent crimes (Morgan & Oudekerk, 2019). Those who report rarely see justice. In response to the #MeToo movement and various institutional scandals, many states are implementing new criminal and civil statutes of limitations focused on sexual violence, because previous and current statutes have been deemed too short (Rhode, 2019). In July 2019, Illinois became just the eighth state to eliminate time restrictions for the prosecution of felony sex crimes (O'Connor, 2019). Kentucky, Maryland, North Carolina, South Carolina, Virginia, West Virginia, and Wyoming are the other states (RAINN, 2019). These new policies align with the empirical evidence on sexual violence trauma and delayed reporting. Other states should eliminate time restrictions as well.

Regarding civil law, there have been recent policies enacted that give victims options and empower them (Anderson & Associates, 2019). For example, "look-back" windows have been created to give victims the ability to hold institutions accountable (Crary, 2019), and other states are contemplating such laws. "Look-back" windows allow adult survivors to come forward with allegations of abuse from their childhood. Institutions like the Catholic Church have spoken out against these laws, arguing that decades-old allegations limit their ability to defend themselves (Crary, 2019). More states should consider laws like these to hold organizations and personnel within them accountable.

Mandatory Reporting

The strictest mandatory reporting laws in the United States focus on violence toward minors, though each state has its own interpretation on who is a mandated reporter. Eighteen states and Puerto Rico require anyone to report child abuse (including sexual abuse) and neglect. Most states designate only certain professionals like teachers, physicians, and social workers as mandatory reporters

(U.S. Department of Health and Human Services, 2019b). Since 2019, a little more than half of all states include clergy as mandatory reporters (U.S. Department of Health and Human Services, 2019a); however, some states make an exception for "clergy-penitent" communications (Wagenmaker & Oberly, 2019). At the time of this writing, lawmakers in some of these states, such as California and Illinois, have introduced bills to eliminate these exceptions. As discussed in this edited volume, states should require all practitioners, including clergy, who work with children to be mandatory reporters. In addition, these individuals need to receive training on laws, on working with victims of abuse, and on the best-practices approach with victims disclosing abuse.

Mandatory reporting regarding adult victims of sexual violence is quite different. According to the last comprehensive legal study on the topic, only three states mandate rape reporting (National District Attorney Association, 2016). Because we know the realities of sexual assault for young adults, universities have been the primary institutions that lawmakers have focused on when implementing mandatory reporting policies during the last decade. In university settings, Title IX and the Clery Act have guided mandatory reporting. Many schools interpret these laws broadly and include all faculty and staff as mandatory reporters, with the exception of those designated as victim advocates, counselors, and health services staff (Gronert, 2019). Students can take a more formal approach by reporting a sex crime to campus police, the Title IX office, or faculty or staff mandated reporters. The less formal approach includes reporting to victim advocates, counselors, or health services staff. A 2015 study found that approximately 55 percent of colleges from a nationally representative sample employed victim advocates, but two-year colleges were less likely to have victim advocates and counseling services for students compared with four-year universities (Richards, 2016), thereby limiting the informal option.

Of these reporters, students have the most interaction with faculty, though they may not know that faculty are mandatory reporters. The U.S. Department of Education advises faculty to immediately warn a student about the faculty member's obligation to report if a student discloses sexual victimization (Wilson, 2014). Many faculty are not skilled or appropriately trained in the best practices for handling such a report. In addition, it may be demoralizing for a student who has gathered the confidence to disclose to a faculty member—perhaps opening up for the first time—to have that trusted professor interrupt or explain that they are a mandatory reporter. This is only one of many issues surrounding mandatory reporting on college campuses (Brown, 2018). Policy should be created that guides consistent mandatory reporting best practices in colleges and universities throughout the United States. This also should include training for all mandatory reporters, which should focus on evidence-based practices for assisting students who report allegations of abuse.

Institutional Hierarchy and Commitment to Change

As of 2018, a record number of women were serving as U.S. senators and in the House of Representatives; still, those percentages are only 25 percent and 24 percent, respectively (Desilver, 2018). The numbers are more diversified in higher education, where minorities represent approximately 13 percent of faculty jobs but only 10 percent of tenured jobs, while women hold approximately 49 percent of faculty jobs but only 38 percent of tenured jobs (Flaherty, 2016). Women do represent approximately half of all administrators in higher education; however, minorities account for only approximately 16 percent (Pritchard et al., 2019). Overall, most of the institutions discussed in this volume are largely run by men.

Women in male-dominated workforces often encounter harassment and discrimination (Kolko & Miller, 2018). Research has found that sexual harassment is prevalent in the workforce today, with approximately 38 percent of women disclosing they have experienced it (Chatterjee, 2018). Institutions should be committed to hiring a diverse workforce that is representative of broader society, including women and people of color. Dobbin and Kaley (2019) have noted that women administrators are more likely to believe harassment complaints and that sexual harassment programming is likely to see greater levels of effectiveness when implemented by women managers. This is partly because women managers are not as likely as men to react negatively to training. Thus, we argue that hiring more women in administrative roles should reduce the level of sexual harassment and discrimination of women in organizational settings.

Additionally, a system of checks and balances is key for hierarchical institutions to reduce sexual violence. Spraitz (2018) has suggested that institutional hierarchy helps determine the level of support for sexual abuse, harassment, and violence prevention programming and that those at the top of the hierarchy must want to make changes; otherwise, there will be institutional silence at best and cover-up at worst. This has been exemplified in the case studies throughout this volume. The #MeToo movement was a response to the inadequate handling of sexual violence in American institutions (Rhode, 2019). All institutions must have policies with strong stances regarding the intolerance of sexual violence.

Wurtele (2012) has written on the sexual exploitation of minors in youth organizations and offered several risk management strategies and ideas for sexual boundary education. Although these policy ideas are focused on youths, they can be amended and applied to many situations in which sexual abuse, harassment, and violence may occur. Risk management strategies discussed by Wurtele include screening; protection policies; monitoring and supervision; electronic communication and social media use; codes of conduct; child sexual abuse education for staff, youths, and families; and training programs for staff. Further, Wurtele provided several topics to cover in sexual boundary education programming, including types of violations, how to avoid crossing boundaries, and how to recognize when boundaries have been crossed.

Wurtele (2012) noted that one of the most obvious strategies for preventing institutional sexual abuse is screening, though it must be done properly. Multiple tools exist to assist in this process, such as criminal background checks and sex offender registries. However, these are not catch-alls for identifying potential abusers, because most people who commit sexual offenses are not reported, caught, or convicted. They may help recognize red flags in rare situations, but as stand-alone policies, they would not help prevent sexual abuse in many of the institutions covered throughout this book. This is why institutions should use a mix of strategies that fit their needs. In these instances, agencies should couple monitoring and supervision with institutional codes of conduct.

In terms of monitoring, Wurtele implored supervisors to "maintain close scrutiny of staff-youth relationships and pay attention to rumors, gossip, or indirect complaints" as methods for identifying potential problem situations (2012, p. 2447). This should be coupled with supervision, evaluation, and accountability measures. In addition, there must be a willingness by supervisory personnel to protect victims and other vulnerable populations when abuse is reported. Institutional codes of conduct should include suspension and termination language focused on anyone who has violated such policies. Additionally, these individuals should be reported to law enforcement if criminal conduct has taken place. Institutions should stand by these policies, even when formerly untouchable CEOs, celebrities, or high-level administrators are at the center of these situations, such as Bill Cosby, Harvey Weinstein, Larry Nassar, and Roger Ailes. Unfortunately, these individuals are the exception. Few high-profile people who have had allegations levied against them are held accountable.

Rather, the contributing authors provided numerous examples of administrative personnel who protected the institution, the accused, or both. Institutional policy must be utilized systematically and justly to hold perpetrators accountable within the institution while appropriate actions are taken. An organizational code of conduct should also outline consequences for administrators who fail to adequately investigate reports of misconduct in order to protect the institution, the accused, or both. Institutional codes of conduct, supervision plans, and background checks are essentially meaningless if the right people are not in charge and if those people do not follow the guidelines.

Firing or disciplining perpetrators only goes so far. It does not repair the damage done to victims (Schultz, 2018). Consequently, these victims are at risk of retaliation or may have to seek new jobs altogether. Therefore, these institutions must also make genuine attempts to repair the harm done to victims within their organization. To do so, institutions should offer treatment options and reparations to victims as helpful good faith measures. Many institutions, including the ones discussed here, have a widespread problem that must be tackled to eliminate sexual violence. Adding these small victim-centered approaches may help with morale, especially when coupled with the institutional-level policies discussed above and outlined below.

Additionally, we suggest enhanced education in multiple areas that may help alleviate risk of sexual victimization in institutional settings. More specifically, sexual boundary training and preventive education training are good areas in which to start. These training exercises should convey the complexities associated with sexual abuse and how deeply traumatized victims may become after enduring abuse (Wurtele, 2012). Further, there should be training that helps one recognize the warning signs of abuse and emphasizes the importance of recognizing, resisting, and reporting abuse (Wurtele, 2009). Without training on these issues, some people may not recognize that behaviors are against policy or against the law (Schulz, 2018).

Several ethical principles that have been applied to the prevention of child sexual abuse can also be applied to institutional sexual abuse. These principles should be covered in any pre-service or in-service employment training:

- knowing the difference between personal and professional boundaries;
- recognizing power dynamics;
- understanding the need to avoid sexual boundary violations;
- understanding the serious harm resulting from sexual boundary violations;
- knowing what constitutes staff sexual misconduct;
- recognizing the red flags . . . in themselves or others of potential boundary violations, and;
- acknowledging the barriers that make intervening difficult. (Wurtele 2012, p. 2449)

This content can be covered through in-person daylong coursework or via online training modules and tutorials. While each of the ideas conveyed above are important, enhanced attention should be given to the last point—the barriers to successful intervention—with a discussion of the myriad strategies for overcoming these barriers.

Institutional Transparency

A common theme among the institutions discussed in this volume is the lack of organizational transparency. The opaqueness of these institutions reduces their credibility (Ridolfi-Starr, 2016). Responses to reports of sexual violence usually remain undisclosed to the public, which immediately discredits the institution.

Agencies must provide clarity. Any code of conduct, reporting policy or procedure, or investigation strategy that institutions have regarding sexual violence should be available on their website and in employee handbooks or other easily accessible places. Additionally, institutions should create annual reports that are available to employees and other stakeholders; these reports should be publicly available for all government organizations. Transparency increases trust, provides clarity, and reduces the chances of ongoing misconduct.

Conclusion: Breaking Barriers and Speaking Out

The #MeToo movement is one of the most prominent examples of how social media plays a role in awareness (see Anderson et al., 2018). Pessimists point out that we have been at similar crossroads before in society with disappointing results (see Schultz, 2018). However, the uniqueness of the #MeToo movement makes it different. Increased attention to the #MeToo movement resulted because of a viral online campaign, but it has transformed into an off-line movement. No matter what the future holds, #MeToo has given victims a voice that most of society has heard.

As seen throughout this text, victim-survivors of sexual abuse and misconduct have faced tremendous barriers to reporting, to being believed, to not being stigmatized and shamed, and to justice. Despite all that #MeToo has already achieved, these barriers still exist. Therefore, it is important to understand that new protocols and trainings will not be a cure-all. Rather, as Spraitz (2018, p. 236) claimed, "It is a challenge to enact recommended policies in a way that they cannot be circumvented by abusers," and Carcara (2009, para. 34) warned that "sexual predators will gravitate to activities and organizations where fewer protective measures are in place." Thus, it can be demoralizing when one realizes that many institutions are autonomous and, because of that, universal implementation of policy solutions is nearly impossible. Even organizations such as university systems, churches, foster care systems, and sports leagues may see inconsistent application by member institutions. This does not help mitigate risk to potential victims. Yet, evidence-based research supports the practices presented in this chapter and throughout this text. Best practices research must continue. Advocates and allies are needed to champion these policies. Those in positions of power should implement the policies that will keep the greatest number of people safe. In the meantime, we all should believe victims when they courageously speak out and step up to tell us their stories.

Tarana Burke spoke out and stepped up. As did Marreka Beckett. And Jen Brockman. Kim Brown. Gretchen Carlson. Andrea Constand. Terry Crews. Jamie Dantzscher. Rachael Denhollander. Lin Farley. Christine Blasey Ford. Cindy

Gallop. Kirsten Gillibrand. Anita Hill. Erin Johnson. Emily Joy. Julie Libarkin. Rose McGowan. Jerry Metcalf. Alyssa Milano. Hannah Paasch. Ayanna Pressley. Stacy Rojas. Alex Story. Emma Sulkowicz. Brianna Wu. Mary Wyandt. They all spoke out and stepped up, as did countless others. Who will be next to speak out, step up, and carry the #MeToo movement forward?

References

Anderson & Associates. (2019, May 13). *Childhood sexual abuse survivors given more time to seek justice, healing: Two-year window allows survivors of any age to file lawsuits.* https://www.andersonadvocates.com/Home/Details/2386

Anderson, M., & Toor, S. (2018, October 11). *How social media users have discussed sexual harassment since #MeToo went viral.* Pew Research Center. https://www.pewresearch.org/fact-tank/2018/10/11/how-social-media-users-have-discussed -sexual-harassment-since-metoo-went-viral/

Anderson, M., Toor, S., Rainie, L., & Smith, A. (2018, July 11). *Activism in the social media age.* Pew Research Center. https://www.pewresearch.org/internet /2018/07/11/public-attitudes-toward-political-engagement-on-social-media/

Brown, S. (2018, August 16). Many professors have to report sexual misconduct. How should they tell their students that? *Chronicle of Higher Education.* https:// www.chronicle.com/article/Many-Professors-Have-to-Report/244294

Carcara, W. S. (2009). Advising houses of worship on a comprehensive and balanced security plan. *Police Chief, 76*(7), 54–57.

Chatterjee, R. (2018, February 21). *A new survey finds 81 percent of women have experienced sexual harassment.* NPR. https://www.npr.org/sections/thetwo -way/2018/02/21/587671849/a-new-survey-finds-eighty-percent-of-women -have-experienced-sexual-harassment

Clark, R. (2016). "Hope in a hashtag": The discursive activism of #WhyIStayed. *Feminist Media Studies, 16*(5), 788–804. https://doi.org/10.1080/14680777.2016 .1138235

Crary, D. (2019a, January 23). *States consider easing statute of limitations on child sex-abuse cases.* Associated Press. https://www.pbs.org/newshour/nation /states-consider-easing-statute-of-limitations-on-child-sex-abuse-cases

Desilver, D. (2018, December 18). *A record number of women will be serving in the new Congress.* Pew Research Center. https://www.pewresearch.org/fact-tank /2018/12/18/record-number-women-in-congress/

Dobbin, F., & Kalev, A. (2019). The promise and peril of sexual harassment programs. *PNAS, 116*(25), 12255–12260.

Dockterman, E. (2014, March 14). Rape survivors talk about why they tweeted their stories. *Time.* https://time.com/25150/rape-victims-talk-about-tweeting-their -experiences-publicly/

Flaherty, C. (2016, August 22). More faculty diversity, not on tenure track. *Inside Higher Ed.* https://www.insidehighered.com/news/2016/08/22/study-finds -gains-faculty-diversity-not-tenure-track

Fortin, J. (2018, September 23). #WhyIDidntReport: Survivors of sexual assault share their stories after Trump tweet. *New York Times.* https://www.nytimes .com/2018/09/23/us/why-i-didnt-report-assault-stories.html

Gronert, N. M. (2019). Law, campus policy, social movements, and sexual violence: Where do we stand in the #MeToo movement? *Sociology Compass,* 1–20. Advance online publication. https://doi.org/10.1111/soc4.12694

Haselton, T. (2018, December 10). *More Americans now get news from social media than from newspapers, says survey.* CNBC. https://www.cnbc.com/2018/12/10 /social-media-more-popular-than-newspapers-for-news-pew.html

Kolko, J., & Miller, C. C. (2018, December 14). As labor market tightens, women are moving into male-dominated jobs. *New York Times.* https://www.nytimes.com /2018/12/14/upshot/as-labor-market-tightens-women-are-moving-into-male -dominated-jobs.html?auth=login-email&login=email

Morgan, R. E., & Oudekerk, B. A. (2019). *Criminal victimization, 2018.* NCJ Publication No. 253043. Bureau of Justice Statistics. https://www.bjs.gov/content/pub /pdf/cv18.pdf

National District Attorney Association. (2016). *Reporting requirements related to rape of competent adult victims.* https://ndaa.org/wp-content/uploads/Rape -Reporting-Requirement-for-Competent-Adult-Victims_Compilation.pdf

O'Connor, J. (2019, July 29). *Illinois becomes 8th state to lift statute of limitation for sex-crimes.* NBC Chicago. https://www.nbcchicago.com/news/local/illinois -becomes-8th-state-to-lift-sex-crime-prosecution-time-limit/129576/

Perrin, A. (2015, October 8). *Social media usage: 2005–2015.* Pew Research Center. https://www.pewresearch.org/internet/2015/10/08/social-networking-usage -2005–2015/

Pew Research Center. (2019, June 12). *Social media fact sheet.* https://www. pewresearch.org/internet/fact-sheet/social-media/

Pflum, M. (2018, October 15). *A year ago, Alyssa Milano started a conversation about #MeToo. These women replied.* NBC News. https://www.nbcnews.com /news/us-news/year-ago-alyssa-milano-started-conversation-about-metoo -these-women-n920246

Pritchard, A., Li, J., McChesney, J., & Bichsel, J. (2019, April). *Administrators in higher education annual report: Key findings, trends, and comprehensive tables for the 2019–2019 academic year.* CUPA-HR. https://www.cupahr.org/wp -content/uploads/surveys/Results/2019-Administrators-Report-Overview.pdf

RAINN. (2019). *State by state guide on statutes of limitations.* https://www.rainn .org/state-state-guide-statutes-limitations

RAINN. (2020a). *Campus sexual violence: Statistics.* https://www.rainn.org
/statistics/campus-sexual-violence

RAINN. (2020b). *The criminal justice system: Statistics.* https://www.rainn.org
/statistics/criminal-justice-system

Rhode, D. L. (2019). #MeToo: Why now? What next? *Duke Law Journal, 69,*
377–428.

Richards, T. N. (2016). An updated review of institutions of higher education's responses to sexual assault: Results from a nationally representative sample. *Journal of Interpersonal Violence, 34,* 1983–2012. https://doi.org/0886260516658757

Ridolfi-Starr, Z. (2016). Transformation requires transparency: Critical policy reforms
to advance campus sexual violence response. *Yale Law Journal, 7*(125), 2156–2181.

Schultz, V. (2018). Reconceptualizing sexual harassment, again. *Yale Law Journal
Forum,* 22–66. https://digitalcommons.law.yale.edu/cgi/viewcontent.cgi
?article=6374&context=fss_papers

Spraitz, J. D. (2018). Institutional sexual abuse. In C. M. Hilinski-Rosick & D. Lee
(Eds.), *Contemporary issues in victimology: Identifying patterns and trends* (pp.
225–244). Lexington Books.

Suk, J., Abhishek, A., Zhang, Y., Ahn, S. Y., Correa, T., Garlough, C., & Shah, D.
V. (2019). #MeToo, networked acknowledgment, and connective action: How
"empowerment through empathy" launched a social movement. *Social Science
Computer Review,* 1–19. Advance online publication. https://doi.org/10.1177
/0894439319864882

Tuerkheimer, D. (2019). Beyond #MeToo. *New York University Law Review, 94*(5),
1146–1208.

U.S. Department of Health and Human Services. (2019a). *Clergy as mandatory
reporters of child abuse and neglect.* https://www.childwelfare.gov/pubPDFs
/clergymandated.pdf

U.S. Department of Health and Human Services. (2019b). *Mandatory reporters of
child abuse and neglect.* https://www.childwelfare.gov/pubPDFs/manda.pdf

Wagenmaker & Oberly. (2019, May 30). *Clergy as mandated reporters, without
exception.* Wagenmaker & Oberly. https://wagenmakerlaw.com/blog/clergy
-mandated-reporters-without-exception

Wilson, R. (2014, November 6). When a student confides a rape, should a professor
have to report it? *Chronicle of Higher Education.* https://www.chronicle.com
/article/When-a-Student-Confides-a/149855

Wurtele, S. K. (2009). Preventing sexual abuse of children in the 21st century: Pre-
paring for challenges and opportunities. *Journal of Child Sexual Abuse, 18,* 1–18.

Wurtele, S. K. (2012). Preventing the sexual exploitation of minors in youth-serving
organizations. *Children and Youth Services Review, 34*(12), 2442–2453. https://
doi.org/10.1016/j.childyouth.2012.09.009

Contributors

Index

Contributors

Nicole Bedera is a doctoral candidate of sociology at the University of Michigan–Ann Arbor. Her research focuses on sexual violence and masculinity, particularly on how both are shaped by organizations such as universities. Her most recent work includes an organizational ethnography of one university's response to campus violence and an interview-based study of queer women's experiences with college sexual violence.

Kendra N. Bowen is an associate professor of criminal justice at Texas Christian University. Her current research primarily focuses on sexual assaults, crimes against children, and various aspects of the sexual abuse scandal in the Catholic Church. Recent publications have appeared in *Corrections: Policy, Practice and Research*; *Sexual Abuse*; the *International Journal for Crime, Justice and Social Democracy*; and the *Journal of Offender Rehabilitation*.

Carolyn Bronstein is the Vincent de Paul Professor of Media Studies and an associate dean for research and strategic initiatives in the College of Communication at DePaul University in Chicago. She is the author of *Battling Pornography: The American Feminist Anti-Pornography Movement, 1976–1986* and a coeditor of *Porno Chic and the Sex Wars: American Sexual Representation and the Sex Wars*.

Shelly Clevenger is the department chair and an associate professor in the Victim Studies Department at Sam Houston State University. She has authored peer-reviewed journal publications, book chapters, and books on the connection between sexual assault, intimate partner abuse, and cybervictimization. She had the honor of presenting her research about cybervictimization at United Nations Women in 2016 and at a U.S. congressional briefing in 2018.

Tracy Everbach is a professor of journalism and a feminist scholar in the Mayborn School of Journalism at the University of North Texas. Her research focuses on women's work and leadership in journalism and on media representations of gender and race. She is a coauthor of *Mediating Misogyny: Gender, Technology, and Harassment.*

Pamela J. Forman teaches gender and public sociology and chairs the Department of Sociology at the University of Wisconsin–Eau Claire. She also conducts qualitative research on gender, cisgender privilege, heterosexism, and sport.

Mia Gilliam is an assistant professor of criminal justice at the University of Wisconsin–Eau Claire. She is currently completing her dissertation as a doctoral candidate in the Department of Criminal Justice at Indiana University. Her primary research interests are gender-based crimes, intimate partner violence, sexual assault, victimology, cultural criminology, and popular culture and crime.

Matthew Hassett is an assistant professor in the Department of Sociology and Criminal Justice at the University of North Carolina at Pembroke. His primary research interests include criminological theory and criminal justice policy.

Jacqueline Lambiase is a professor in and the chair of the Department of Strategic Communication in Texas Christian University's Bob Schieffer College of Communication. For three decades she has scrutinized gendered images and sexuality in advertising and other media forms. In 2016 she won the Jean Giles-Sims Wise Woman Award, and in 2018 she published, with Carolyn Bronstein, the article "#WomenNotObjects: Madonna Badger Takes on Objectification."

Reneè Lamphere is an associate professor of criminal justice in the Department of Sociology and Criminal Justice at the University of North Carolina at Pembroke. Her areas of academic interest include corrections, mixed-methods research, sexual violence and victimization, family violence, teaching and pedagogy, and cyber and digital-media crimes.

Tania G. Levey is a professor of sociology at York College, City University of New York. Research and teaching interests include gender, sexuality, sex work, social media, and research methods. Levey recently published *Sexual Harassment Online: Shaming and Silencing Women in the Digital Age.*

Lake D. Montie is a graduate of the University of Wisconsin–Eau Claire, their love for humanistic, data-driven advocacy has led them to pursue a dual degree in sociology and information systems. Their passion for highlighting the voices of marginalized communities and addressing social injustices is reflected in their past research on the university honors program and surrounding policies that regulate the participation of transgender athletes in elite cycling.

Anne M. Nurse is a professor of sociology at the College of Wooster in Ohio. She has published multiple articles about child sexual abuse prevention and is the author of *Locked Up, Locked Out: Young Men in the Juvenile Justice System* and a coauthor of *Social Inequality: Forms, Causes, and Consequences,* now in a 10th edition.

Jason D. Spraitz is an associate professor and the coordinator of the criminal justice program at the University of Wisconsin–Eau Claire. Recently, he and his research team analyzed sexual grooming patterns and neutralization techniques used by clergy who have been accused of sexual misconduct. This work has appeared in several journals, including *Sexual Abuse,* the *Journal of Interpersonal Violence,* the *Journal of Crime and Justice,* and the *Journal of Sexual Aggression.*

Ashley Wellman is an instructor of criminal justice at Texas Christian University. Her primary research focuses on violent victimization, including families of cold case homicides and sexual assault survivors. Wellman's work has been published in an array of scholarly journals, including *Violence and Victims,* the *Journal of Loss and Trauma,* and *Police Quarterly.*

Amina Zarrugh is an assistant professor of sociology at Texas Christian University. Her research focuses on state violence, gender, race and ethnicity, and social movements in the United States and in the broader Middle East and North Africa.

Index

corrections system: LGBTQ inmate victimization, 105; #MeToo stories in, 108–111; prevalence of sexual violence in, 101–112; Prison Rape Elimination Act (PREA), 106–108, 112; rates of victimization in, 104–106; sex and sexuality in, 102–103, 106; sexual violence training for officers and administrators, 111; treatment protocols, 112

Cosby, Bill, 5, 101, 125–126, 129, 200

Cotton, Donald J., 103

Crabb, Stephen, 48

Crews, Terry, 5, 127–128, 202

Criado-Perez, Caroline, 178

Crime Awareness and Campus Security Act, 17

Crosset, Todd W., 146

Curley, Tim, 139–140

Dantzscher, Jamie, 142, 202

Davis, David, 48

"Dear Colleague Letter," 28

"Dear Sisters" ad, 129

"Declaration of Sentiments and Principles," 43

Denhollander, Rachel, 142, 202

Denney, Andrew S., 71

DePalma, Anthony, 63

Devanny, Joe, 51

DeVaul, Richard, 166

DeVos, Betsy, 4, 25, 29

Dhrodia, Asmina, 187

DiCaprio, Leonardo, 124

Dickey, R. A., 110

DiGiuseppe, David L., 88

Dobbin, Frank, 199

Dolan, Timothy, 75, 76

Doocy, Steve, 164

Dowdell, Elizabeth Burgess, 88, 95

doxing, 178

Doyle, T. P., 74

Dr Pepper, 168

Drummond, David, 166

Dubick, Stephanie, 72

due process, 34n1

Easteal, Patricia, 162

echo chambers, 177

Elephant in the Valley (Vassallo et al.), 163

emphasized femininity, 135–136

Endicott, Marisa, 108

Engler, John, 144

Enloe, Cynthia, 133

Erickson, Rodney, 139

Eshoo, Anna G., 52

eugenics movement, 42

Euser, Saskia, 89

evangelical communities, 4, 72–73, 75, 77–78

Everbach, Tracy, 6

Facebook, 6, 175, 176, 177, 179–181, 182–183, 184, 188n1

Fallon, Michael, 49

Family and Community Development Committee, 64

Farley, Lin, 159, 160, 164, 165, 202

Farrow, Ronan, 187

Feinstein, Dianne, 52

Feminist Media Studies, 184, 186

Ferraro, Geraldine, 45

Field, Valorie Kondos, 143

Financial Times, 49–50

Fisher, Bonnie S., 13

Fishman, Joseph Fulling, 103

Fitzgerald, Patrick, 145

Fleury, Theo, 110

"Flip the Script," 4, 33

Fontes, Lisa Aronson, 68–69

"forced homosexuality," 103

Ford, Christine Blasey, 4, 20, 47, 52–55, 202

PERSPECTIVES ON CRIME AND JUSTICE

Open, inclusive, and broad in focus, the series covers scholarship on a wide range of crime and justice issues, including the exploration of understudied subjects relating to crime, its causes, and attendant social responses. Of particular interest are works that examine emerging topics or shed new light on more richly studied subjects. Volumes in the series explore emerging forms of deviance and crime, critical perspectives on crime and justice, international and transnational considerations of and responses to crime, innovative crime reduction strategies, and alternate forms of response by the community and justice system to disorder, delinquency, and criminality. Both single-authored studies and collections of original edited content are welcome.

Series Editor
Joseph A. Schafer is a professor of criminology and criminal justice at St. Louis University. His research considers issues of police behavior, police organizations, and citizen perceptions of crime. He is the author, coauthor, or coeditor of several books, including *Effective Leadership in Policing: Successful Traits and Habits* and *Contemporary Research on Police Organizations*, and he has written more than fifty scholarly journal articles and more than two dozen book chapters and essays.

OTHER BOOKS IN THE PERSPECTIVES ON CRIME AND JUSTICE SERIES

Dilemma of Duties: The Conflicted Role of Juvenile Defenders
Anne M. Corbin

Demystifying the Big House: Exploring Prison Experience and Media Representations
Edited by Katherine A. Foss